BLUEPRINTS: A PROBLEM NOTEBOOK

Fundamentals of Financial Management

Tenth Edition

Eugene F. Brigham
University of Florida

Michael C. Ehrhardt
University of Tennessee

SOUTH-WESTERN
THOMSON LEARNING

Australia · Canada · Mexico · Singapore · Spain · United Kingdom · United States

Blue Prints: A Problem Notebook to accompany Financial Management: Theory and Practice, 10e, by Eugene F. Brigham and Michael C. Ehrhardt

Printer: Edwards Brothers

Printed in the United States of America
3 4 5 04

For more information contact South-Western, 5191 Natorp Boulevard, Mason, Ohio 45040 or find us on the Internet at http://www.swcollege.com

For permission to use material from this text or product, contact us by
- **telephone: 1-800-730-2214**
- **fax: 1-800-730-2215**
- **web: http://www.thomsonrights.com**

ISBN: 0-03-033568-X

PREFACE

Blueprints has become an integral part of the material we provide to students. To get students more involved, we have developed a set of Mini Cases which cover the key points in each chapter and which we use as the basis for our lectures. For our classes, we use the computer slideshow to present the material that is summarized in each Mini Case. Early on, students began asking us to make copies of the slides available to them. We did so, and that improved the class considerably. With paper copies of the slides, students could focus on what was being said in the lecture without having to copy things down for later review. *Blueprints* includes a copy of each Mini Case, copies of the slides, and space to write down additional notes. Since, we frequently use the blackboard, both to explain the calculations which lie behind some of the numbers and to provide different examples, our students end up with lots of marginal notes which clarify various points.

We consider the current version quite complete. However, the optimal product varies from instructor to instructor, depending on how the class is conducted. Therefore, instructors are encouraged to modify *Blueprints* to suit their own styles and interests. For example, if one covers chapters in a different order, or does not cover certain chapters, or covers only part of some chapters, or has additional materials not covered in the text, or anything else, the *Blueprints* chapters can be rearranged, added to or subtracted from, or modified in any other way.

One thing has become crystal clear over the years—the best lecture notes, and materials related thereto, are instructor-specific. It is difficult to use someone else's notes verbatim. However, there is no point in reinventing the wheel, and if the *Blueprints* wheel fits a particular instructor's wagon, he or she might do well to use it, spending time adapting it to his or her own style and coverage rather than taking the time to develop lectures notes *de novo*. Therefore, you are encouraged to look over the *Blueprints* package, decide if and how you might use it, and then go to it. If you are like us, you will change things from semester to semester—is no such thing as static optimality!

We would like to thank Dana Aberwald Clark for riding herd on all of us, and making sure *Blueprints* was completed on time and was consistent with the text of *Financial Management*. Susan Purcell Whitman and Tina Goforth took care of the massive typing job; their care and dedication are much appreciated.

If you do use the package, and find some modifications that work well for you, we would very much appreciate hearing from you—your modifications might well help us and others. Please send any comments or suggestions to Michael Ehrhardt at the address given below.

Eugene F. Brigham

P.O. Box 117167
College of Business
University of Florida
Gainesville, Florida 32611-7167

Michael C. Ehrhardt

ehrhardt@utk.edu
Finance Department, SMC 424
University of Tennessee
Knoxville, TN 37996-0540

January 2001

SUGGESTIONS FOR STUDENTS USING BLUEPRINTS

1. Read the textbook chapter first, going through the entire chapter rapidly. Don't expect to understand everything on this first reading, but do try to get a good idea of what the chapter covers, the key terms, and the like. It is useful to read the chapter before the first lecture on it.

2. You could also read the *Blueprints* chapter material before class, but that is not necessary.

3. *Blueprints* was designed as the basis for a lecture—the most important material in each chapter is covered, and the material most likely to give you trouble is emphasized. As your instructor goes through *Blueprints*, you should (1) see what we regard as the most important material and (2) get a better feel for how to think about issues and work relevant problems.

4. You could read *Blueprints*, in connection with the text, and get a reasonably good idea of what is going on in the course. However, the real value of *Blueprints* is as a vehicle to help the class lecture make more sense and to help you get a good set of notes. In class, your instructor will discuss various points raised in *Blueprints* and elaborate on different issues. Also, he or she will explain how formulas are used, where data in tables come from, and the like. You will end up with lots of marginal notes on your copy if you use *Blueprints* as it is supposed to be used. Indeed, these marginal notes will constitute your class notes.

BLUEPRINTS

TABLE OF CONTENTS

BLUEPRINTS: CHAPTER 1
AN OVERVIEW OF FINANCIAL MANAGEMENT

Take a Walk on the Wild Side

Joe Birdsong opened Take A Walk on the Wild Side 17 years ago; the store is located in Nantahala, North Carolina, and sells hiking, rafting, and kayaking equipment. Today, Joe has 50 employees including his daughter Anne, who works part time in the store to help pay for her college education.

Joe's business has boomed in recent years, and he is looking for new ways to take advantage of his increasing business opportunities. Although Joe's formal business training is limited, Anne will soon graduate with an MBA. Joe has offered her the opportunity to join the business as a full-fledged partner. Anne is interested, but she is also considering other career opportunities in finance.

Right now, Anne is leaning toward staying with the family business, partly because she thinks it faces a number of interesting challenges and opportunities. Anne is particularly interested in further expanding the business and then incorporating it. Joe is intrigued by her ideas, but he is also concerned that her plans might change the way in which he does business. In particular, Joe has a strong commitment to social activism, and he has always tried to strike a balance between work and pleasure. He is worried that these goals will be compromised if the company incorporates and brings in outside shareholders.

Anne and Joe plan to take a long weekend off to sit down and think about all of these issues. Anne, who is highly organized, has outlined a series of questions for them to address:

a. What three questions does financial management seek to answer?

b. What kinds of career opportunities are open to finance majors?

c. (1) What are the alternative forms of business organization?

   (2) What are their advantages and disadvantages?

d. What is the primary goal of the corporation?

   (1) Do firms have any responsibilities to society at large?

   (2) Is stock price maximization good or bad for society?

   (3) Should firms behave ethically?

e. What factors affect stock prices?

f. What determines cash flows?

g. What factors affect the level and risk of cash flows?

h. What are the most important financial management issues of the new millenium?

i. What is an agency relationship?

   (1) What agency relationships exist within a corporation?

   (2) What mechanisms exist to influence managers to act in shareholders' best interests?

   (3) Should shareholders (through managers) take actions that are detrimental to bondholders?

1 - 1

CHAPTER 1
An Overview of Financial Management

- Role of financial management
- Career opportunities
- Forms of business organization
- Goals of the corporation
- Issues of the new millenium
- Agency relationships

1 - 2

What three questions does financial management seek to answer?

- What causes a company to have a particular stock value?
- How can managers make choices that add value to their companies?
- How can managers ensure that their companies don't run out of cash while executing their plans?

1 - 3

Career Opportunities in Finance

- Institutions and capital markets
- Investments
- Financial management

1 - 4

Alternative Forms of Business Organization

- Sole proprietorship
- Partnership
- Corporation

1 - 5

Sole Proprietorship

- Advantages:
  - Ease of formation
  - Subject to few regulations
  - No corporate income taxes
- Disadvantages:
  - Limited life
  - Unlimited liability
  - Difficult to raise capital

1 - 6

Partnership

- A partnership has roughly the same advantages and disadvantages as a sole proprietorship.

1 - 7

Corporation

- Advantages:
  - Unlimited life
  - Easy transfer of ownership
  - Limited liability
  - Ease of raising capital
- Disadvantages:
  - Double taxation
  - Cost of set-up and report filing

1 - 8

Goals of the Corporation

- The primary goal is shareholder wealth maximization, which translates to maximizing stock price.
  - Should firms behave ethically? YES!
  - Do firms have any responsibilities to society at large? YES! Shareholders are also members of society.

1 - 9

Is maximizing stock price good for society, employees, and customers?

- Employment growth is higher in firms that try to maximize stock price. On average, employment goes up in:
  - firms that make managers into owners (such as LBO firms)
  - firms that were owned by the government but that have been sold to private investors

1 - 10

- Consumer welfare is higher in capitalist free market economies than in communist or socialist economies.
- *Fortune* lists the most admired firms. In addition to high stock returns, these firms have:
  - high quality from customers' view
  - employees who like working there

1 - 11

Factors that Affect Stock Price

- Amount of cash flows expected by shareholders
- Timing of the cash flow stream
- Risk of the cash flows

1 - 12

Three Determinants of Cash Flows

- Sales
  - Current level
  - Short-term growth rate in sales
  - Long-term sustainable growth rate in sales
- Operating expenses
- Capital expenses

1 - 13

Factors that Affect the Level and Risk of Cash Flows

- Decisions made by financial managers:
  - Investment decisions (product lines, production processes, geographic market, use of technology, marketing strategy)
  - Financing decisions (choice of debt policy and dividend policy)
- The external environment

1 - 14

Financial Management Issues of the New Millenium

- Use of computers and electronic transfers of information
- The globalization of business

1 - 15

Agency Relationships

- An agency relationship exists whenever a principal hires an agent to act on his or her behalf.
- Within a corporation, agency relationships exist between:
  - Shareholders and managers
  - Shareholders and creditors

1 - 16

Shareholders versus Managers

- Managers are naturally inclined to act in their own best interests.
- But the following factors affect managerial behavior:
  - Managerial compensation plans
  - Direct intervention by shareholders
  - The threat of firing
  - The threat of takeover

1 - 17

Shareholders versus Creditors

- Shareholders (through managers) could take actions to maximize stock price that are detrimental to creditors.
- In the long run, such actions will raise the cost of debt and ultimately lower stock price.

BLUEPRINTS: CHAPTER 2
FINANCIAL STATEMENTS, CASH FLOW, AND TAXES

Donna Jamison, a 1997 graduate of the University of Tennessee with four years of banking experience, was recently brought in as assistant to the chairman of the board of Computron Industries, a manufacturer of electronic calculators.

The company doubled its plant capacity, opened new sales offices outside its home territory, and launched an expensive advertising campaign. Computron's results were not satisfactory, to put it mildly. Its board of directors, which consisted of its president and vice-president plus its major stockholders (who were all local business people), was most upset when directors learned how the expansion was going. Suppliers were being paid late and were unhappy, and the bank was complaining about the deteriorating situation and threatening to cut off credit. As a result, Al Watkins, Computron's president, was informed that changes would have to be made, and quickly, or he would be fired. Also, at the board's insistence Donna Jamison was brought in and given the job of assistant to Fred Campo, a retired banker who was Computron's chairman and largest stockholder. Campo agreed to give up a few of his golfing days and to help nurse the company back to health, with Jamison's help.

Jamison began by gathering financial statements and other data.

Assume that you are Jamison's assistant, and you must help her answer the following questions for Campo. (Note: We will continue with this case in Chapter 3, and you will feel more comfortable with the analysis there, but answering these questions will help prepare you for Chapter 3. Provide clear explanations, not just yes or no answers!)

Balance Sheets

	2001	2000
Assets:		
Cash	$ 7,282	$ 9,000
Short-term investments	0	48,600
Accounts receivable	632,160	351,200
Inventories	1,287,360	715,200
Total current assets	$1,926,802	$1,124,000
Gross fixed assets	1,202,950	491,000
Less accumulated depreciation	263,160	146,200
Net fixed assets	$ 939,790	$ 344,800
Total assets	$2,866,592	$1,468,800
Liabilities and Equity:		
Accounts payable	$ 524,160	$ 145,600
Notes payable	720,000	200,000
Accruals	489,600	136,000
Total current liabilities	$1,733,760	$ 481,600
Long-term debt	1,000,000	323,432
Common stock (100,000 shares)	460,000	460,000
Retained earnings	(327,168)	203,768
Total equity	$ 132,832	$ 663,768
Total liabilities and equity	$2,866,592	$1,468,800

Income Statements

	2001	2000
Sales	$5,834,400	$3,432,000
Cost of goods sold	5,728,000	2,864,000
Other expenses	680,000	340,000
Depreciation	116,960	18,900
Total operating costs	$6,524,960	$3,222,900
EBIT	($ 690,560)	$ 209,100
Interest expense	176,000	62,500
EBT	($ 866,560)	$ 146,600
Taxes (40%)	(346,624)	58,640
Net income	($ 519,936)	$ 87,960
EPS	($5.199)	$0.880
DPS	$0.110	$0.220
Book value per share	$1.328	$6.638
Stock price	$2.250	$8.500
Shares outstanding	100,000	100,000
Tax rate	40.00%	40.00%
Lease payments	40,000	40,000
Sinking fund payments	0	0

Statement of Retained Earnings, 2001

Balance of retained earnings, 12/31/00	$203,768
Add: Net income, 2001	(519,936)
Less: Dividends paid	(11,000)
Balance of retained earnings, 12/31/01	($327,168)

Statement of Cash Flows, 2001

OPERATING ACTIVITIES	
Net income	($ 519,936)
Adjustments:	
Non-cash adjustments:	
Depreciation	116,960
Changes in working capital:	
Change in accounts receivable	(280,960)
Change in inventories	(572,160)
Change in accounts payable	378,560
Change in accruals	353,600
Net cash provided by operating activities	($ 523,936)
LONG-TERM INVESTING ACTIVITIES	
Cash used to acquire fixed assets	($ 711,950)
FINANCING ACTIVITIES	
Change in short-term investments	$ 48,600
Change in notes payable	520,000
Change in long-term debt	676,568
Payment of cash dividends	(11,000)
Net cash provided by financing activities	$1,234,168
Sum: Net change in cash	($ 1,718)
Plus: Cash at beginning of year	9,000
Cash at end of year	$ 7,282

a. What effect did the expansion have on sales, net operating profit after taxes (NOPAT), net operating working capital, capital, and net income?

b. What effect did the expansion have on net cash flow, operating cash flow, and free cash flow?

c. Jamison also has asked you to estimate Computron's EVA. She estimates that the after-tax cost of capital was 11 percent in 2000 and 13 percent in 2001.

d. Looking at Computron's stock price today, would you conclude that the expansion increased or decreased MVA?

e. Computron purchases materials on 30-day terms, meaning that it is supposed to pay for purchases within 30 days of receipt. Judging from its 2001 balance sheet, do you think Computron pays suppliers on time? Explain. If not, what problems might this lead to?

f. Computron spends money for labor, materials, and fixed assets (depreciation) to make products, and still more money to sell those products. Then, it makes sales which result in receivables, which eventually result in cash inflows. Does it appear that Computron's sales price exceeds its costs per unit sold? How does this affect the cash balance?

g. Suppose Computron's sales manager told the sales staff to start offering 60-day credit terms rather than the 30-day terms now being offered. Computron's competitors react by offering similar terms, so sales remain constant. What effect would this have on the cash account? How would the cash account be affected if sales doubled as a result of the credit policy change?

h. Can you imagine a situation in which the sales price exceeds the cost of producing and selling a unit of output, yet a dramatic increase in sales volume causes the cash balance to decline?

i. In general, could a company like Computron increase sales without a corresponding increase in inventory and other assets? Would the asset increase occur before the increase in sales, and, if so, how would that affect the cash account and the statement of cash flows?

j. Did Computron finance its expansion program with internally generated funds (additions to retained earnings plus depreciation) or with external capital? How does the choice of financing affect the company's financial strength?

k. Refer to the income statements and the statement of cash flows. Suppose Computron broke even in 2001 in the sense that sales revenues equaled total operating costs plus interest charges. Would the asset expansion have caused the company to experience a cash shortage which required it to raise external capital?

l. If Computron started depreciating fixed assets over 7 years rather than 10 years, would that affect (1) the physical stock of assets, (2) the balance sheet account for fixed assets, (3) the company's reported net income, and (4) its cash position? Assume the same depreciation method is used for stockholder reporting and for tax calculations, and the accounting change has no effect on assets' physical lives.

m. Explain how (1) inventory valuation methods, (2) the accounting policy regarding expensing versus capitalizing research and development, and (3) the policy with regard to funding future retirement plan costs (retirement pay and retirees' health benefits) could affect the financial statements.

n. Computron's stock sells for $2.25 per share even though the company had large losses. Does the positive stock price indicate that some investors are irrational?

o. Computron followed the standard practice of paying dividends on a quarterly basis. It paid a dividend during the first two quarters of 2001 then eliminated the dividend when management realized that a loss would be incurred for the year. The dividend was cut before the losses were announced, and at that point the stock price fell from $8.50 to $3.50. Why would an $0.11, or even a $0.22, dividend reduction lead to a $5.00 stock price reduction?

p. Explain how earnings per share, dividends per share, and book value per share are calculated, and what they mean. Why does the market price per share *not* equal the book value per share?

q. How much new money did Computron borrow from its bank during 2001? How much additional credit did its suppliers extend? Its employees and the taxing authorities?

r. If you were Computron's banker, or the credit manager of one of its suppliers, would you be worried about your job? If you were a current Computron employee, a retiree, or a stockholder, should you be concerned?

s. The 2001 income statement shows negative taxes, that is, a tax credit. How much taxes would the company have had to pay in the past to actually get this credit? If taxes paid within the last 2 years had been less than $346,624, what would have happened? Would this have affected the statement of cash flows and the ending cash balance?

t. Working with Jamison has required you to put in a lot of overtime, so you have had very little time to spend on your private finances. It's now April 1, and you have only two weeks left to file your income tax return. You have managed to get all the information together that you will need to complete your return. Computron paid you a salary of $45,000, and you received $3,000 in dividends from common stock that you own. You are single, so your personal exemption is $2,800, and your itemized deductions are $4,550.

   (1) On the basis of the information above and the individual tax rate schedule shown in this chapter, what is your tax liability?

   (2) What are your marginal and average tax rates?

u. Assume that a corporation has $100,000 of taxable income from operations plus $5,000 of interest income and $10,000 of dividend income. What is the company's tax liability?

v. Assume that after paying your personal income tax as calculated in Part t, you have $5,000 to invest. You have narrowed your investment choices down to California bonds with a yield of 7 percent or equally risky Exxon bonds with a yield of 10 percent. Which one should you choose and why? At what marginal tax rate would you be indifferent to the choice between California and Exxon bonds?

2 - 1

CHAPTER 2
Financial Statements, Cash Flow, and Taxes

- Balance sheet
- Income statement
- Statement of cash flows
- Accounting income versus cash flow
- MVA and EVA
- Personal taxes
- Corporate taxes

2 - 2

Balance Sheets: Assets

	2001	2000
Cash	7,282	9,000
Short-term inv.	0	48,600
AR	632,160	351,200
Inventories	1,287,360	715,200
Total CA	1,926,802	1,124,000
Gross FA	1,202,950	491,000
Less: Depr.	263,160	146,200
Net FA	939,790	344,800
Total assets	2,866,592	1,468,800

2 - 3

Liabilities and Equity

	2001	2000
Accts payable	524,160	145,600
Notes payable	720,000	200,000
Accruals	489,600	136,000
Total CL	1,733,760	481,600
Long-term debt	1,000,000	323,432
Common stock	460,000	460,000
Retained earnings	(327,168)	203,768
Total equity	132,832	663,768
Total L&E	2,866,592	1,468,800

2 - 4

Income Statement

	2001	2000
Sales	5,834,400	3,432,000
COGS	5,728,000	2,864,000
Other expenses	680,000	340,000
Deprec.	116,960	18,900
Tot. op. costs	6,524,960	3,222,900
EBIT	(690,560)	209,100
Interest exp.	176,000	62,500
EBT	(866,560)	146,600
Taxes (40%)	(346,624)	58,640
Net income	(519,936)	87,960

2 - 5

Other Data

	2001	2000
No. of shares	100,000	100,000
EPS	($5.199)	$0.88
DPS	$0.110	$0.22
Stock price	$2.25	$8.50
Lease pmts	$40,000	$40,000

2 - 6

Statement of Retained Earnings (2001)

Balance of retained earnings, 12/31/00	$203,768
Add: Net income, 2001	(519,936)
Less: Dividends paid	(11,000)
Balance of retained earnings, 12/31/01	($327,168)

2 - 7

Statement of Cash Flows: 2001

OPERATING ACTIVITIES	
Net Income	(519,936)
Adjustments:	
Depreciation	116,960
Change in AR	(280,960)
Change in inventories	(572,160)
Change in AP	378,560
Change in accruals	353,600
Net cash provided by ops.	(523,936)

2 - 8

L-T INVESTING ACTIVITIES	
Investments in fixed assets	(711,950)
FINANCING ACTIVITIES	
Change in s-t investments	48,600
Change in notes payable	520,000
Change in long-term debt	676,568
Payment of cash dividends	(11,000)
Net cash from financing	1,234,168
Sum: net change in cash	(1,718)
Plus: cash at beginning of year	9,000
Cash at end of year	7,282

2 - 9

What can you conclude about the company's financial condition from its statement of cash flows?

- Net cash from operations = -$523,936, mainly because of negative net income.
- The firm borrowed $1,185,568 and sold $48,600 in short-term investments to meet its cash requirements.
- Even after borrowing, the cash account fell by $1,718.

2 - 10

What effect did the expansion have on net operating working capital (NOWC)?

$$NOWC = \text{Operating CA} - \text{Operating CL}$$

$$NOWC_{01} = (\$7,282 + \$632,160 + \$1,287,360) - (\$524,160 + \$489,600) = \$913,042.$$

$$NOWC_{00} = \$793,800.$$

2 - 11

What effect did the expansion have on capital used in operations?

$$\text{Operating capital} = \text{NOWC} + \text{Net fixed assets}.$$

$$\text{Operating capital}_{01} = \$913,042 + \$939,790 = \$1,852,832.$$

$$\text{Operating capital}_{00} = \$1,138,600.$$

2 - 12

Did the expansion create additional net operating profit after taxes (NOPAT)?

$$NOPAT = EBIT(1 - \text{Tax rate})$$

$$NOPAT_{01} = -\$690,560(1 - 0.4) = -\$690,560(0.6) = -\$414,336.$$

$$NOPAT_{00} = \$125,460.$$

2 - 13

What is your initial assessment of the expansion's effect on operations?

	2001	2000
Sales	$5,834,400	$3,432,000
NOPAT	($414,336)	$125,460
NOWC	$913,042	$793,800
Operating capital	$1,852,832	$1,138,600

2 - 14

What effect did the company's expansion have on its net cash flow and operating cash flow?

NCF_{01} = NI + DEP = -$519,936 + $116,960
= -$402,976.

NCF_{00} = $87,960 + $18,900 = $106,860.

OCF_{01} = NOPAT + DEP
= -$414,336 + $116,960
= -$297,376.

OCF_{00} = $125,460 + $18,900
= $144,360.

2 - 15

What was the free cash flow (FCF) for 2001?

FCF = NOPAT - Net capital investment
= -$414,336 - ($1,852,832 - 1,138,600)
= -$414,336 - $714,232
= -$1,128,568.

How do you suppose investors reacted?

2 - 16

What is the company's EVA? Assume the firm's after-tax cost of capital (COC) was 11% in 2000 and 13% in 2001.

EVA_{01} = NOPAT- (COC)(Capital)
= -\$414,336 - (0.13)(\$1,852,832)
= -\$414,336 - \$240,868
= -\$655,204.

EVA_{00} = \$125,460 - (0.11)(\$1,138,600)
= \$125,460 - \$125,246
= \$214.

2 - 17

Would you conclude that the expansion increased or decreased MVA?

MVA = Market value of equity - Equity capital supplied.

During the last year stock price has decreased 73%, so market value of equity has declined. Consequently, MVA has declined.

2 - 18

Does the company pay its suppliers on time?

- Probably not.
- A/P increased 260% over the past year, while sales increased by only 70%.
- If this continues, suppliers may cut off trade credit.

2 - 19

Does it appear that the sales price exceeds the cost per unit sold?

- No, the negative NOPAT shows that the company is spending more on it's operations than it is taking in.

2 - 20

What effect would each of these actions have on the cash account?

1. The company offers 60-day credit terms. The improved terms are matched by its competitors, so sales remain constant.

   - A/R would ↑
   - Cash would ↓

2 - 21

2. Sales double as a result of the change in credit terms.

   - Short-run: Inventory and fixed assets ↑ to meet increased sales. A/R ↑ , Cash ↓. Company may have to seek additional financing.
   - Long-run: Collections increase and the company's cash position would improve.

2 - 22

How was the expansion financed?

- The expansion was financed primarily with external capital.
- The company issued long-term debt which reduced its financial strength and flexibility.

2 - 23

Would external capital have been required if they had broken even in 2001 (Net income = 0)?

- Yes, the company would still have to finance its increase in assets.

2 - 24

What happens if fixed assets are depreciated over 7 years (as opposed to the current 10 years)?

- No effect on physical assets.
- Fixed assets on balance sheet would decline.
- Net income would decline.
- Tax payments would decline.
- Cash position would improve.

2 - 25

Other policies that can affect financial statements

- Inventory valuation methods.
- Capitalization of R&D expenses.
- Policies for funding the company's retirement plan.

2 - 26

Does the company's positive stock price ($2.25), in the face of large losses, suggest that investors are irrational?

- No, it means that investors expect things to get better in the future.

2 - 27

Why did the stock price fall after the dividend was cut?

- Management was "signaling" that the firm's operations were in trouble.
- The dividend cut lowered investors' expectations for future cash flows, which caused the stock price to decline.

2 - 28

What were some other sources of financing used in 2001?

- Selling financial assets: Short term investments decreased by $48,600.
- Bank loans: Notes payable increased by $520,000.
- Credit from suppliers: A/P increased by $378,560.
- Employees: Accruals increased by $353,600.

2 - 29

What is the effect of the $346,624 tax credit received in 2001.

- This suggests the company paid at least $346,624 in taxes during the past 2 years.
- If the payments over the past 2 years were less than $346,624 the firm would have had to carry forward the amount of its loss that was not carried back.
- If the firm did not receive a full refund its cash position would be even worse.

2 - 30

2000 Tax Year Single Individual Tax Rates

Taxable Income	Tax on Base	Rate*
0 - 26,250	0	15%
26,250 - 63,550	3,937.50	28%
63,550 - 132,600	14,381.50	31%
132,600 - 288,350	35,787.00	36%
Over 288,350	91,857.00	39.6%

*Plus this percentage on the amount over the bracket base.

2 - 31

Assume your salary is $45,000, and you received $3,000 in dividends. You are single, so your personal exemption is $2,800 and your itemized deductions are $4,550.

On the basis of the information above and the 2000 tax year tax rate schedule, what is your tax liability?

2 - 32

Calculation of Taxable Income

Salary	$45,000
Dividends	3,000
Personal exemptions	(2,800)
Deductions	(4,550)
Taxable Income	$40,650

2 - 33

$40,650 - $26,250

- **Tax Liability:**
  TL = $3,937.50 + 0.28($14,400)
  = $7,969.50.
- **Marginal Tax Rate =** 28%.
- **Average Tax Rate:**
  Tax rate = $\frac{\$7,969.5}{\$40,650}$ = 19.6%.

2 - 34

2000 Corporate Tax Rates

Taxable Income	Tax on Base	Rate*
0 - 50,000	0	15%
50,000 - 75,000	7,500	25%
75,000 - 100,000	13,750	34%
100,000 - 335,000	22,250	39%
...	...	...
Over 18.3M	6.4M	35%

*Plus this percentage on the amount over the bracket base.

2 - 35

Assume a corporation has $100,000 of taxable income from operations, $5,000 of interest income, and $10,000 of dividend income.

What is its tax liability?

2 - 36

Operating income	$100,000
Interest income	5,000
Taxable dividend income	3,000*
Taxable income	$108,000

Tax = $22,250 + 0.39 ($8,000)
= $25,370.

*Dividends - Exclusion
= $10,000 - 0.7($10,000) = $3,000.

2 - 37

Taxable versus Tax Exempt Bonds

State and local government bonds (municipals, or "munis") are generally exempt from federal taxes.

2 - 38

- Exxon bonds at 10% versus California muni bonds at 7%.
- T = Tax rate = 28%.
- After-tax interest income:

  Exxon = 0.10($5,000) - 0.10($5,000)(0.28)

  = 0.10($5,000)(0.72) = $360.

  CAL = 0.07($5,000) - 0 = $350.

2 - 39

At what tax rate would you be indifferent between the muni and the corporate bonds?

Solve for T in this equation:

Muni yield = Corp Yield(1-T)

7.00% = 10.0%(1-T)

T = 30.0%.

2 - 40

Implications

- If T > 30%, buy tax exempt munis.
- If T < 30%, buy corporate bonds.
- Only high income, and hence high tax bracket, individuals should buy munis.

BLUEPRINTS: CHAPTER 3
ANALYSIS OF FINANCIAL STATEMENTS

The first part of the case, presented in Chapter 2, discussed the situation that Computron Industries was in after an expansion program. Thus far, sales have not been up to the forecasted level, costs have been higher than were projected, and a large loss occurred in 2001 rather than the expected profit. As a result, its managers, directors, and investors are concerned about the firm's survival.

Donna Jamison was brought in as assistant to Fred Campo, Computron's chairman, who had the task of getting the company back into a sound financial position. Computron's 2000 and 2001 balance sheets and income statements, together with projections for 2002, are shown in the following tables. Also, the tables show the 2000 and 2001 financial ratios, along with industry average data. The 2002 projected financial statement data represent Jamison's and Campo's best guess for 2002 results, assuming that some new financing is arranged to get the company "over the hump."

Jamison examined monthly data for 2001 (not given in the case), and she detected an improving pattern during the year. Monthly sales were rising, costs were falling, and large losses in the early months had turned to a small profit by December. Thus, the annual data look somewhat worse than final monthly data. Also, it appears to be taking longer for the advertising program to get the message across, for the new sales offices to generate sales, and for the new manufacturing facilities to operate efficiently. In other words, the lags between spending money and deriving benefits were longer than Computron's managers had anticipated. For these reasons, Jamison and Campo see hope for the company—provided it can survive in the short run.

Jamison must prepare an analysis of where the company is now, what it must do to regain its financial health, and what actions should be taken. Your assignment is to help her answer the following questions. Provide clear explanations, not yes or no answers.

Balance Sheets

	2002E	2001	2000
Assets:			
Cash	$ 14,000	$ 7,282	$ 9,000
Short-term investments	71,632	0	48,600
Accounts receivable	878,000	632,160	351,200
Inventories	1,716,480	1,287,360	715,200
Total current assets	$2,680,112	$1,926,802	$1,124,000
Gross fixed assets	1,197,160	1,202,950	491,000
Less accumulated depreciation	380,120	263,160	146,200
Net fixed assets	$ 817,040	$ 939,790	$ 344,800
Total assets	$3,497,152	$2,866,592	$1,468,800
Liabilities and Equity:			
Accounts payable	$ 436,800	$ 524,160	$ 145,600
Notes payable	600,000	720,000	200,000
Accruals	408,000	489,600	136,000
Total current liabilities	$1,444,800	$1,733,760	$ 481,600
Long-term debt	500,000	1,000,000	323,432
Common stock	1,680,936	460,000	460,000
Retained earnings	(128,584)	(327,168)	203,768
Total equity	$1,552,352	$ 132,832	$ 663,768
Total liabilities and equity	$3,497,152	$2,866,592	$1,468,800

Note: "E" indicates estimated. The 2002 data are forecasts.

Income Statements

	2002E	2001	2000
Sales	$7,035,600	$5,834,400	$3,432,000
Cost of goods sold	6,100,000	5,728,000	2,864,000
Other expenses	312,960	680,000	340,000
Depreciation	120,000	116,960	18,900
Total operating costs	$6,532,960	$6,524,960	$3,222,900
EBIT	$ 502,640	($ 690,560)	$ 209,100
Interest expense	80,000	176,000	62,500
EBT	$ 422,640	($ 866,560)	$ 146,600
Taxes (40%)	169,056	(346,624)	58,640
Net income	$ 253,584	($ 519,936)	$ 87,960
EPS	$ 1.014	($5.199)	$0.880
DPS	$ 0.220	$0.110	$0.220
Book value per share	$ 6.209	$1.328	$6.638
Stock price	$12.17	$2.250	$8.500
Shares outstanding	250,000	100,000	100,000
Tax rate	40.00%	40.00%	40.00%
Lease payments	40,000	40,000	40,000
Sinking fund payments	0	0	0

Note: "E" indicates estimated. The 2002 data are forecasts.

Ratio Analysis

	2002E	2001	2000	Industry Average
Current		1.1×	2.3×	2.7×
Quick		0.4×	0.8×	1.0×
Inventory turnover		4.5×	4.8×	6.1×
Days sales outstanding (DSO)		39.0	36.8	32.0
Fixed assets turnover		6.2×	10.0×	7.0×
Total assets turnover		2.0×	2.3×	2.5×
Debt ratio		95.4%	54.8%	50.0%
TIE		-3.9×	3.3×	6.2×
EBITDA coverage		-2.5×	2.6×	8.0×
Profit margin		-8.9%	2.6%	3.6%
Basic earning power		-24.1%	14.2%	17.8%
ROA		-18.1%	6.0%	9.0%
ROE		-391.4%	13.3%	18.0%
Price/earnings		-0.4×	9.7×	14.2×
Price/cash flow		-0.6×	8.0×	7.6×
Market/book		1.7×	1.3×	2.9×
Book value per share		$1.33	$6.64	n.a.

Note: "E" indicates estimated. The 2002 data are forecasts.

a. Why are ratios useful? What are the five major categories of ratios?

b. Calculate the 2002 current and quick ratios based on the projected balance sheet and income statement data. What can you say about the company's liquidity position in 2000, 2001, and as projected for 2002? We often think of ratios as being useful (1) to managers to help run the business, (2) to bankers for credit analysis, and (3) to stockholders for stock valuation. Would these different types of analysts have an equal interest in the liquidity ratios?

c. Calculate the 2002 inventory turnover, days sales outstanding (DSO), fixed assets turnover, operating capital requirement, and total assets turnover. How does Computron's utilization of assets stack up against other firms in its industry?

d. Calculate the 2002 debt, times-interest-earned, and EBITDA coverage ratios. How does Computron compare with the industry with respect to financial leverage? What can you conclude from these ratios?

e. Calculate the 2002 profit margin, basic earning power (BEP), return on assets (ROA), and return on equity (ROE). What can you say about these ratios?

f. Calculate the 2002 price/earnings ratio, price/cash flow ratio, and market/book ratio. Do these ratios indicate that investors are expected to have a high or low opinion of the company?

g. Perform a common size analysis and percent change analysis. What do these analyses tell you about Computron?

h. Use the extended Du Pont equation to provide a summary and overview of Computron's financial condition as projected for 2002. What are the firm's major strengths and weaknesses?

h. Use the following simplified 2002 balance sheet to show, in general terms, how an improvement in the DSO would tend to affect the stock price. For example, if the company could improve its collection procedures and thereby lower its DSO from 44.9 days to the 32-day industry average without affecting sales, how would that change "ripple through" the financial statements (shown in thousands below) and influence the stock price?

Accounts receivable	$ 878	Debt	$1,945
Other current assets	1,802		
Net fixed assets	817	Equity	1,552
Total assets	$3,497	Liabilities plus equity	$3,497

j. Does it appear that inventories could be reduced, and, if so, how should that adjustment affect profitability and stock price?

k. In 2001, the company paid its suppliers much later than the due dates, and it was not maintaining financial ratios at levels called for in its bank loan agreements. Therefore, suppliers could cut the company off, and its bank could refuse to renew the loan when it comes due in 90 days. On the basis of data provided, would you, as a credit manager, continue to sell to Computron on credit? (You could demand cash on delivery, that is, sell on terms of COD, but that might cause Computron to stop buying from your company.) Similarly, if you were the bank loan officer, would you recommend renewing the loan or demand its repayment? Would your actions be influenced if, in early 2002, Computron showed you its 2002 projections plus proof that it was going to raise over $1.2 million of new equity capital?

l. In hindsight, what should Computron have done back in 2000?

m. What are some potential problems and limitations of financial ratio analysis?

n. What are some qualitative factors analysts should consider when evaluating a company's likely future financial performance?

3 - 1

CHAPTER 3
Analysis of Financial Statements

- Ratio analysis
- Du Pont system
- Effects of improving ratios
- Limitations of ratio analysis
- Qualitative factors

3 - 2

Balance Sheet: Assets

	2002E	2001
Cash	14,000	7,282
ST investments	71,632	0
AR	878,000	632,160
Inventories	1,716,480	1,287,360
Total CA	2,680,112	1,926,802
Gross FA	1,197,160	1,202,950
Less: Deprec.	380,120	263,160
Net FA	817,040	939,790
Total assets	3,497,152	2,866,592

3 - 3

Liabilities and Equity

	2002E	2001
Accounts payable	436,800	524,160
Notes payable	600,000	720,000
Accruals	408,000	489,600
Total CL	1,444,800	1,733,760
Long-term debt	500,000	1,000,000
Common stock	1,680,936	460,000
Retained earnings	(128,584)	(327,168)
Total equity	1,552,352	132,832
Total L & E	3,497,152	2,866,592

3 - 4

Income Statement

	2002E	2001
Sales	7,035,600	5,834,400
COGS	6,100,000	5,728,000
Other expenses	312,960	680,000
Depreciation	120,000	116,960
Tot. op. costs	6,532,960	6,524,960
EBIT	502,640	(690,560)
Interest exp.	80,000	176,000
EBT	422,640	(866,560)
Taxes (40%)	169,056	(346,624)
Net income	253,584	(519,936)

3 - 5

Other Data

	2002E	2001
Shares out.	250,000	100,000
EPS	$1.014	($5.199)
DPS	$0.220	$0.110
Stock price	$12.17	$2.25
Lease pmts	$40,000	$40,000

3 - 6

Why are ratios useful?

- Standardize numbers; facilitate comparisons
- Used to highlight weaknesses and strengths

3 - 7

What are the five major categories of ratios, and what questions do they answer?

- **Liquidity: Can we make required payments as they fall due?**
- **Asset management: Do we have the right amount of assets for the level of sales?**

(More...)

3 - 8

- **Debt management: Do we have the right mix of debt and equity?**
- **Profitability: Do sales prices exceed unit costs, and are sales high enough as reflected in PM, ROE, and ROA?**
- **Market value: Do investors like what they see as reflected in P/E and M/B ratios?**

3 - 9

Calculate the firm's forecasted current and quick ratios for 2002.

$$CR_{02} = \frac{CA}{CL} = \frac{\$2,680}{\$1,445} = 1.85x.$$

$$QR_{02} = \frac{CA - Inv.}{CL}$$

$$= \frac{\$2,680 - \$1,716}{\$1,445} = 0.67x.$$

3 - 10

Comments on CR and QR

	2002E	2001	2000	Ind.
CR	1.85x	1.1x	2.3x	2.7x
QR	0.67x	0.4x	0.8x	1.0x

- Expected to improve but still below the industry average.
- Liquidity position is weak.

3 - 11

What is the inventory turnover ratio as compared to the industry average?

$$\text{Inv. turnover} = \frac{\text{Sales}}{\text{Inventories}} = \frac{\$7,036}{\$1,716} = 4.10\text{x}.$$

	2002E	2001	2000	Ind.
Inv. T.	4.1x	4.5x	4.8x	6.1x

3 - 12

Comments on Inventory Turnover

- Inventory turnover is below industry average.
- Firm might have old inventory, or its control might be poor.
- No improvement is currently forecasted.

3 - 13

DSO is the average number of days after making a sale before receiving cash.

$$\text{DSO} = \frac{\text{Receivables}}{\text{Average sales per day}}$$

$$= \frac{\text{Receivables}}{\text{Sales/360}} = \frac{\$878}{\$7{,}036/360}$$

= 44.9 days.

3 - 14

Appraisal of DSO

	2002	2001	2000	Ind.
DSO	44.9	39.0	36.8	32.0

- Firm collects too slowly, and situation is getting worse.
- Poor credit policy.

3 - 15

Fixed Assets and Total Assets Turnover Ratios

$$\text{Fixed assets turnover} = \frac{\text{Sales}}{\text{Net fixed assets}}$$

$$= \frac{\$7{,}036}{\$817} = 8.61\text{x.}$$

$$\text{Total assets turnover} = \frac{\text{Sales}}{\text{Total assets}}$$

$$= \frac{\$7{,}036}{\$3{,}497} = 2.01\text{x.}$$

(More...)

3 - 16

	2002E	2001	2000	Ind.
FA TO	8.6x	6.2x	10.0x	7.0x
TA TO	2.0x	2.0x	2.3x	2.5x

- FA turnover is expected to exceed industry average. Good.
- TA turnover not up to industry average. Caused by excessive current assets (A/R and inventory).

3 - 17

Calculate the debt, TIE, and EBITDA coverage ratios.

$$\text{Debt ratio} = \frac{\text{Total debt}}{\text{Total assets}} = \frac{\$1{,}445 + \$500}{\$3{,}497} = 55.6\%.$$

$$\text{TIE} = \frac{\text{EBIT}}{\text{Int. expense}} = \frac{\$502.6}{\$80} = 6.3\text{x}.$$

(More...)

3 - 18

$$\text{EBITDA coverage} = \text{EC} = \frac{\text{EBIT + Depr. \& Amort. + Lease payments}}{\text{Interest expense} + \text{Lease pmt.} + \text{Loan pmt.}}$$

$$= \frac{\$502.6 + \$120 + \$40}{\$80 + \$40 + \$0} = 5.5\text{x}.$$

All three ratios reflect use of debt, but focus on different aspects.

3 - 19

How do the debt management ratios compare with industry averages?

	2002E	2001	2000	Ind.
D/A	55.6%	95.4%	54.8%	50.0%
TIE	5.8x	-3.9x	3.3x	6.2x
EC	4.3x	-2.5x	2.6x	8.0x

Too much debt, but projected to improve.

3 - 20

Profit Margin (PM)

$$PM = \frac{NI}{Sales} = \frac{\$253.6}{\$7,036} = 3.6\%.$$

	2002E	2001	2000	Ind.
PM	3.6%	-8.9%	2.6%	3.6%

Very bad in 2001, but projected to meet industry average in 2002. Looking good.

3 - 21

Basic Earning Power (BEP)

$$BEP = \frac{EBIT}{Total\ assets}$$

$$= \frac{\$502.6}{\$3,497} = 14.4\%.$$

(More...)

3 - 22

	2002E	2001	2000	Ind.
BEP	14.4%	-24.1%	14.2%	17.8%

- BEP removes effect of taxes and financial leverage. Useful for comparison.
- Projected to be below average.
- Room for improvement.

3 - 23

Return on Assets (ROA) and Return on Equity (ROE)

$$ROA = \frac{\text{Net income}}{\text{Total assets}}$$

$$= \frac{\$253.6}{\$3,497} = 7.3\%.$$

(More…)

3 - 24

$$ROE = \frac{\text{Net income}}{\text{Common equity}}$$

$$= \frac{\$253.6}{\$1,552} = 16.3\%.$$

	2002E	2001	2000	Ind.
ROA	7.3%	-18.1%	6.0%	9.0%
ROE	16.3%	-391.0%	13.3%	18.0%

Both below average but improving.

3 - 25

Effects of Debt on ROA and ROE

- ROA is lowered by debt--interest expense lowers net income, which also lowers ROA.
- However, the use of debt lowers equity, and if equity is lowered more than net income, ROE would increase.

3 - 26

Calculate and appraise the P/E, P/CF, and M/B ratios.

Price = $12.17.

$$\text{EPS} = \frac{\text{NI}}{\text{Shares out.}} = \frac{\$253.6}{250} = \$1.01.$$

$$\text{P/E} = \frac{\text{Price per share}}{\text{EPS}} = \frac{\$12.17}{\$1.01} = 12x.$$

(More...)

3 - 27

Typical industry average P/E ratios

Industry	P/E ratio
Banking	17.15
Computer Software Services	33.01
Drug	41.81
Electric Utilities (Eastern U.S.)	19.40
Internet Services*	290.35
Semiconductors	78.41
Steel	12.71
Tobacco	11.59
Water Utilities	21.84

* Because many internet companies have negative earnings and no P/E, there was only a small sample of internet companies.

3 - 28

$$\text{CF per share} = \frac{\text{NI + Depr.}}{\text{Shares out.}}$$

$$= \frac{\$253.6 + \$120.0}{250} = \$1.49.$$

$$\text{P/CF} = \frac{\text{Price per share}}{\text{Cash flow per share}}$$

$$= \frac{\$12.17}{\$1.49} = 8.2\text{x}.$$

3 - 29

$$\text{BVPS} = \frac{\text{Com. equity}}{\text{Shares out.}}$$

$$= \frac{\$1{,}552}{250} = \$6.21.$$

$$\text{M/B} = \frac{\text{Mkt. price per share}}{\text{Book value per share}}$$

$$= \frac{\$12.17}{\$6.21} = 2.0\text{x}.$$

(More...)

3 - 30

	2002E	2001	2000	Ind.
P/E	12.0x	-0.4x	9.7x	14.2x
P/CF	8.2x	-0.6x	8.0x	7.6x
M/B	2.0x	1.7x	1.3x	2.9x

- P/E: How much investors will pay for $1 of earnings. High is good.
- M/B: How much paid for $1 of book value. Higher is good.
- P/E and M/B are high if ROE is high, risk is low.

3 - 31

Common Size Balance Sheets: Divide all items by Total Assets

Assets	2000	2001	2002E	Ind.
Cash	0.6%	0.3%	0.4%	0.3%
ST Invest.	3.3%	0.0%	2.0%	0.3%
AR	23.9%	22.1%	25.1%	22.4%
Invent.	48.7%	44.9%	49.1%	41.2%
Total CA	76.5%	67.2%	76.6%	64.1%
Net FA	23.5%	32.8%	23.4%	35.9%
TA	100.0%	100.0%	100.0%	100.0%

3 - 32

Divide all items by Total Liabilities & Equity

	2000	2001	2002E	Ind.
AP	9.9%	18.3%	12.5%	11.9%
Notes pay.	13.6%	25.1%	17.2%	2.4%
Accruals	9.3%	17.1%	11.7%	9.5%
Total CL	32.8%	60.5%	41.3%	23.7%
LT Debt	22.0%	34.9%	14.3%	26.3%
Total equ.	45.2%	4.6%	44.4%	50.0%
Total L&E	100.0%	100.0%	100.0%	100.0%

3 - 33

Analysis of Common Size Balance Sheets

- Computron has higher proportion of inventory and current assets than Industry.
- Computron has slightly less equity (which means more debt) than Industry.
- Computron has more short-term debt than industry, but less long-term debt than industry.

3 - 34

Common Size Income Statement: Divide all items by Sales

	2000	2001	2002E	Ind.
Sales	100.0%	100.0%	100.0%	100.0%
COGS	83.4%	98.2%	86.7%	84.5%
Other exp.	9.9%	11.7%	4.4%	4.4%
Depr.	0.6%	2.0%	1.7%	4.0%
EBIT	6.1%	-11.8%	7.1%	7.1%
Int. Exp.	1.8%	3.0%	1.1%	1.1%
EBT	4.3%	-14.9%	6.0%	5.9%
Taxes	1.7%	-5.9%	2.4%	2.4%
NI	2.6%	-8.9%	3.6%	3.6%

3 - 35

Analysis of Common Size Income Statements

- Computron has higher COGS (86.7) than industry (84.5), but lower depreciation. Result is that Computron has similar EBIT (7.1) as industry.

3 - 36

Percentage Change Analysis: Find Percentage Change from First Year (2000)

Income St.	2000	2001	2002E
Sales	0.0%	70.0%	105.0%
COGS	0.0%	100.0%	113.0%
Other exp.	0.0%	100.0%	-8.0%
Depr.	0.0%	518.8%	534.9%
EBIT	0.0%	-430.3%	140.4%
Int. Exp.	0.0%	181.6%	28.0%
EBT	0.0%	-691.1%	188.3%
Taxes	0.0%	-691.1%	188.3%
NI	0.0%	-691.1%	188.3%

3 - 37

Analysis of Percent Change Income Statement

- We see that 2002 sales grow 105% from 2000, and that NI grows 188% from 2000.
- So Computron has become more profitable.

3 - 38

Percentage Change Balance Sheets

Assets	2000	2001	2002E
Cash	0.0%	-19.1%	55.6%
ST Invest.	0.0%	-100.0%	47.4%
AR	0.0%	80.0%	150.0%
Invent.	0.0%	80.0%	140.0%
Total CA	0.0%	71.4%	138.4%
Net FA	0.0%	172.6%	137.0%
TA	0.0%	95.2%	138.1%

3 - 39

Liab. & Eq.	2000	2001	2002E
AP	0.0%	260.0%	200.0%
Notes pay.	0.0%	260.0%	200.0%
Accruals	0.0%	260.0%	200.0%
Total CL	0.0%	260.0%	200.0%
LT Debt	0.0%	209.2%	54.6%
Total equity	0.0%	-80.0%	133.9%
Total L&E	0.0%	95.2%	138.1%

3 - 40

Analysis of Percent Change Balance Sheets

- We see that total assets grow at a rate of 138%, while sales grow at a rate of only 105%. So asset utilization remains a problem.

3 - 41

Explain the Du Pont System

$$\begin{pmatrix}\text{Profit}\\ \text{margin}\end{pmatrix}\begin{pmatrix}\text{TA}\\ \text{turnover}\end{pmatrix}\begin{pmatrix}\text{Equity}\\ \text{multiplier}\end{pmatrix} = \text{ROE}$$

$$\frac{\text{NI}}{\text{Sales}} \times \frac{\text{Sales}}{\text{TA}} \times \frac{\text{TA}}{\text{CE}} = \text{ROE.}$$

2000	2.6%	x	2.3	x	2.2	=	13.2%
2001	-8.9%	x	2.0	x	21.6	=	-391.0%
2002	3.6%	x	2.0	x	2.3	=	16.3%
Ind.	3.6%	x	2.5	x	2.0	=	18.0%

3 - 42

The Du Pont system focuses on:

- Expense control (PM)
- Asset utilization (TATO)
- Debt utilization (EM)

It shows how these factors combine to determine the ROE.

3 - 43

Simplified Firm Data

A/R	$ 878	Debt	$1,945
Other CA	1,802	Equity	1,552
Net FA	817		
Total assets	$3,497	L&E	$3,497

$$\text{Sales/day} = \frac{\$7{,}035{,}600}{360} = \$19{,}543.$$

Q. How would reducing DSO to 32 days affect the company?

3 - 44

Effect of reducing DSO from 44.9 days to 32 days:

Old A/R = $19,543 x 44.9= $878,000

New A/R = $19,543 x 32.0= 625,376

Cash freed up: $252,624

Initially shows up as additional cash.

3 - 45

New Balance Sheet

Added cash	$ 253	Debt	$1,945
A/R	625	Equity	1,552
Other CA	1,802		
Net FA	817		
Total assets	$3,497	Total L&E	$3,497

What could be done with the new cash? Effect on stock price and risk?

3 - 46

Potential use of freed up cash

- Repurchase stock. Higher ROE, higher EPS.
- Expand business. Higher profits.
- Reduce debt. Better debt ratio; lower interest, hence higher NI.

(More...)

3 - 47

- Inventories are also too high. Could analyze the effect of an inventory reduction on freeing up cash and increasing the quick ratio and asset management ratios. Such an analysis would be similar to what was done with DSO in previous slides.
- All these actions would likely improve stock price.

3 - 48

Would you lend money to this company?

- Maybe. The situation could improve, and the loan, with a high interest rate to reflect the risk, could be a good investment.
- However, company should not have relied so heavily on debt financing in the past.

3 - 49

What are some potential problems and limitations of financial ratio analysis?

- Comparison with industry averages is difficult if the firm operates many different divisions.
- "Average" performance is not necessarily good.
- Seasonal factors can distort ratios.

(More...)

3 - 50

- Window dressing techniques can make statements and ratios look better.
- Different accounting and operating practices can distort comparisons.
- Sometimes it is difficult to tell if a ratio value is "good" or "bad."
- Often, different ratios give different signals, so it is difficult to tell, on balance, whether a company is in a strong or weak financial condition.

3 - 51

What are some qualitative factors analysts should consider when evaluating a company's likely future financial performance?

- Are the company's revenues tied to a single customer?
- To what extent are the company's revenues tied to a single product?
- To what extent does the company rely on a single supplier?

(More...)

3 - 52

- What percentage of the company's business is generated overseas?
- What is the competitive situation?
- What does the future have in store?
- What is the company's legal and regulatory environment?

BLUEPRINTS: CHAPTER 4

FINANCIAL PLANNING AND FORECASTING FINANCIAL STATEMENTS

Sue Wilson, the new financial manager of Northwest Chemicals (NWC), an Oregon producer of specialized chemicals for use in fruit orchards, must prepare a financial forecast for 2002. NWC's 2001 sales were $2 billion, and the marketing department is forecasting a 25 percent increase for 2002. Wilson thinks the company was operating at full capacity in 2001, but she is not sure about this. The 2001 financial statements, plus some other data, are shown below.

A. 2001 Balance Sheet (millions of dollars)

		Percent of Sales			Percent of Sales
Cash & securities	$ 20	1%	Accounts payable and accruals	$ 100	5%
Accounts receivable	240	12%	Notes payable	100	
Inventory	240	12%	Total current liabilities	$ 200	
Total current assets	$ 500		Long-term debt	100	
Net fixed assets	500	25%	Common stock	500	
			Retained earnings	200	
Total assets	$1,000		Total liabilities and equity	$1,000	

B. 2001 Income Statement (millions of dollars)

		Percent of Sales
Sales	$2,000.00	
Cost of Goods Sold (COGS)	1,200.00	60%
Sales, general, and administrative costs (SGA)	700.00	35%
Earnings before interest and taxes	$ 100.00	
Interest	16.00	
Earnings before taxes	$ 84.00	
Taxes (40%)	33.60	
Net income	$ 50.40	
Dividends (30%)	$ 15.12	
Addition to retained earnings	$ 35.28	

C. Key ratios

	NWC	Industry
Basic earning power	10.00%	20.00%
Profit margin	2.52	4.00
Return on equity	7.20	15.60
Days sales outstanding (360 days)	43.20 days	32.00 days
Inventory turnover	8.33X	11.00X
Fixed assets turnover	4.00	5.00
Total assets turnover	2.00	2.50
Debt/assets	30.00%	36.00%
Times interest earned	6.25X	9.40X
Current ratio	2.50	3.00
Payout ratio	30.00%	30.00%
Operating profit margin after taxes (NOPAT/Sales)	3.00%	5.00%
Operating capital requirement (Operating capital/Sales)	45.00	35.00
Return on invested capital (NOPAT/Operating capital)	6.67	14.00

Assume that you were recently hired as Wilson's assistant, and your first major task is to help her develop the forecast. She asked you to begin by answering the following set of questions.

a. Assume (1) that NWC was operating at full capacity in 2001 with respect to all assets, (2) that all assets must grow proportionally with sales, (3) that accounts payable and accruals will also grow in proportion to sales, and (4) that the 2001 profit margin and dividend payout will be maintained. Under these conditions, what will the company's financial requirements be for the coming year? Use the AFN equation to answer this question.

b. Now estimate the 2002 financial requirements using the percent of sales approach, making an initial forecast plus one additional "pass" to determine the effects of "financing feedbacks." Assume (1) that each type of asset, as well as payables, accruals, and fixed and variable costs, will be the same percent of sales in 2002 as in 2001; (2) that the payout ratio is held constant at 30 percent; (3) that external funds needed are financed 50 percent by notes payable and 50 percent by long-term debt (no new common stock will be issued); and (4) that all debt carries an interest rate of 8 percent.

c. Why do the two methods produce somewhat different AFN forecasts? Which method provides the more accurate forecast?

d. Calculate NWC's forecasted ratios, and compare them with the company's 2001 ratios and with the industry averages. How does NWC compare with the average firm in its industry, and is the company expected to improve during the coming year?

e. Calculate NWC's free cash flow for 2002.

f. Suppose you now learn that NWC's 2001 receivables and inventories were in line with required levels, given the firm's credit and inventory policies, but that excess capacity existed with regard to fixed assets. Specifically, fixed assets were operated at only 75 percent of capacity.

   (1) What level of sales could have existed in 2001 with the available fixed assets? What would the fixed assets/sales ratio have been if NWC had been operating at full capacity?

   (2) How would the existence of excess capacity in fixed assets affect the additional funds needed during 2002?

g. Without actually working out the numbers, how would you expect the ratios to change in the situation where excess capacity in fixed assets exists? Explain your reasoning.

h. Based on comparisons between NWC's days sales outstanding (DSO) and inventory turnover ratios with the industry average figures, does it appear that NWC is operating efficiently with respect to its inventory and accounts receivable? If the company were able to bring these ratios into line with the industry averages, what effect would this have on its AFN and its financial ratios? What effect would this have on free cash flow? (Note: Inventories and receivables will be discussed in detail in Chapter 22.)

i. The relationship between sales and the various types of assets is important in financial forecasting. The percent of sales approach, under the assumption that each asset item grows at the same rate as sales, leads to an AFN forecast that is reasonably close to the forecast using the AFN equation. Explain how each of the following factors would affect the accuracy of financial forecasts based on the AFN equation: (1) excess capacity, (2) base stocks of assets, such as shoes in a shoe store, (3) economies of scale in the use of assets, and (4) lumpy assets.

j. (1) How could regression analysis be used to detect the presence of the situations described above and then to improve the financial forecasts? Plot a graph of the following data, which is for a typical well-managed company in NWC's industry, to illustrate your answer.

	Sales	Inventories
1999	$1,280	$118
2000	1,600	138
2001	2,000	162
2002 (est.)	2,500	192

(2) On the same graph that plots the above data, draw a line which shows how the regression line must appear to justify the use of the AFN formula and the percent of sales forecasting procedure. As a part of your answer, show the growth rate in inventories that results from a 10 percent increase in sales from a sales level of (a) $200 and (b) $2,000 based on both the actual regression line and a *hypothetical* regression line which is linear and which goes through the origin.

k. How would changes in these items affect the AFN? (1) The dividend payout ratio, (2) the profit margin, (3) the capital intensity ratio, and (4) NWC begins buying from its suppliers on terms which permit it to pay after 60 days rather than after 30 days. (Consider each item separately and hold all other things constant.)

4 - 1

CHAPTER 4
Financial Planning and Forecasting Financial Statements

- Plans: strategic, operating, and financial
- Pro forma financial statements
  - Sales forecasts
  - Percent of sales method
- Additional Funds Needed (AFN) formula

4 - 2

Pro Forma Financial Statements

- Three important uses:
  - Forecast the amount of external financing that will be required
  - Evaluate the impact that changes in the operating plan have on the value of the firm
  - Set appropriate targets for compensation plans

4 - 3

Steps in Financial Forecasting

- Forecast sales
- Project the assets needed to support sales
- Project internally generated funds
- Project outside funds needed
- Decide how to raise funds
- See effects of plan on ratios and stock price

4 - 4

2001 Balance Sheet (Millions of $)

Cash & sec.	$ 20	Accts. pay. & accruals	$ 100
Accounts rec.	240	Notes payable	100
Inventories	240	Total CL	$ 200
Total CA	$ 500	L-T debt	100
		Common stk	500
Net fixed assets	500	Retained earnings	200
Total assets	$1,000	Total claims	$1,000

4 - 5

2001 Income Statement (Millions of $)

Sales	$2,000.00
Less: COGS (60%)	1,200.00
SGA costs	700.00
EBIT	$ 100.00
Interest	16.00
EBT	$ 84.00
Taxes (40%)	33.60
Net income	$ 50.40
Dividends (30%)	$15.12
Add'n to RE	$35.28

4 - 6

Key Ratios

	NWC	Industry	Condition
BEP	10.00%	20.00%	Poor
Profit Margin	2.52%	4.00%	"
ROE	7.20%	15.60%	"
DSO	43.20 days	32.00 days	"
Inv. turnover	8.33x	11.00x	"
F.A. turnover	4.00x	5.00x	"
T.A. turnover	2.00x	2.50x	"
Debt/ assets	30.00%	36.00%	Good
TIE	6.25x	9.40x	Poor
Current ratio	2.50x	3.00x	"
Payout ratio	30.00%	30.00%	O.K.

4 - 7

Key Ratios (Continued)

	NWC	Ind.	Cond.
Net oper. prof. margin after taxes (NOPAT/Sales)	3.00%	5.00%	Poor
Oper. capital requirement (Net oper. capital/Sales)	45.00%	35.00%	Poor
Return on invested capital (NOPAT/Net oper. capital)	6.67%	14.00%	Poor

4 - 8

AFN (Additional Funds Needed): Key Assumptions

- Operating at full capacity in 2001.
- Each type of asset grows proportionally with sales.
- Payables and accruals grow proportionally with sales.
- 2001 profit margin (2.52%) and payout (30%) will be maintained.
- Sales are expected to increase by $500 million. (%ΔS = 25%)

4 - 9

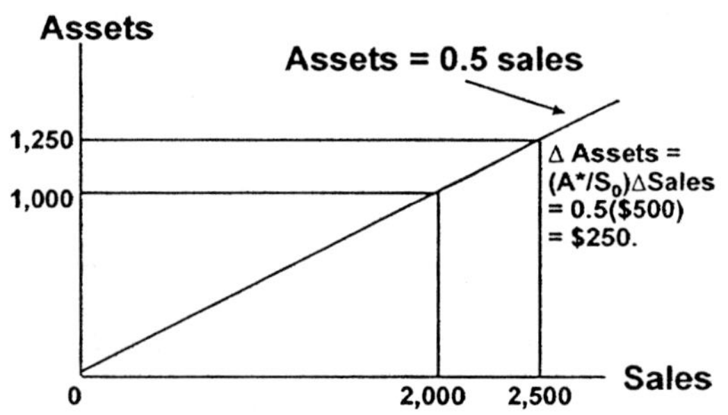

A^*/S_0 = $1,000/$2,000 = 0.5 = $1,250/$2,500.

4 - 10

Assets must increase by $250 million. What is the AFN, based on the AFN equation?

$$AFN = (A^*/S_0)\Delta S - (L^*/S_0)\Delta S - M(S_1)(1 - d)$$
$$= (\$1{,}000/\$2{,}000)(\$500)$$
$$- (\$100/\$2{,}000)(\$500)$$
$$- 0.0252(\$2{,}500)(1 - 0.3)$$
$$= \$180.9 \text{ million.}$$

4 - 11

Projecting Pro Forma Statements with the Percent of Sales Method

- Project sales based on forecasted growth rate in sales
- Forecast some items as a percent of the forecasted sales
  - Costs
  - Cash
  - Accounts receivable

(More...)

4 - 12

- Items as percent of sales (Continued...)
  - Inventories
  - Net fixed assets
  - Accounts payable and accruals
- Choose other items
  - Debt (which determines interest)
  - Dividends (which determines retained earnings)
  - Common stock

4 - 13

Percent of Sales: Inputs

	2001 Actual	2002 Proj.
COGS/Sales	60%	60%
SGA/Sales	35%	35%
Cash/Sales	1%	1%
Acct. rec./Sales	12%	12%
Inv./Sales	12%	12%
Net FA/Sales	25%	25%
AP & accr./Sales	5%	5%

4 - 14

Other Inputs

Percent growth in sales	25%
Growth factor in sales (g)	1.25
Interest rate on debt	8%
Tax rate	40%
Dividend payout rate	30%

4 - 15

2002 1st Pass Income Statement

	2001	Factor	2002 1st Pass
Sales	$2,000	g=1.25	$2,500
Less: COGS		Pct=60%	1,500
SGA		Pct=35%	875
EBIT			$125
Interest	16	→	16
EBT			$109
Taxes (40%)			44
Net. income			$65
Div. (30%)			$19
Add. to RE			$46

4 - 16

2002 1st Pass Balance Sheet (Assets)

Forecasted assets are a percent of forecasted sales.

	2002 Sales = $2,500 Factor	2002 1st Pass
Cash	Pct= 1%	$25
Accts. rec.	Pct=12%	300
Inventories	Pct=12%	300
Total CA		$625
Net FA	Pct=25%	625
Total assets		$1,250

4 - 17

2002 1st Pass Balance Sheet (Claims)

	2001	2002 Sales = $2,500 Factor	2002 1st Pass
AP/accruals		Pct=5%	$125
Notes payable	100	→	100
Total CL			$225
L-T debt	100	→	100
Common stk.	500	→	500
Ret. earnings	200	+46*	246
Total claims			$1,071

*From 1st pass income statement.

4 - 18

What are the additional funds needed (AFN)?

- Forecasted total assets = $1,250
- Forecasted total claims = $1,071
- Forecast AFN = $ 179

NWC must have the assets to make forecasted sales. The balance sheets must balance. So, we must raise $179 externally.

4 - 19

Assumptions about How AFN Will Be Raised

- No new common stock will be issued.
- Any external funds needed will be raised as debt, 50% notes payable, and 50% L-T debt.

4 - 20

How will the AFN be financed?

Additional notes payable =
0.5 ($179) = $89.50 ≈ $90.

Additional L-T debt =
0.5 ($179) = $89.50 ≈ $89.

But this financing will add 0.08($179) = $14.32 to interest expense, which will lower NI and retained earnings.

4 - 21

2002 2nd Pass Income Statement

	1st Pass	Feedback	2nd Pass
Sales	$2,500	→	
$2,500		→	
Less: COGS	1,500	→	
1,500		→	
SGA	875		875
EBIT	$ 125		$ 125
Interest	16	+14	
30			
EBT	$ 109		$ 95
Taxes (40%)	44		38
Net income	$ 65		$ 57
Div. (30%)	$ 19		$ 17

4 - 22

2002 2nd Pass Balance Sheet (Assets)

	1st Pass	AFN	2nd Pass
Cash	$25	→	$25
Accts. rec.	300	→	300
Inventories	300	→	300
Total CA	$625	→	$625
Net FA	625	→	625
Total assets	$1,250	→	$1,250

No change in asset requirements.

4 - 23

2002 2nd Pass Balance Sheet (Claims)

	1st Pass	Feedback	2nd Pass
AP/accruals	$ 125	→	$ 125
Notes payable	100	+90	
190			
Total CL	$ 225		$ 315
L-T debt	100	+89	
189			
Common stk.	500		500
Ret. earnings	246	-6	
240			
Total claims	$1,071		$1,244

4 - 24

Results After the Second Pass

- Forecasted assets = $1,250 (no change)
- Forecasted claims = $1,244 (higher)
- 2nd pass AFN = $ 6 (short)
- Cumulative AFN = $179 + $6 = $185.
- The $6 shortfall came from the $6 reduction in retained earnings. Additional passes could be made until assets exactly equal claims. $6(0.08) = $0.48 interest on 3rd pass.

4 - 25

Equation AFN = $181 vs. Pro Forma AFN = $185. Why are they different?

- Equation method assumes a constant profit margin.
- Pro forma method is more flexible. More important, it allows different items to grow at different rates.

4 - 26

Ratios After 2nd Pass

	2001	2002(E)	Industry	Cond.
BEP	10.00%	10.00%	20.00%	Poor
Profit Margin	2.52%	2.27%	4.00%	Poor
ROE	7.20%	7.68%	15.60%	Poor
DSO (days)	43.20	43.20	32.00	Poor
Inv. turnover	8.33x	8.33x	11.00x	Poor
FA turnover	4.00x	4.00x	5.00x	Poor
TA turnover	2.00x	2.00x	2.50x	Poor
D/A ratio	30.00%	40.34%	36.00%	Good
TIE	6.25x	4.12x	9.40x	Poor
Current ratio	2.50x	1.99x	3.00x	Poor
Payout ratio	30.00%	30.00%	30.00%	OK

4 - 27

Ratios after 2nd Pass (Continued)

	NWC	Ind.	Cond.
Net oper. prof. margin after taxes (NOPAT/Sales)	3.00%	5.00%	Poor
Oper. capital requirement (Net oper. capital/Sales)	45.00%	35.00%	Poor
Return on invested capital (NOPAT/Net oper. capital)	6.67%	14.00%	Poor

Note: These are the same as in 2001 (see slide 14-7), because there have been no improvements in operations (i.e., all percent of sales items have same percentages in 2001 and 2002). Also, there are no differences between 1st pass and 2nd pass because changes in financing do not affect measures of operating performance.

4 - 28

What is the forecasted free cash flow for 2002?

	2001	2002(E)
Net operating WC (CA - AP & accruals)	$400	$500
Total operating capital (Net op. WC + net FA)	$900	$1,125
NOPAT (EBITx(1-T))	$60	$75
Less Inv. in op. capital		$225
Free cash flow		-$150

4 - 29

Suppose in 2001 fixed assets had been operated at only 75% of capacity.

$$\text{Capacity sales} = \frac{\text{Actual sales}}{\text{\% of capacity}}$$

$$= \frac{\$2,000}{0.75} = \$2,667.$$

With the existing fixed assets, sales could be $2,667. Since sales are forecasted at only $2,500, no new fixed assets are needed.

4 - 30

How would the excess capacity situation affect the 2002 AFN?

- The projected increase in fixed assets was $125, the AFN would decrease by $125.
- Since no new fixed assets will be needed, AFN (based on second pass) will fall by $125, to

  $185 - $125 = $60.

4 - 31

Q. If sales went up to $3,000, not $2,500, what would the F.A. requirement be?

A. Target ratio = FA/Capacity sales
= $500/$2,667 = 18.75%.

Have enough F.A. for sales up to $2,667, but need F.A. for another $333 of sales:

ΔFA = 0.1875($333) = $62.4.

4 - 32

How would excess capacity affect the forecasted ratios?

1. Sales wouldn't change but assets would be lower, so turnovers would be better.
2. Less new debt, hence lower interest, so higher profits, EPS, ROE (when financing feedbacks considered).
3. Debt ratio, TIE would improve.

4 - 33

2002 Forecasted Ratios: S_{02} = $2,500

	% of 2001 Capacity		
	100%	75%	Industry
BEP	10.00%	11.11%	20.00%
Profit Margin	2.27%	2.51%	4.00%
ROE	7.68%	8.44%	15.60%
DSO (days)	43.20	43.20	32.00
Inv. turnover	8.33x	8.33x	11.00x
F.A. turnover	4.00x	5.00x	5.00x
T.A. turnover	2.00x	2.22x	2.50x
D/A ratio	40.34%	33.71%	36.00%
TIE	4.12x	6.15x	9.40x
Current ratio	1.99x	2.48x	3.00x

4 - 34

How is NWC performing with regard to its receivables and inventories?

- DSO is higher than the industry average, and inventory turnover is lower than the industry average.
- Improvements here would lower current assets, reduce capital requirements, and further improve profitability and other ratios.

4 - 35

Improvements in Working Capital Management

	Before	After
DSO (days)	43.20	32.00
Accts. rec./Sales	12.00%	8.89%
Inventory turnover	8.33x	11.00x
Inventory/Sales	12.00%	9.09%

4 - 36

Impact of Improvements in Working Capital Management

	Before	After
Free cash flow (1999)	-$150.0	$0.5
ROIC (NOPAT/Capital)	6.7%	7.7%
ROE	7.7%	8.59%

4 - 37

Declining A/S Ratio

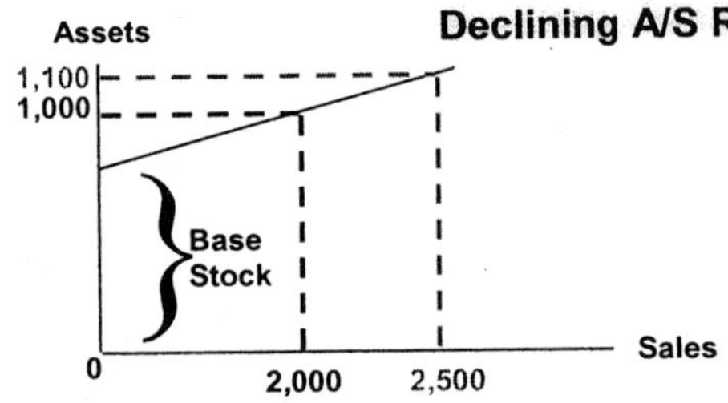

$1,000/$2,000 = 0.5; $1,100/$2,500 = 0.44. Declining ratio shows economies of scale. **Going from S = $0 to S = $2,000 requires $1,000 of assets. Next $500 of sales requires only $100 of assets.**

4 - 38

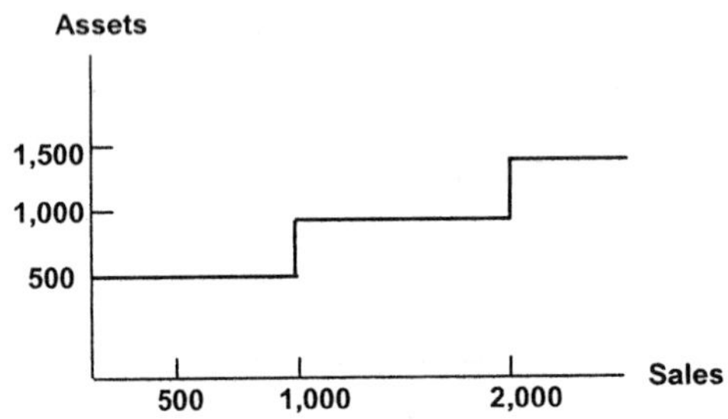

A/S changes if assets are lumpy. Generally will have excess capacity, but eventually a small ΔS leads to a large ΔA.

4 - 39

Summary: How different factors affect the AFN forecast.

- Excess capacity:
  - Existence lowers AFN.
- Base stocks of assets:
  - Leads to less-than-proportional asset increases.
- Economies of scale:
  - Also leads to less-than-proportional asset increases.
- Lumpy assets:
  - Leads to large periodic AFN requirements, recurring excess capacity.

4 - 40

Regression Analysis for Asset Forecasting

- Get historical data on a good company, then fit a regression line to see how much a given sales increase will require in way of asset increase.

4 - 41

Example of Regression

For a Well-Managed Co.

Year	Sales	Inv.
1999	$1,280	$118
2000	1,600	138
2001	2,000	162
2002E	2,500E	192E

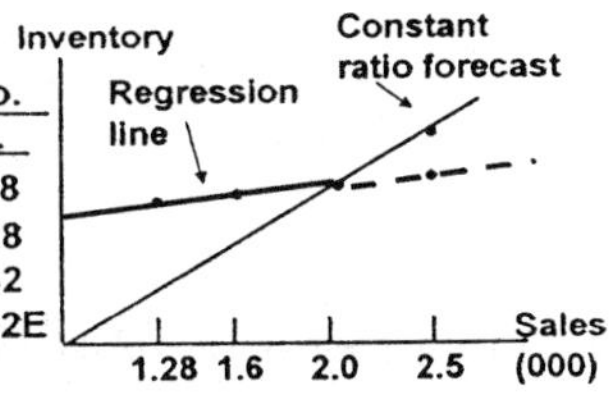

Constant ratio overestimates inventory required to go from S_1 = \$2,000 to S_2 = \$2,500.

4 - 42

Regression with 10B for Our Example

- Same as finding beta coefficients.
- Clear all

1280 Input 118Σ+
1600 Input 138Σ+
2000 Input 162Σ+
0 ■ ŷ, m → 40.0 = Inventory at sales = 0.
■ SWAP → 0.0611 = Slope coefficient.
Inventory = 40.0 + 0.0611 Sales.
LEAVE CALCULATOR ALONE!

4 - 43

Equation is now in the calculator. Let's use it by inputting new sales of $2,500 and getting forecasted inventory:

2500 ■ $\hat{y}$, m ⟶ 192.66.

The constant ratio forecast was inventory = $300, so the regression forecast is lower by $107. This would free up $107 for use elsewhere, which would improve profitability and raise P_0.

4 - 44

How would increases in these items affect the AFN?

- Higher dividend payout ratio?

  Increase AFN: Less retained earnings.

- Higher profit margin?

  Decrease AFN: Higher profits, more retained earnings.

(More...)

4 - 45

- Higher capital intensity ratio, A^*/S_0?

  Increase AFN: Need more assets for given sales increase.

- Pay suppliers in 60 days rather than 30 days?

  Decrease AFN: Trade creditors supply more capital, i.e., L^*/S_0 increases.

BLUEPRINTS: CHAPTER 5

THE FINANCIAL ENVIRONMENT: MARKETS, INSTITUTIONS, AND INTEREST RATES

Assume that you recently graduated with a degree in finance and have just reported to work as an investment advisor at the brokerage firm of Balik and Kiefer Inc. Your first assignment is to explain the nature of the U.S. financial markets to Michelle DellaTorre, a professional tennis player who has just come to the United States from Chile. DellaTorre is a highly ranked tennis player who expects to invest substantial amounts of money through Balik and Kiefer. She is also very bright, and, therefore, she would like to understand in general terms what will happen to her money. Your boss has developed the following set of questions which you must ask and answer to explain the U.S. financial system to DellaTorre.

a. What is a market? How are physical asset markets differentiated from financial markets?

b. Differentiate between money markets and capital markets.

c. Differentiate between a primary market and a secondary market. If Apple Computer decided to issue additional common stock, and DellaTorre purchased 100 shares of this stock from Merrill Lynch, the underwriter, would this transaction be a primary market transaction or a secondary market transaction? Would it make a difference if DellaTorre purchased previously outstanding Apple stock in the Nasdaq market?

d. Describe the three primary ways in which capital is transferred between savers and borrowers.

e. Securities can be traded on organized exchanges or in the over-the-counter market. Define each of these markets, and describe how stocks are traded in each of them.

f. What do we call the price that a borrower must pay for debt capital? What is the price of equity capital? What are the four most fundamental factors that affect the cost of money, or the general level of interest rates, in the economy?

g. What is the real risk-free rate of interest (k^*) and the nominal risk-free rate (k_{RF})? How are these two rates measured?

h. Define the terms inflation premium (IP), default risk premium (DRP), liquidity premium (LP), and maturity risk premium (MRP). Which of these premiums is included when determining the interest rate on (1) short-term U.S. Treasury securities, (2) long-term U.S. Treasury securities, (3) short-term corporate securities, and (4) long-term corporate securities? Explain how the premiums would vary over time and among the different securities listed above.

i. What is the term structure of interest rates? What is a yield curve?

j. Suppose most investors expect the inflation rate to be 5 percent next year, 6 percent the following year, and 8 percent thereafter. The real risk-free rate is 3 percent. The maturity risk premium is zero for securities that mature in 1 year or less, 0.1 percent for 2-year securities, and then the MRP increases by 0.1 percent per year thereafter for 20 years, after which it is stable. What is the interest rate on 1-year, 10-year, and 20-year Treasury securities? Draw a yield curve with these data. What factors can explain why this constructed yield curve is upward sloping?

k. At any given time, how would the yield curve facing an AAA-rated company compare with the yield curve for U.S. Treasury securities? At any given time, how would the yield curve facing a BB-rated company compare with the yield curve for U.S. Treasury securities? Draw a graph to illustrate your answer.

l. What is the pure expectations theory? What does the pure expectations theory imply about the term structure of interest rates?

m. Suppose that you observe the following term structure for Treasury securities:

Maturity	Yield
1 year	6.0%
2 years	6.2
3 years	6.4
4 years	6.5
5 years	6.5

Assume the pure expectations theory of the term structure is correct. This implies that you can use the yield curve given above to "back out" the market's expectations about future interest rates. What does the market expect will be the interest rate on 3-year securities, two years from now?

n. Finally, DellaTorre is also interested in investing in countries other than the United States. Describe the various types of risks that arise when investing overseas.

5 - 1

CHAPTER 5
The Financial Environment: Markets, Institutions, and Interest Rates

- Financial markets
- Types of financial institutions
- Determinants of interest rates
- Yield curves

5 - 2

Define these markets

- Markets in general
- Markets for physical assets
- Markets for financial assets
- Money versus capital markets
- Primary versus secondary markets
- Spot versus future markets

5 - 3

Three Primary Ways Capital Is Transferred Between Savers and Borrowers

- Direct transfer
- Through an investment banking house
- Through a financial intermediary

5 - 4

The Top 5 Banking Companies in the World, 1999

Bank Name	Country	Total assets
Deutsche Bank AG	Germany	$735 billion
UBS Group	Switzerland	$687 billion
Citigroup	United States	$669 billion
Bank of America	United States	$618 billion
Bank of Tokyo	Japan	$580 billion

5 - 5

Organized Exchanges versus Over-the-Counter Market

- Auction markets versus dealer markets (exchanges versus the OTC market)
- NYSE versus Nasdaq system
- Differences are narrowing
- Nasdaq vs. true OTC

5 - 6

- What do we call the price, or cost, of debt capital?

The interest rate

- What do we call the price, or cost, of equity capital?

Required return = Dividend yield + Capital gain.

5 - 7

What four factors affect the cost of money?

- Production opportunities
- Time preferences for consumption
- Risk
- Expected inflation

5 - 8

Real versus Nominal Rates

k^* = Real risk-free rate. T-bond rate if no inflation; 1% to 4%.

k = Any nominal rate.

k_{RF} = Rate on Treasury securities.

5 - 9

$$k = k^* + IP + DRP + LP + MRP.$$

Here:

k = Required rate of return on a debt security.

k^* = Real risk-free rate.

IP = Inflation premium.

DRP = Default risk premium.

LP = Liquidity premium.

MRP = Maturity risk premium.

5 - 10

Premiums Added to k* for Different Types of Debt

- ST Treasury: only IP for ST inflation
- LT Treasury: IP for LT inflation, MRP
- ST corporate: ST IP, DRP, LP
- LT corporate: IP, DRP, MRP, LP

5 - 11

What is the "term structure of interest rates"? What is a "yield curve"?

- Term structure: the relationship between interest rates (or yields) and maturities.
- A graph of the term structure is called the yield curve.

5 - 12

Treasury Yield Curve

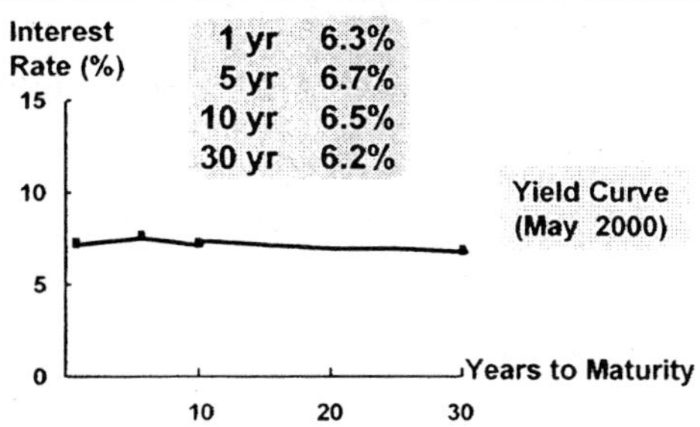

5 - 13

Yield Curve Construction

Step 1: Find the average expected inflation rate over years 1 to n:

$$IP_n = \frac{\sum_{t=1}^{n} INFL_t}{n}.$$

5 - 14

$IP_1 = 5\%/1.0 = 5.00\%$.

$IP_{10} = [5 + 6 + 8(8)]/10 = 7.5\%$.

$IP_{20} = [5 + 6 + 8(18)]/20 = 7.75\%$.

Must earn these IPs to break even versus inflation; that is, these IPs would permit you to earn k* (before taxes).

5 - 15

Step 2: Find MRP based on this equation:

$$MRP_t = 0.1\%(t - 1).$$

$MRP_1 = 0.1\% \times 0 = 0.0\%$.

$MRP_{10} = 0.1\% \times 9 = 0.9\%$.

$MRP_{20} = 0.1\% \times 19 = 1.9\%$.

5 - 16

Step 3: Add the IPs and MRPs to k*:

$$k_{RF_t} = k^* + IP_t + MRP_t.$$

k_{RF} = Quoted market interest rate on treasury securities.

Assume k* = 3%:

k_{RF1} = 3% + 5% + 0.0% = 8.0%.
k_{RF10} = 3% + 7.5% + 0.9% = 11.4%.
k_{RF20} = 3% + 7.75% + 1.9% = 12.65%.

5 - 17

Hypothetical Treasury Yield Curve

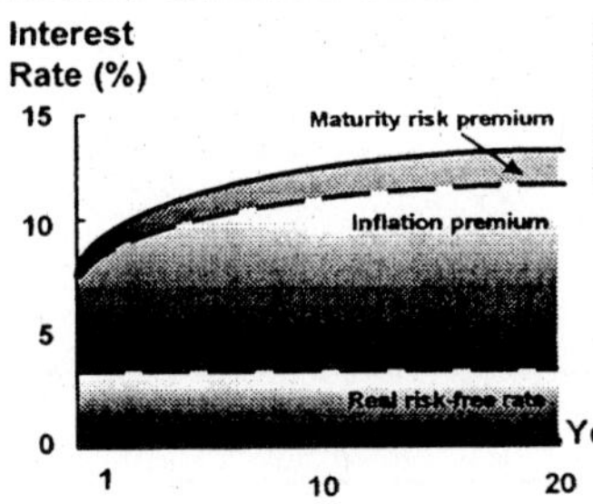

Years to Maturity

1 yr	8.0%
10 yr	11.4%
20 yr	12.65%

5 - 18

What factors can explain the shape of this yield curve?

- This constructed yield curve is upward sloping.
- This is due to increasing expected inflation and an increasing maturity risk premium.

5 - 19

What kind of relationship exists between the Treasury yield curve and the yield curves for corporate issues?

- Corporate yield curves are higher than that of the Treasury bond. However, corporate yield curves are not necessarily parallel to the Treasury curve.
- The spread between a corporate yield curve and the Treasury curve widens as the corporate bond rating decreases.

5 - 20

Hypothetical Treasury and Corporate Yield Curves

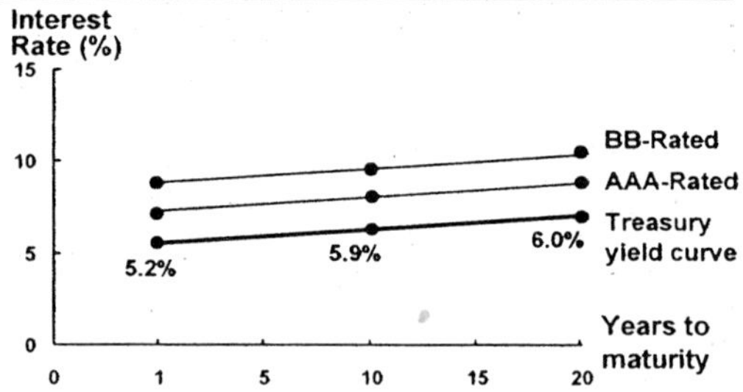

5 - 21

How does the volume of corporate bond issues compare to that of Treasury securities?

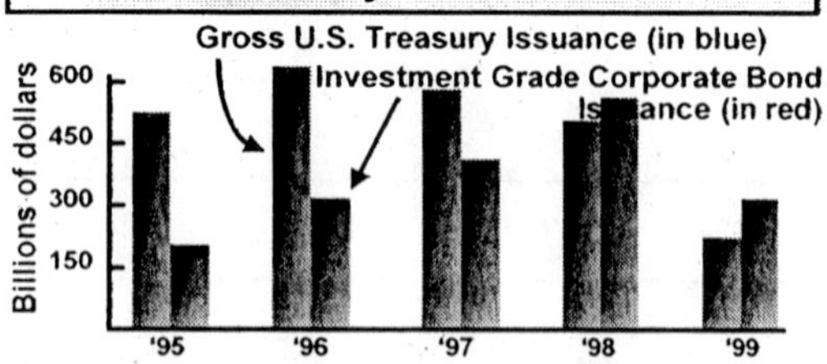

Recently, the volume of investment grade corporate bond issues has overtaken Treasury issues.

5 - 22

The Pure Expectations Hypothesis (PEH)

- Shape of the yield curve depends on the investors' expectations about future interest rates.
- If interest rates are expected to increase, L-T rates will be higher than S-T rates and vice versa. Thus, the yield curve can slope up or down.

5 - 23

- PEH assumes that MRP = 0.
- Long-term rates are an average of current and future short-term rates.
- If PEH is correct, you can use the yield curve to "back out" expected future interest rates.

5 - 24

Observed Treasury Rates

Maturity	Yield
1 year	6.0%
2 years	6.2%
3 years	6.4%
4 years	6.5%
5 years	6.5%

If PEH holds, what does the market expect will be the interest rate on one-year securities, one year from now? Three-year securities, two years from now?

5 - 25

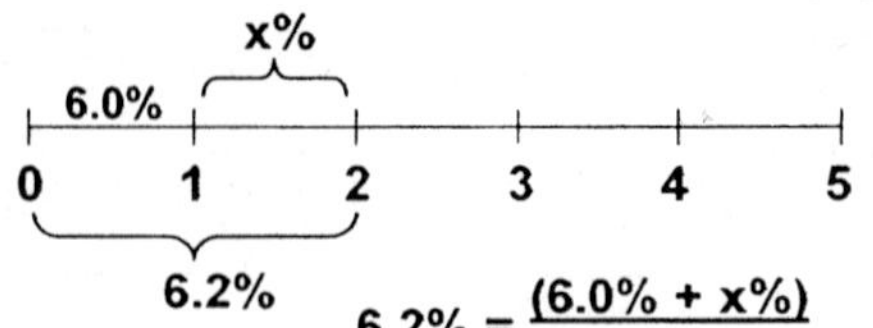

$$6.2\% = \frac{(6.0\% + x\%)}{2}$$

$$12.4\% = 6.0 + x\%$$

$$6.4\% = x\%.$$

PEH tells us that one-year securities will yield 6.4%, one year from now (x%).

5 - 26

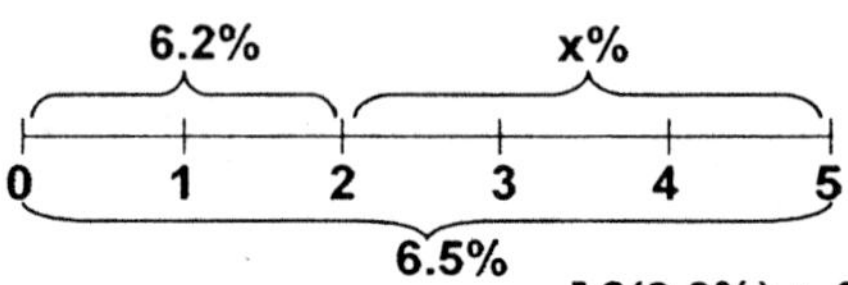

$$6.5\% = \frac{[\,2(6.2\%) + 3(x\%)\,]}{5}$$

$$32.5\% = 12.4\% + 3(x\%)$$

$$20.1\% = 3(x\%)$$

$$6.7\% = x\%.$$

PEH tells us that three-year securities will yield 6.7%, two years from now (x%).

5 - 27

Conclusions about PEH

- **Some argue that the PEH isn't correct, because securities of different maturities have different risk.**
- **General view (supported by most evidence) is that lenders prefer S-T securities, and view L-T securities as riskier.**
- **Thus, investors demand a MRP to get them to hold L-T securities (i.e., MRP > 0).**

5 - 28

What various types of risks arise when investing overseas?

Country risk: Arises from investing or doing business in a particular country. It depends on the country's economic, political, and social environment.

Exchange rate risk: If investment is denominated in a currency other than the dollar, the investment's value will depend on what happens to exchange rate.

5 - 29

Two Factors Lead to Exchange Rate Fluctuations

- Changes in relative inflation will lead to changes in exchange rates.
- An increase in country risk will also cause that country's currency to fall.

BLUEPRINTS: CHAPTER 6

RISK AND RETURN: THE BASICS

Assume that you recently graduated with a major in finance, and you just landed a job as a financial planner with Merrill Finch Inc., a large financial services corporation. Your first assignment is to invest $100,000 for a client. Because the funds are to be invested in a business at the end of one year, you have been instructed to plan for a one-year holding period. Further, your boss has restricted you to the following investment alternatives, shown with their probabilities and associated outcomes. (Disregard for now the items at the bottom of the data; you will fill in the blanks later.)

		Returns on Alternative Investments					
		Estimated Rate of Return					
State of the Economy	Prob.	T-Bills	High Tech	Collections	U.S. Rubber	Market Portfolio	2-stock Portfolio
Recession	0.1	8.0%	-22.0%	28.0%	10.0%*	-13.0%	3.0%
Below avg	0.2	8.0	-2.0	14.7	-10.0	1.0	
Average	0.4	8.0	20.0	0.0	7.0	15.0	10.0%
Above avg	0.2	8.0	35.0	-10.0	45.0	29.0	
Boom	0.1	8.0	50.0	-20.0	30.0	43.0	15.0
k-Hat ($\hat{k}$)				1.7%	13.8%	15.0%	
Std dev (σ)		0.0		13.4	18.8	15.3	
Coef of var (CV)				7.9	1.4	1.0	
Beta (b)				-0.86	0.68		

* Note that the estimated returns of U.S. Rubber do not always move in the same direction as the overall economy. For example, when the economy is below average, consumers purchase fewer tires than they would if the economy was stronger. However, if the economy is in a flat-out recession, a large number of consumers who were planning to purchase a new car may choose to wait and instead purchase new tires for the car they currently own. Under these circumstances, we would expect U.S. Rubber's stock price to be higher if there is a recession than if the economy was just below average.

Merrill Finch's economic forecasting staff has developed probability estimates for the state of the economy, and its security analysts have developed a sophisticated computer program which was used to estimate the rate of return on each alternative under each state of the economy. High Tech Inc. is an electronics firm; Collections Inc. collects past-due debts; and U.S. Rubber manufactures tires and various other rubber and plastics products. Merrill Finch also maintains an "index fund" which owns a market-weighted fraction of all publicly traded stocks; you can invest in that fund, and thus obtain average stock market results. Given the situation as described, answer the following questions.

a. What are investment returns? What is the return on an investment that costs $1,000 and is sold after one year for $1,100?

b. (1) Why is the T-bill's return independent of the state of the economy? Do T-bills promise a completely risk-free return?

(2) Why are High Tech's returns expected to move with the economy whereas Collections' are expected to move counter to the economy?

c. Calculate the expected rate of return on each alternative and fill in the blanks on the row for $\hat{k}$ in the table above.

d. You should recognize that basing a decision solely on expected returns is only appropriate for risk-neutral individuals. Since your client, like virtually everyone, is risk averse, the riskiness of each alternative is an important aspect of the decision. One possible measure of risk is the standard deviation of returns.

(1) Calculate this value for each alternative, and fill in the blank on the row for σ in the table above.

(2) What type of risk is measured by the standard deviation?

(3) Draw a graph which shows *roughly* the shape of the probability distributions for High Tech, U.S. Rubber, and T-bills.

e. Suppose you suddenly remembered that the coefficient of variation (CV) is generally regarded as being a better measure of stand-alone risk than the standard deviation when the alternatives being considered have widely differing expected returns. Calculate the missing CVs and fill in the blanks on the row for CV in the table above. Does the CV produce the same risk rankings as the standard deviation?

f. Suppose you created a 2-stock portfolio by investing $50,000 in High Tech and $50,000 in Collections.

(1) Calculate the expected return $(\hat{k}_p)$, the standard deviation (σ_p), and the coefficient of variation (CV_p) for this portfolio and fill in the appropriate blanks in the table above.

(2) How does the risk of this 2-stock portfolio compare with the risk of the individual stocks if they were held in isolation?

g. Suppose an investor starts with a portfolio consisting of one randomly selected stock. What would happen (1) to the risk and (2) to the expected return of the portfolio as more and more randomly selected stocks were added to the portfolio? What is the implication for investors? Draw a graph of the two portfolios to illustrate your answer.

h. (1) Should portfolio effects impact the way investors think about the risk of individual stocks?

(2) If you decided to hold a 1-stock portfolio, and consequently were exposed to more risk than diversified investors, could you expect to be compensated for all of your risk; that is, could you earn a risk premium on that part of your risk that you could have eliminated by diversifying?

i. How is risk measured for individual securities? How are beta coefficients calculated?

j. Suppose you have the following historical returns for the stock market and for another company, K. W. Enterprises. Explain how to calculate beta, and use the historical stock returns to calculate the beta for KWE. Interpret your results.

Year	Market	KWE
1	25.7%	40.0%
2	8.0	-15.0
3	-11.0	-15.0
4	15.0	35.0
5	32.5	10.0
6	13.7	30.0
7	40.0	42.0
8	10.0	-10.0
9	-10.8	25.0
10	-13.1	25.0

k. The expected rates of return and the beta coefficients of the alternatives as supplied by Merrill Finch's computer program are as follows:

Security	Return ($\hat{k}$)	Risk (Beta)
High Tech	17.4%	1.29
Market	15.0	1.00
U.S. Rubber	13.8	0.68
T-bills	8.0	0.00
Collections	1.7	(0.86)

(1) Do the expected returns appear to be related to each alternative's market risk?

(2) Is it possible to choose among the alternatives on the basis of the information developed thus far?

l. (1) Write out the Security Market Line (SML) equation, use it to calculate the required rate of return on each alternative, and then graph the relationship between the expected and required rates of return.

(2) How do the expected rates of return compare with the required rates of return?

(3) Does the fact that Collections has an expected return which is less than the T-bill rate make any sense?

(4) What would be the market risk and the required return of a 50-50 portfolio of High Tech and Collections? Of High Tech and U.S. Rubber?

m. (1) Suppose investors raised their inflation expectations by 3 percentage points over current estimates as reflected in the 8 percent T-bill rate. What effect would higher inflation have on the SML and on the returns required on high- and low-risk securities?

(2) Suppose instead that investors' risk aversion increased enough to cause the market risk premium to increase by 3 percentage points. (Inflation remains constant.) What effect would this have on the SML and on returns of high- and low-risk securities?

6 - 1

CHAPTER 6
Risk and Return: The Basics

- Basic return concepts
- Basic risk concepts
- Stand-alone risk
- Portfolio (market) risk
- Risk and return: CAPM/SML

6 - 2

What are investment returns?

- Investment returns measure the financial results of an investment.
- Returns may be historical or prospective (anticipated).
- Returns can be expressed in:
  - Dollar terms.
  - Percentage terms.

6 - 3

What is the return on an investment that costs $1,000 and is sold after 1 year for $1,100?

- Dollar return:

  $ Received - $ Invested
  $1,100 - $1,000 = $100.

- Percentage return:

  $ Return/$ Invested
  $100/$1,000 = 0.10 = 10%.

6 - 4

What is investment risk?

- Typically, investment returns are not known with certainty.
- Investment risk pertains to the probability of earning a return less than that expected.
- The greater the chance of a return far below the expected return, the greater the risk.

6 - 5

Probability distribution

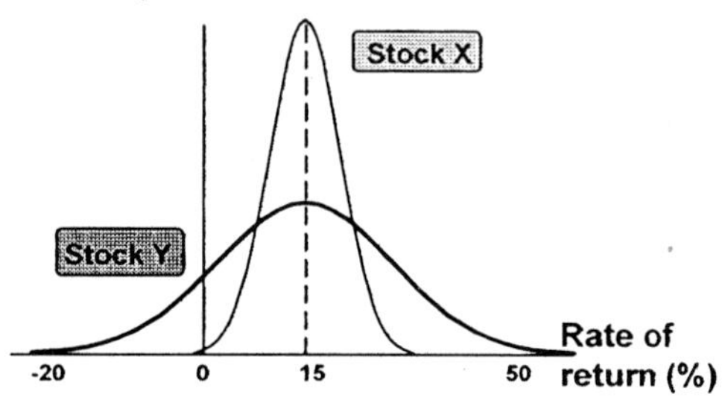

- Which stock is riskier? Why?

6 - 6

Assume the Following Investment Alternatives

Economy	Prob.	T-Bill	HT	Coll	USR	MP
Recession	0.10	8.0%	-22.0%	28.0%	10.0%	-13.0%
Below avg.	0.20	8.0	-2.0	14.7	-10.0	1.0
Average	0.40	8.0	20.0	0.0	7.0	15.0
Above avg.	0.20	8.0	35.0	-10.0	45.0	29.0
Boom	0.10	8.0	50.0	-20.0	30.0	43.0
	1.00					

6 - 7

What is unique about the T-bill return?

- The T-bill will return 8% regardless of the state of the economy.
- Is the T-bill riskless? Explain.

6 - 8

Do the returns of HT and Collections move with or counter to the economy?

- HT moves with the economy, so it is positively correlated with the economy. This is the typical situation.
- Collections moves counter to the economy. Such negative correlation is unusual.

6 - 9

Calculate the expected rate of return on each alternative.

$\hat{k}$ = expected rate of return.

$$\hat{k} = \sum_{i=1}^{n} k_i P_i.$$

$$\hat{k}_{HT} = 0.10(-22\%) + 0.20(-2\%) + 0.40(20\%) + 0.20(35\%) + 0.10(50\%) = 17.4\%.$$

6 - 10

	$\hat{k}$
HT	17.4%
Market	15.0
USR	13.8
T-bill	8.0
Collections	1.7

- HT has the highest rate of return.
- Does that make it best?

6 - 11

What is the standard deviation of returns for each alternative?

σ = Standard deviation

$$\sigma = \sqrt{\text{Variance}} = \sqrt{\sigma^2} = \sqrt{\sum_{i=1}^{n}\left(k_i - \hat{k}\right)^2 P_i}.$$

6 - 12

$$\sigma = \sqrt{\sum_{i=1}^{n}\left(k_i - \hat{k}\right)^2 P_i}.$$

HT:

$\sigma = ((-22 - 17.4)^2 0.10 + (-2 - 17.4)^2 0.20 + (20 - 17.4)^2 0.40 + (35 - 17.4)^2 0.20 + (50 - 17.4)^2 0.10)^{1/2} = 20.0\%.$

$\sigma_{T\text{-bills}} = 0.0\%.$ $\sigma_{Coll} = 13.4\%.$
$\sigma_{HT} = 20.0\%.$ $\sigma_{USR} = 18.8\%.$
$\sigma_M = 15.3\%.$

6 - 13

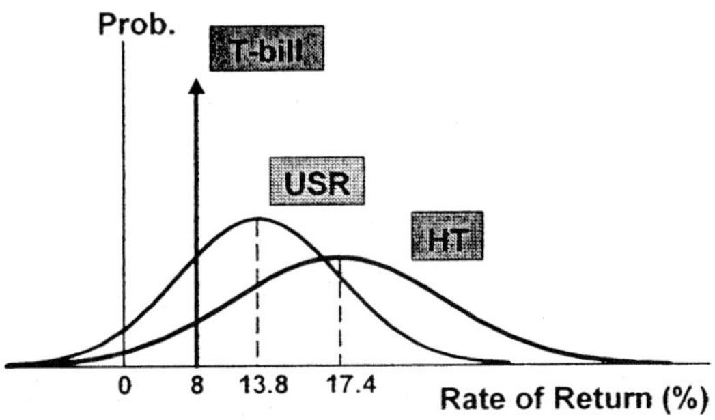

6 - 14

- Standard deviation measures the stand-alone risk of an investment.
- The larger the standard deviation, the higher the probability that returns will be far below the expected return.
- Coefficient of variation is an alternative measure of stand-alone risk.

6 - 15

Expected Return versus Risk

Security	Expected return	Risk, σ
HT	17.4%	20.0%
Market	15.0	15.3
USR	13.8	18.8
T-bills	8.0	0.0
Collections	1.7	13.4

- Which alternative is best?

6 - 16

Portfolio Risk and Return

Assume a two-stock portfolio with \$50,000 in HT and \$50,000 in Collections.

Calculate $\hat{k}_p$ and σ_p.

6 - 17

Portfolio Return, $\hat{k}_p$

$\hat{k}_p$ is a weighted average:

$$\hat{k}_p = \sum_{i=1}^{n} w_i \hat{k}_i.$$

$\hat{k}_p = 0.5(17.4\%) + 0.5(1.7\%) = 9.6\%.$

$\hat{k}_p$ is between $\hat{k}_{HT}$ and $\hat{k}_{Coll}$.

6 - 18

Alternative Method

		Estimated Return		
Economy	Prob.	HT	Coll.	Port.
Recession	0.10	-22.0%	28.0%	3.0%
Below avg.	0.20	-2.0	14.7	6.4
Average	0.40	20.0	0.0	10.0
Above avg.	0.20	35.0	-10.0	12.5
Boom	0.10	50.0	-20.0	15.0

$\hat{k}_p = (3.0\%)0.10 + (6.4\%)0.20 + (10.0\%)0.40 + (12.5\%)0.20 + (15.0\%)0.10 = 9.6\%.$

(More...)

6 - 19

- $\sigma_p = ((3.0 - 9.6)^2 0.10 + (6.4 - 9.6)^2 0.20 + (10.0 - 9.6)^2 0.40 + (12.5 - 9.6)^2 0.20 + (15.0 - 9.6)^2 0.10)^{1/2} = 3.3\%$.
- σ_p is much lower than:
  - either stock (20% and 13.4%).
  - average of HT and Coll (16.7%).
- The portfolio provides average return but much lower risk. The key here is negative correlation.

6 - 20

Two-Stock Portfolios

- Two stocks can be combined to form a riskless portfolio if r = -1.0.
- Risk is not reduced at all if the two stocks have r = +1.0.
- In general, stocks have $r \approx 0.65$, so risk is lowered but not eliminated.
- Investors typically hold many stocks.
- What happens when r = 0?

6 - 21

What would happen to the risk of an average 1-stock portfolio as more randomly selected stocks were added?

- σ_p would decrease because the added stocks would not be perfectly correlated, but $\hat{k}_p$ would remain relatively constant.

6 - 22

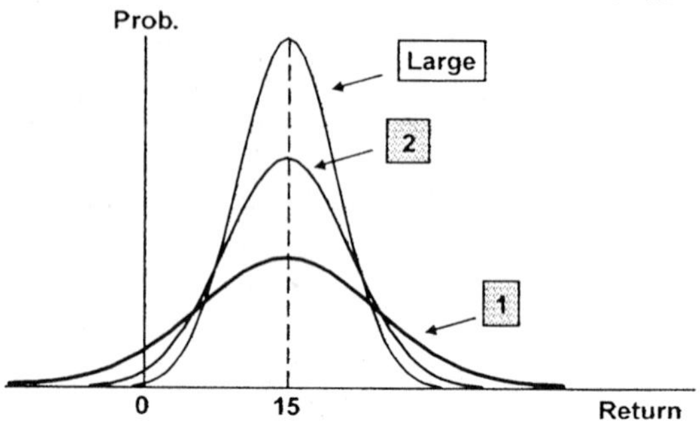

$\sigma_1 \approx 35\%$; $\sigma_{Large} \approx 20\%$.

6 - 23

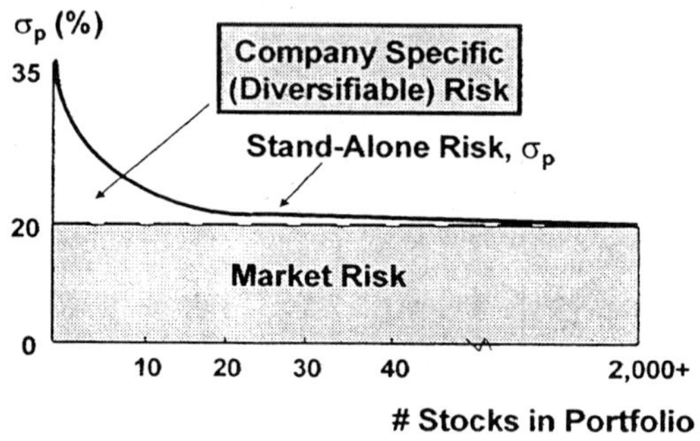

6 - 24

Stand-alone risk = Market risk + Diversifiable risk.

Market risk is that part of a security's stand-alone risk that *cannot* be eliminated by diversification.

Firm-specific, or diversifiable, risk is that part of a security's stand-alone risk that *can* be eliminated by diversification.

6 - 25

Conclusions

- As more stocks are added, each new stock has a smaller risk-reducing impact on the portfolio.
- σ_p falls very slowly after about 40 stocks are included. The lower limit for σ_p is about 20% = σ_M .
- By forming well-diversified portfolios, investors can eliminate about half the riskiness of owning a single stock.

6 - 26

Can an investor holding one stock earn a return commensurate with its risk?

- No. Rational investors will minimize risk by holding portfolios.
- They bear only market risk, so prices and returns reflect this lower risk.
- The one-stock investor bears higher (stand-alone) risk, so the return is less than that required by the risk.

6 - 27

How is market risk measured for individual securities?

- Market risk, which is relevant for stocks held in well-diversified portfolios, is defined as the contribution of a security to the overall riskiness of the portfolio.
- It is measured by a stock's beta coefficient, which measures the stock's volatility relative to the market.
- What is the relevant risk for a stock held in isolation?

6 - 28

How are betas calculated?

- Run a regression with returns on the stock in question plotted on the Y axis and returns on the market portfolio plotted on the X axis.
- The slope of the regression line, which measures relative volatility, is defined as the stock's beta coefficient, or b.

6 - 29

Use the historical stock returns to calculate the beta for KWE.

Year	Market	KWE
1	25.7%	40.0%
2	8.0%	-15.0%
3	-11.0%	-15.0%
4	15.0%	35.0%
5	32.5%	10.0%
6	13.7%	30.0%
7	40.0%	42.0%
8	10.0%	-10.0%
9	-10.8%	-25.0%
10	-13.1%	25.0%

6 - 30

Calculating Beta for KWE

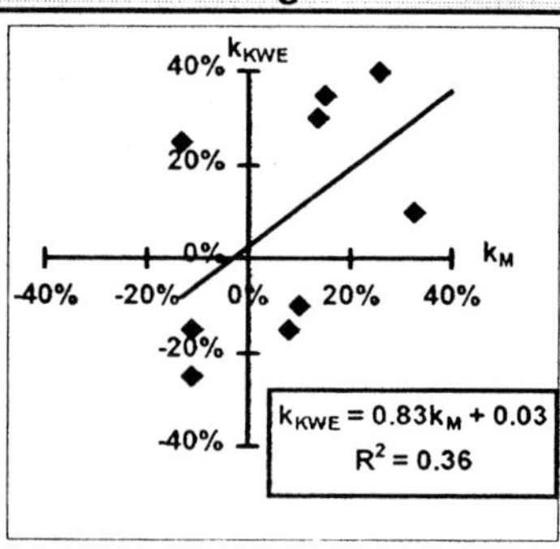

6 - 31

How is beta calculated?

- The regression line, and hence beta, can be found using a calculator with a regression function or a spreadsheet program. In this example, b = 0.83.
- Analysts typically use four or five years' of monthly returns to establish the regression line. Some use 52 weeks of weekly returns.

6 - 32

How is beta interpreted?

- If b = 1.0, stock has average risk.
- If b > 1.0, stock is riskier than average.
- If b < 1.0, stock is less risky than average.
- Most stocks have betas in the range of 0.5 to 1.5.
- Can a stock have a negative beta?

6 - 33

Expected Return versus Market Risk

Security	Expected return	Risk, b
HT	17.4%	1.29
Market	15.0	1.00
USR	13.8	0.68
T-bills	8.0	0.00
Collections	1.7	-0.86

- Which of the alternatives is best?

6 - 34

Use the SML to calculate each alternative's required return.

- The Security Market Line (SML) is part of the Capital Asset Pricing Model (CAPM).
- SML: $k_i = k_{RF} + (RP_M)b_i$.
- Assume $k_{RF} = 8\%$; $\hat{k}_M = k_M = 15\%$.
- $RP_M = (k_M - k_{RF}) = 15\% - 8\% = 7\%$.

6 - 35

Required Rates of Return

$$k_{HT} = 8.0\% + (7\%)(1.29)$$
$$= 8.0\% + 9.0\% = 17.0\%.$$
$$k_M = 8.0\% + (7\%)(1.00) = 15.0\%.$$
$$k_{USR} = 8.0\% + (7\%)(0.68) = 12.8\%.$$
$$k_{T\text{-}bill} = 8.0\% + (7\%)(0.00) = 8.0\%.$$
$$k_{Coll} = 8.0\% + (7\%)(-0.86) = 2.0\%.$$

6 - 36

Expected versus Required Returns

	$\hat{k}$	k	
HT	17.4%	17.0%	Undervalued
Market	15.0	15.0	Fairly valued
USR	13.8	12.8	Undervalued
T-bills	8.0	8.0	Fairly valued
Coll	1.7	2.0	Overvalued

6 - 37

k_i (%) SML: $k_i = k_{RF} + (RP_M)\, b_i$
$k_i = 8\% + (7\%)\, b_i$

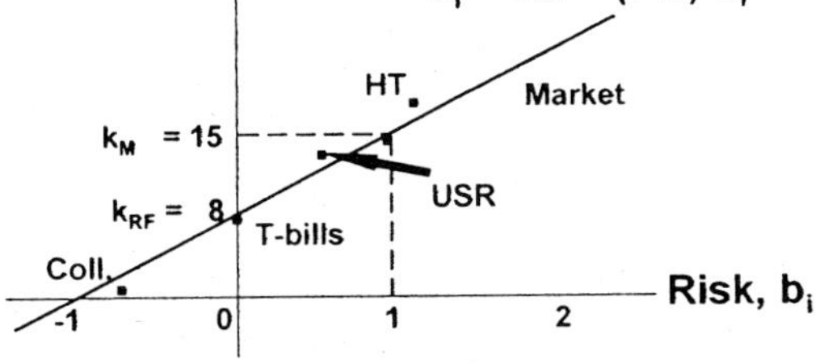

SML and Investment Alternatives

6 - 38

Calculate beta for a portfolio with 50% HT and 50% Collections

$$
\begin{aligned}
b_p &= \text{Weighted average} \\
&= 0.5(b_{HT}) + 0.5(b_{Coll}) \\
&= 0.5(1.29) + 0.5(-0.86) \\
&= 0.22.
\end{aligned}
$$

6 - 39

What is the required rate of return on the HT/Collections portfolio?

$$
\begin{aligned}
k_p &= \text{Weighted average } k \\
&= 0.5(17\%) + 0.5(2\%) = 9.5\%.
\end{aligned}
$$

Or use SML:

$$
\begin{aligned}
k_p &= k_{RF} + (RP_M)\, b_p \\
&= 8.0\% + 7\%(0.22) = 9.5\%.
\end{aligned}
$$

6 - 40

Impact of Inflation Change on SML

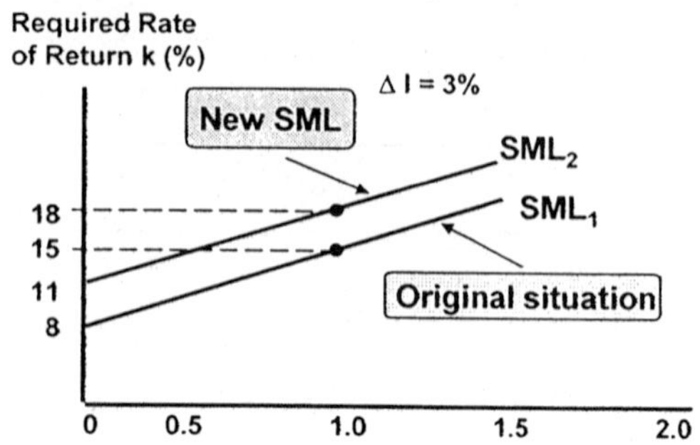

6 - 41

Impact of Risk Aversion Change

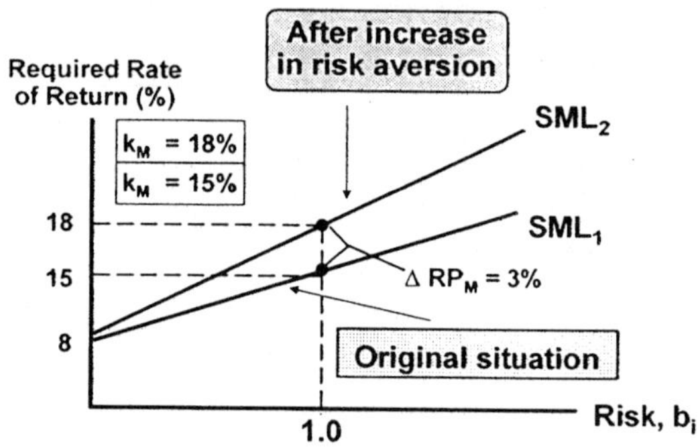

6 - 42

Has the CAPM been verified through empirical tests?

- No. The statistical tests have problems that make empirical verification virtually impossible.
- Investors may be concerned about both stand-alone risk and market risk.
- Furthermore, investors' required returns are based on future risk, but betas are based on historical data.

BLUEPRINTS: CHAPTER 7

RISK AND RETURN: PORTFOLIO THEORY AND ASSET PRICING MODELS

To begin, briefly review the Chapter 6 Mini Case. Then, extend your knowledge or risk and return by answering the following questions.

a. What is the Capital Asset Pricing Model (CAPM)? What are the assumptions that underlie the model?

b. Construct a reasonable, but hypothetical, graph which shows risk, as measured by portfolio standard deviation, on the X axis and expected rate of return on the Y axis. Now add an illustrative feasible (or attainable) set of portfolios, and show what portion of the feasible set is efficient. What makes a particular portfolio efficient? Don't worry about specific values when constructing the graph--merely illustrate how things look with "reasonable" data.

c. Now add a set of indifference curves to the graph created for Part b. What do these curves represent? What is the optimal portfolio for this investor? Finally, add a second set of indifference curves which leads to the selection of a different optimal portfolio. Why do the two investors choose different portfolios?

d. Now add the risk-free asset. What impact does this have on the efficient frontier?

e. Write out the equation for the Capital Market Line (CML) and draw it on the graph. Interpret the CML. Now add a set of indifference curves, and illustrate how an investor's optimal portfolio is some combination of the risky portfolio and the risk-free asset. What is the composition of the risky portfolio?

f. What is a characteristic line? How is this line used to estimate a stock's beta coefficient? Write out and explain the formula that relates total risk, market risk, and diversifiable risk.

g. What are two potential tests that can be conducted to verify the CAPM? What are the results of such tests? What is Roll's critique of CAPM tests?

h. Briefly explain the difference between the CAPM and the Arbitrage Pricing Theory (APT).

i. What is the current status of the APT?

j. Suppose you are given the following information. The beta of company, b_i, is 0.9, the risk free rate, k_{RF}, is 6.8%, and the expected market premium, k_M-k_{RF}, is 6.3%. Because your company is larger than average and more successful than average (i.e., it has a lower book-to-market ratio), you think the Fama-French 3-factor model might be more appropriate than the CAPM. You estimate the additional coefficients from the Fama-French 3-factor model: the coefficient for the size effect, c_i, is -0.5, and the coefficient for the book-to-market effect, d_i, is –0.3. If the expected value of the size factor is 4% and the expected value of the book-to-market factor is 5%, what is the required return using the Fama-French 3-factor model? (Assume that a_i = 0.0.) What is the required return using CAPM?

7 - 1

CHAPTER 7
Risk and Return: Portfolio Theory and Asset Pricing Models

- Capital Asset Pricing Model (CAPM)
  - Efficient frontier
  - Capital Market Line (CML)
  - Security Market Line (SML)
  - Beta calculation
- Arbitrage pricing theory
- Fama-French 3-factor model

7 - 2

What is the CAPM?

- The CAPM is an equilibrium model that specifies the relationship between risk and required rate of return for assets held in well-diversified portfolios.
- It is based on the premise that only one factor affects risk.
- What is that factor?

7 - 3

What are the assumptions of the CAPM?

- Investors all think in terms of a single holding period.
- All investors have identical expectations.
- Investors can borrow or lend unlimited amounts at the risk-free rate.

(More...)

7 - 4

- All assets are perfectly divisible.
- There are no taxes and no transactions costs.
- All investors are price takers, that is, investors' buying and selling won't influence stock prices.
- Quantities of all assets are given and fixed.

7 - 5

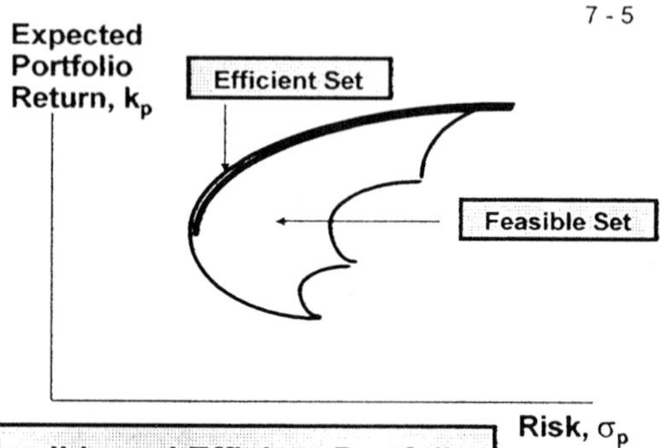

Feasible and Efficient Portfolios

7 - 6

- The feasible set of portfolios represents all portfolios that can be constructed from a given set of stocks.
- An efficient portfolio is one that offers:
  - the most return for a given amount of risk, or
  - the least risk for a give amount of return.
- The collection of efficient portfolios is called the efficient set or efficient frontier.

7 - 7

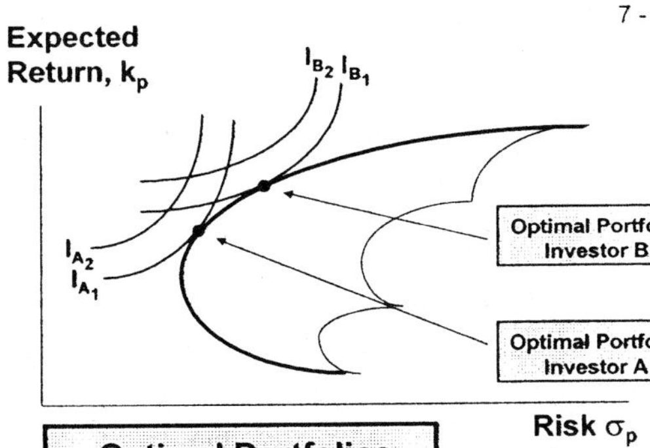

Optimal Portfolios

7 - 8

- Indifference curves reflect an investor's attitude toward risk as reflected in his or her risk/return tradeoff function. They differ among investors because of differences in risk aversion.
- An investor's optimal portfolio is defined by the tangency point between the efficient set and the investor's indifference curve.

7 - 9

What impact does k_{RF} have on the efficient frontier?

- When a risk-free asset is added to the feasible set, investors can create portfolios that combine this asset with a portfolio of risky assets.
- The straight line connecting k_{RF} with M, the tangency point between the line and the old efficient set, becomes the new efficient frontier.

7 - 10

Efficient Set with a Risk-Free Asset

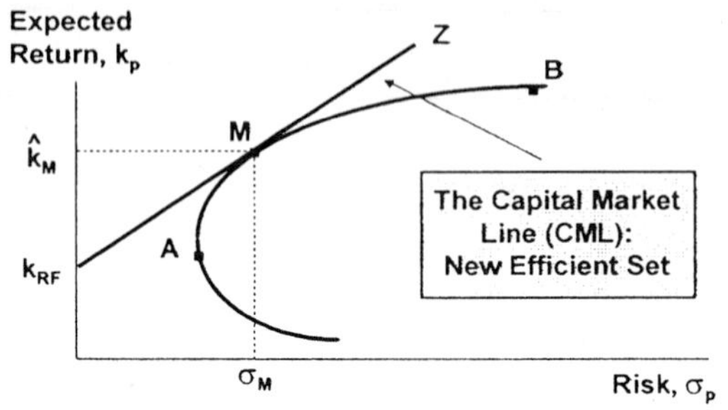

7 - 11

What is the Capital Market Line?

- The Capital Market Line (CML) is all linear combinations of the risk-free asset and Portfolio M.
- Portfolios below the CML are inferior.
  - The CML defines the new efficient set.
  - All investors will choose a portfolio on the CML.

7 - 12

The CML Equation

$$\hat{k}_p = k_{RF} + \left[\frac{\hat{k}_M - k_{RF}}{\sigma_M}\right]\sigma_p.$$

Intercept (k_{RF})   Slope   Risk measure (σ_p)

7 - 13

What does the CML tell us?

- The expected rate of return on any efficient portfolio is equal to the risk-free rate plus a risk premium.
- The optimal portfolio for any investor is the point of tangency between the CML and the investor's indifference curves.

7 - 14

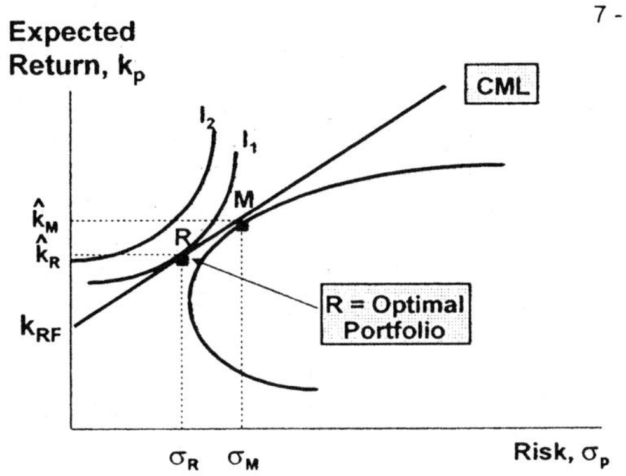

7 - 15

What is the Security Market Line (SML)?

- The CML gives the risk/return relationship for efficient portfolios.
- The Security Market Line (SML), also part of the CAPM, gives the risk/return relationship for individual stocks.

7 - 16

The SML Equation

- The measure of risk used in the SML is the beta coefficient of company i, b_i.
- The SML equation:

$$k_i = k_{RF} + (RP_M)\, b_i$$

7 - 17

How are betas calculated?

- Run a regression line of past returns on Stock i versus returns on the market.
- The regression line is called the characteristic line.
- The slope coefficient of the characteristic line is defined as the beta coefficient.

7 - 18

Illustration of beta calculation

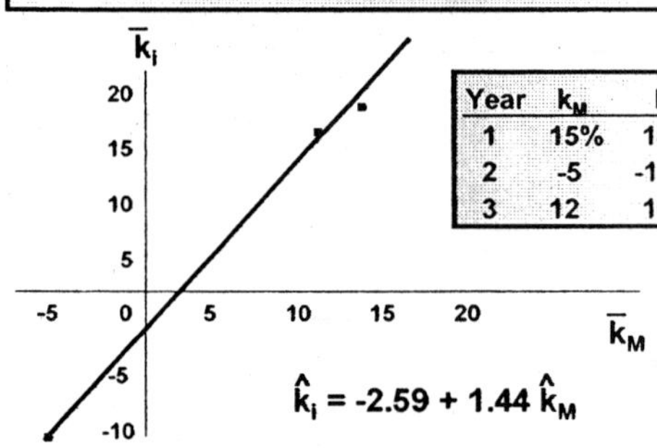

Year	k_M	k_i
1	15%	18%
2	-5	-10
3	12	16

7 - 19

Method of Calculation

- Analysts use a computer with statistical or spreadsheet software to perform the regression.
  - At least 3 year's of monthly returns or 1 year's of weekly returns are used.
  - Many analysts use 5 years of monthly returns.

(More...)

7 - 20

- If beta = 1.0, stock is average risk.
- If beta > 1.0, stock is riskier than average.
- If beta < 1.0, stock is less risky than average.
- Most stocks have betas in the range of 0.5 to 1.5.

7 - 21

Interpreting Regression Results

- The R^2 measures the percent of a stock's variance that is explained by the market. The typical R^2 is:
  - 0.3 for an individual stock
  - over 0.9 for a well diversified portfolio

7 - 22

Interpreting Regression Results (Continued)

- The 95% confidence interval shows the range in which we are 95% sure that the true value of beta lies. The typical range is:
  - from about 0.5 to 1.5 for an individual stock
  - from about .92 to 1.08 for a well diversified portfolio

7 - 23

What is the relationship between stand-alone, market, and diversifiable risk.

$\sigma_j^2 = b_j^2 \sigma_M^2 + \sigma_{e_j}^2.$

σ_j^2 = variance
= stand-alone risk of Stock j.

$b_j^2 \sigma_M^2$ = market risk of Stock j.

$\sigma_{e_j}^2$ = variance of error term
= diversifiable risk of Stock j.

7 - 24

What are two potential tests that can be conducted to verify the CAPM?

- Beta stability tests
- Tests based on the slope of the SML

7 - 25

Tests of the SML indicate:

- A more-or-less linear relationship between realized returns and market risk.
- Slope is less than predicted.
- Irrelevance of diversifiable risk specified in the CAPM model can be questioned.

(More...)

7 - 26

- Betas of individual securities are not good estimators of future risk.
- Betas of portfolios of 10 or more randomly selected stocks are reasonably stable.
- Past portfolio betas are good estimates of future portfolio volatility.

7 - 27

Are there problems with the CAPM tests?

- Yes.
    - Richard Roll questioned whether it was even conceptually possible to test the CAPM.
    - Roll showed that it is virtually impossible to prove investors behave in accordance with CAPM theory.

7 - 28

What are our conclusions regarding the CAPM?

- It is impossible to verify.
- Recent studies have questioned its validity.
- Investors seem to be concerned with both market risk and stand-alone risk. Therefore, the SML may not produce a correct estimate of k_i.

(More...)

7 - 29

- CAPM/SML concepts are based on expectations, yet betas are calculated using historical data. A company's historical data may not reflect investors' expectations about future riskiness.
- Other models are being developed that will one day replace the CAPM, but it still provides a good framework for thinking about risk and return.

7 - 30

What is the difference between the CAPM and the Arbitrage Pricing Theory (APT)?

- The CAPM is a single factor model.
- The APT proposes that the relationship between risk and return is more complex and may be due to multiple factors such as GDP growth, expected inflation, tax rate changes, and dividend yield.

7 - 31

Required Return for Stock i under the APT

$$k_i = k_{RF} + (k_1 - k_{RF})b_1 + (k_2 - k_{RF})b_2 + ... + (k_j - k_{RF})b_j.$$

k_j = required rate of return on a portfolio sensitive only to economic Factor j.

b_j = sensitivity of Stock i to economic Factor j.

7 - 32

What is the status of the APT?

- The APT is being used for some real world applications.
- Its acceptance has been slow because the model does not specify what factors influence stock returns.
- More research on risk and return models is needed to find a model that is theoretically sound, empirically verified, and easy to use.

7 - 33

Fama-French 3-Factor Model

- Fama and French propose three factors:
  - The excess market return, k_M-k_{RF}.
  - the return on, S, a portfolio of small firms (where size is based on the market value of equity) minus the return on B, a portfolio of big firms. This return is called k_{SMB}, for S minus B.

7 - 34

Fama-French 3-Factor Model (Continued)

- the return on, H, a portfolio of firms with high book-to-market ratios (using market equity and book equity) minus the return on L, a portfolio of firms with low book-to-market ratios. This return is called k_{HML}, for H minus L.

7 - 35

Required Return for Stock i under the Fama-French 3-Factor Model

$k_i = k_{RF} + (k_M - k_{RF})b_i + (k_{SMB})c_i + (k_{HMB})d_i$

b_i = sensitivity of Stock i to the market return.

c_j = sensitivity of Stock i to the size factor.

d_j = sensitivity of Stock i to the book-to-market factor.

7 - 36

Required Return for Stock i: b_i=0.9, k_{RF}=6.8%, the market risk premium is 6.3%, c_i=-0.5, the expected value for the size factor is 4%, d_i=-0.3, and the expected value for the book-to-market factor is 5%.

$k_i = k_{RF} + (k_M - k_{RF})b_i + (k_{SMB})c_i + (k_{HMB})d_i$

k_i = 6.8% + (6.3%)(0.9) + (4%)(-0.5) + (5%)(-0.3)
= 8.97%

7 - 37

CAPM Required Return for Stock i

CAPM:

$k_i = k_{RF} + (k_M - k_{RF})b_i$

$k_i = 6.8\% + (6.3\%)(0.9)$
$= 12.47\%$

Fama-French (previous slide):

$k_i = 8.97\%$

BLUEPRINTS: CHAPTER 8
TIME VALUE OF MONEY

Assume that you are nearing graduation and that you have applied for a job with a local bank. As part of the bank's evaluation process, you have been asked to take an examination which covers several financial analysis techniques. The first section of the test addresses discounted cash flow analysis. See how you would do by answering the following questions.

a. Draw time lines for (1) a $100 lump sum cash flow at the end of year 2, (2) an ordinary annuity of $100 per year for 3 years, and (3) an uneven cash flow stream of -$50, $100, $75, and $50 at the end of Years 0 through 3.

b. (1) What is the future value of an initial $100 after 3 years if it is invested in an account paying 10 percent annual interest?

(2) What is the present value of $100 to be received in 3 years if the appropriate interest rate is 10 percent?

c. We sometimes need to find how long it will take a sum of money (or anything else) to grow to some specified amount. For example, if a company's sales are growing at a rate of 20 percent per year, how long will it take sales to double?

d. What is the difference between an ordinary annuity and an annuity due? What type of annuity is shown below? How would you change it to the other type of annuity?

0	1	2	3
	100	100	100

e. (1) What is the future value of a 3-year ordinary annuity of $100 if the appropriate interest rate is 10 percent?

(2) What is the present value of the annuity?

(3) What would the future and present values be if the annuity were an annuity due?

f. What is the present value of the following uneven cash flow stream? The appropriate interest rate is 10 percent, compounded annually.

0	1	2	3	4 Years
0	100	300	300	-50

g. What annual interest rate will cause \$100 to grow to \$125.97 in 3 years?

h. (1) Will the future value be larger or smaller if we compound an initial amount more often than annually, for example, every 6 months, or *semiannually*, holding the stated interest rate constant? Why?

(2) Define (a) the stated, or quoted, or nominal, rate (i_{Nom}), (b) the periodic rate (i_{Per}), and (c) the effective annual rate (EAR).

(3) What is the effective annual rate for a nominal rate of 10 percent, compounded semiannually? Compounded quarterly? Compounded daily?

(4) What is the future value of \$100 after 3 years under 10 percent semiannual compounding? Quarterly compounding?

i. Will the effective annual rate ever be equal to the nominal (quoted) rate?

j. (1) What is the value at the end of Year 3 of the following cash flow stream if the quoted interest rate is 10 percent, compounded semiannually?

0		1		2		3 Years
0		100		100		100

(2) What is the PV of the same stream?

(3) Is the stream an annuity?

(4) An important rule is that you should *never* show a nominal rate on a time line or use it in calculations unless what condition holds? (Hint: Think of annual compounding, when i_{Nom} = EAR = i_{Per}.) What would be wrong with your answer to questions j(1) and j(2) if you used the nominal rate (10 %) rather than the periodic rate ($i_{Nom}/2$ = 10%/2 = 5%)?

k. (1) Construct an amortization schedule for a \$1,000, 10 percent annual rate loan with 3 equal installments.

(2) What is the annual interest expense for the borrower, and the annual interest income for the lender, during Year 2?

l. Suppose on January 1, 2002, you deposit $100 in an account that pays a nominal, or quoted, interest rate of 11.33463 percent, with interest added (compounded) daily. How much will you have in your account on October 1, or after 9 months?

m. Now, suppose you leave your money in the bank for 21 months. Thus, on January 1, 2002, you deposit $100 in an account that pays a 12 percent effective annual interest rate. How much will be in your account on October 1, 2003?

n. Suppose someone offered to sell you a note calling for the payment of $1,000 15 months from today. They offer to sell it to you for $850. You have $850 in a bank time deposit which pays a 6.76649 percent nominal rate with daily compounding, which is a 7 percent effective annual interest rate, and you plan to leave the money in the bank unless you buy the note. The note is not risky—you are sure it will be paid on schedule. Should you buy the note? Check the decision in three ways: (1) by comparing your future value if you buy the note versus leaving your money in the bank, (2) by comparing the PV of the note with your current bank account, and (3) by comparing the EAR on the note versus that of the bank account.

o. Suppose the note discussed in Part n had a cost of $850, but called for 5 quarterly payments of $190 each, with the first payment due in 3 months rather than $1,000 at the end of 15 months. Would it be a good investment for you?

8 - 1

CHAPTER 8
Time Value of Money

- Future value
- Present value
- Rates of return
- Amortization

8 - 2

Time lines show timing of cash flows.

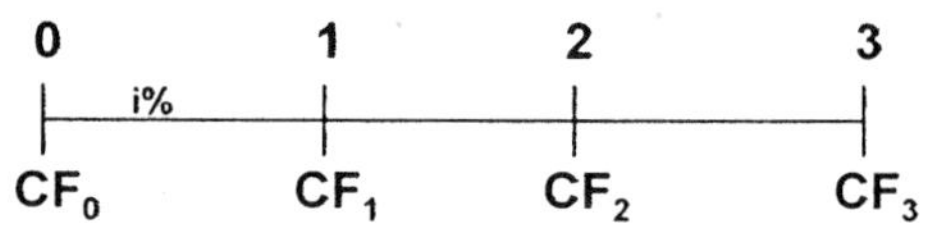

Tick marks at ends of periods, so Time 0 is today; Time 1 is the end of Period 1; or the beginning of Period 2.

8 - 3

Time line for a $100 lump sum due at the end of Year 2.

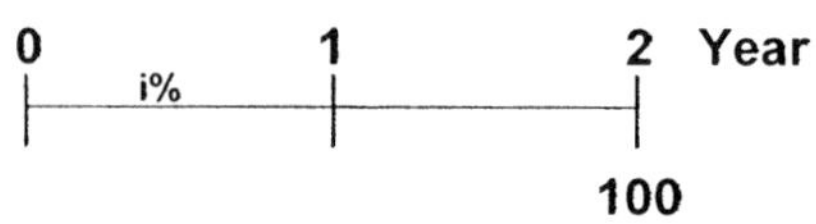

8 - 4

Time line for an ordinary annuity of $100 for 3 years.

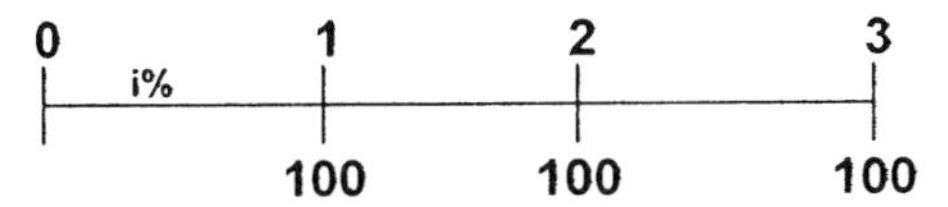

8 - 5

Time line for uneven CFs: -$50 at t = 0 and $100, $75, and $50 at the end of Years 1 through 3.

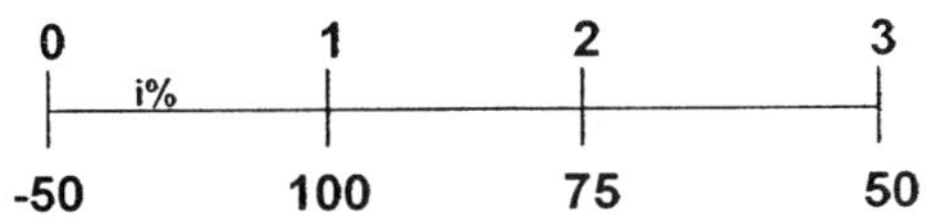

8 - 6

What's the FV of an initial $100 after 3 years if i = 10%?

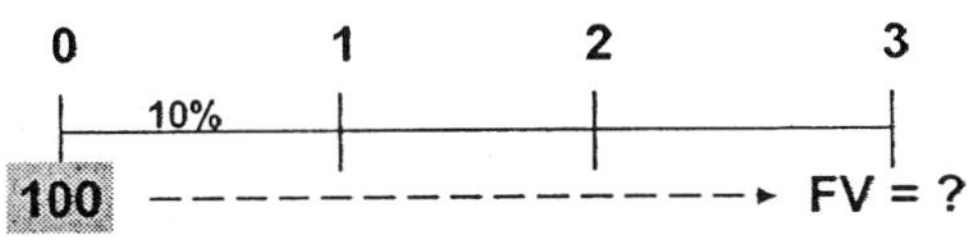

Finding FVs (moving to the right on a time line) is called compounding.

8 - 7

After 1 year:

$$FV_1 = PV + INT_1 = PV + PV(i)$$
$$= PV(1 + i)$$
$$= \$100(1.10)$$
$$= \$110.00.$$

After 2 years:

$$FV_2 = PV(1 + i)^2$$
$$= \$100(1.10)^2$$
$$= \$121.00.$$

8 - 8

After 3 years:

$$FV_3 = PV(1 + i)^3$$
$$= \$100(1.10)^3$$
$$= \$133.10.$$

In general,

$$FV_n = PV(1 + i)^n.$$

8 - 9

Three Ways to Find FVs

- Solve the equation with a regular calculator.
- Use a financial calculator.
- Use a spreadsheet.

8 - 10

Financial Calculator Solution

Financial calculators solve this equation:

$$FV_n = PV(1+i)^n.$$

There are 4 variables. If 3 are known, the calculator will solve for the 4th.

8 - 11

Here's the setup to find FV:

INPUTS	3	10	-100	0	
	N	I/YR	PV	PMT	FV
OUTPUT					133.10

Clearing automatically sets everything to 0, but for safety enter PMT = 0.

Set: P/YR = 1, END.

8 - 12

What's the PV of $100 due in 3 years if i = 10%?

Finding PVs is discounting, and it's the reverse of compounding.

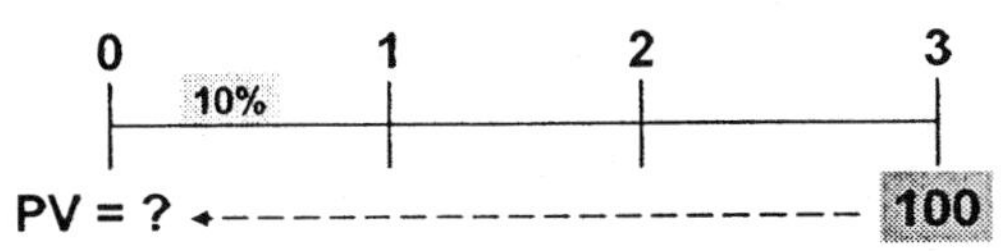

8 - 13

Solve $FV_n = PV(1 + i)^n$ for PV:

$$V = \frac{FV_n}{(1+i)^n} = FV_n\left(\frac{1}{1+i}\right)^n$$

$$PV = \$100\left(\frac{1}{1.10}\right)^3$$
$$= \$100(0.7513) = \$75.13.$$

8 - 14

Financial Calculator Solution

INPUTS	3	10		0	100
	N	I/YR	PV	PMT	FV
OUTPUT			-75.13		

Either PV or FV must be negative. Here PV = -75.13. Put in \$75.13 today, take out \$100 after 3 years.

8 - 15

Finding the Time to Double

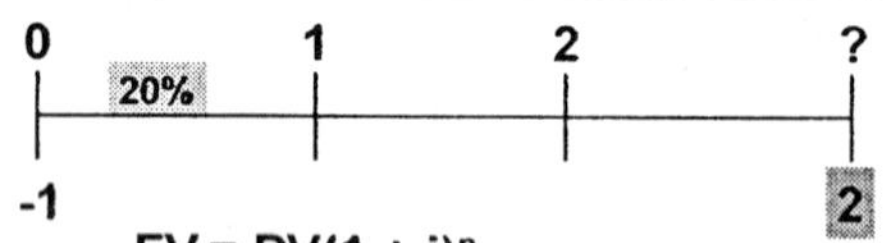

$$FV = PV(1 + i)^n$$
$$\$2 = \$1(1 + 0.20)^n$$
$$(1.2)^n = \$2/\$1 = 2$$
$$nLN(1.2) = LN(2)$$
$$n = LN(2)/LN(1.2)$$
$$n = 0.693/0.182 = 3.8.$$

8 - 16

Financial Calculator

INPUTS		20	-1	0	2
	N	I/YR	PV	PMT	FV
OUTPUT	3.8				

8 - 17

What's the difference between an ordinary annuity and an annuity due?

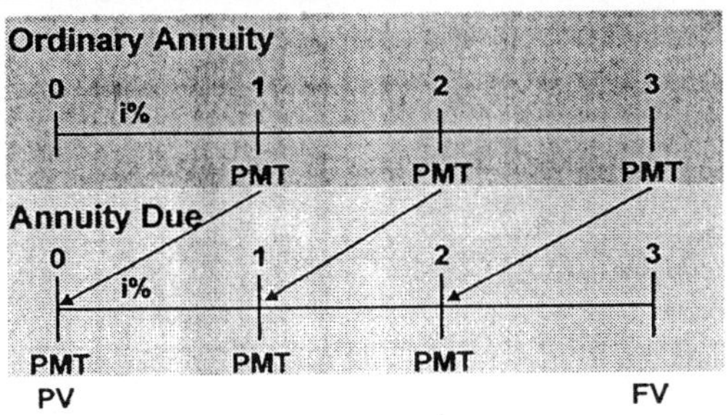

8 - 18

What's the FV of a 3-year ordinary annuity of $100 at 10%?

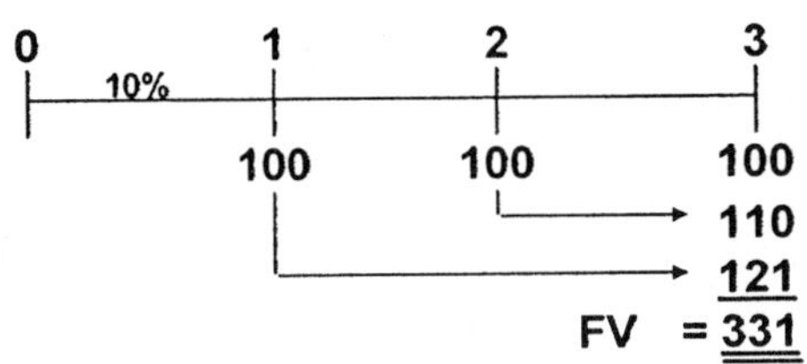

8 - 19

Financial Calculator Solution

INPUTS	3	10	0	-100	
	N	I/YR	PV	PMT	FV
OUTPUT					331.00

Have payments but no lump sum PV, so enter 0 for present value.

8 - 20

What's the PV of this ordinary annuity?

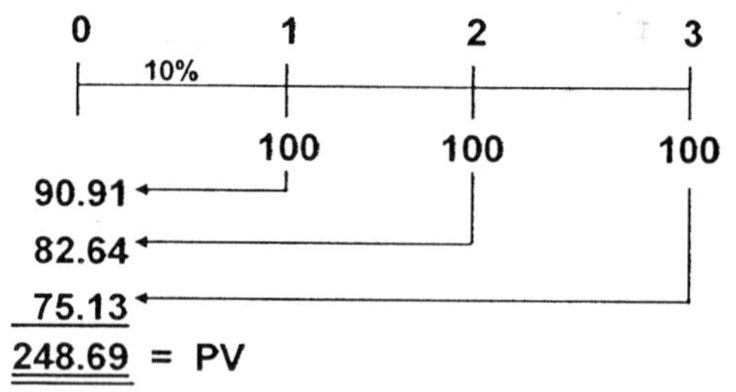

8 - 21

INPUTS	3	10		100	0
	N	I/YR	PV	PMT	FV
OUTPUT			-248.69		

Have payments but no lump sum FV, so enter 0 for future value.

8 - 22

Spreadsheet Solution

	A	B	C	D
1	0	1	2	3
2		100	100	100
3	248.69			

Excel Formula in cell A3:

=NPV(10%,B2:D2)

8 - 23

Special Function for Annuities

For ordinary annuities, this formula in cell A3 gives 248.96:

=PV(10%,3,-100)

A similar function gives the future value of 331.00:

=FV(10%,3,-100)

8 - 24

Find the FV and PV if the annuity were an annuity due.

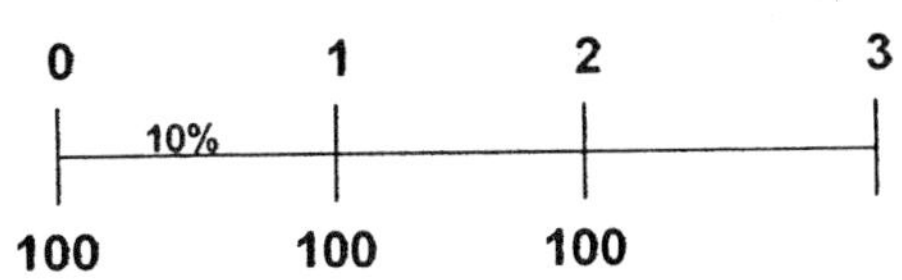

8 - 25

Switch from "End" to "Begin". Then enter variables to find PVA_3 = $273.55.

INPUTS	3	10		100	0
	N	I/YR	PV	PMT	FV
OUTPUT			-273.55		

Then enter PV = 0 and press FV to find FV = $364.10.

8 - 26

Excel Function for Annuities Due

Change the formula to:

=PV(10%,3,-100,0,1)

The fourth term, 0, tells the function there are no other cash flows. The fifth term tells the function that it is an annuity due. A similar function gives the future value of an annuity due:

=FV(10%,3,-100,0,1)

8 - 27

What is the PV of this uneven cash flow stream?

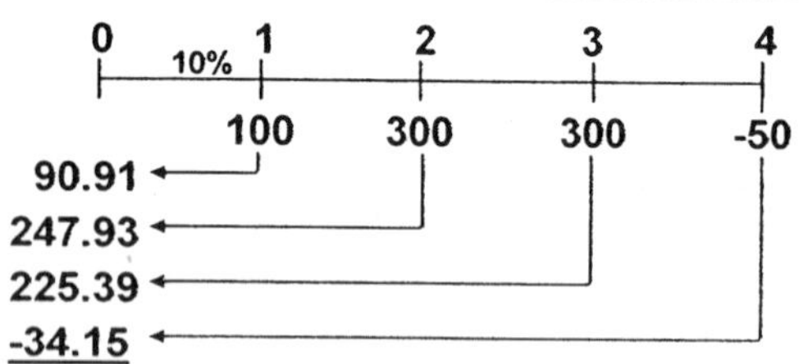

530.08 = PV

8 - 28

- Input in "CFLO" register:

  CF_0 = 0

  CF_1 = 100

  CF_2 = 300

  CF_3 = 300

  CF_4 = -50

- Enter I = 10%, then press NPV button to get NPV = 530.09. (Here NPV = PV.)

8 - 29

Spreadsheet Solution

	A	B	C	D	E
1	0	1	2	3	4
2		100	300	300	-50
3	530.09				

Excel Formula in cell A3:

=NPV(10%,B2:E2)

8 - 30

What interest rate would cause $100 to grow to $125.97 in 3 years?

$\$100(1 + i)^3 = \$125.97.$

$(1 + i)^3 = \$125.97/\$100 = 1.2597$

$1 + i = (1.2597)^{1/3} = 1.08$

$i = 8\%.$

INPUTS	3		-100	0	125.97
	N	I/YR	PV	PMT	FV
OUTPUT		8%			

8 - 31

Will the FV of a lump sum be larger or smaller if we compound more often, holding the stated I% constant? Why?

LARGER! If compounding is more frequent than once a year--for example, semiannually, quarterly, or daily--interest is earned on interest more often.

8 - 32

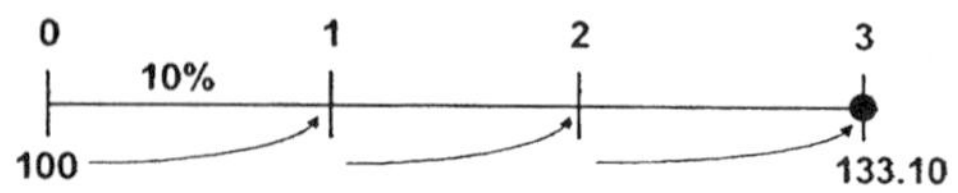

Annually: $FV_3 = \$100(1.10)^3 = \$133.10.$

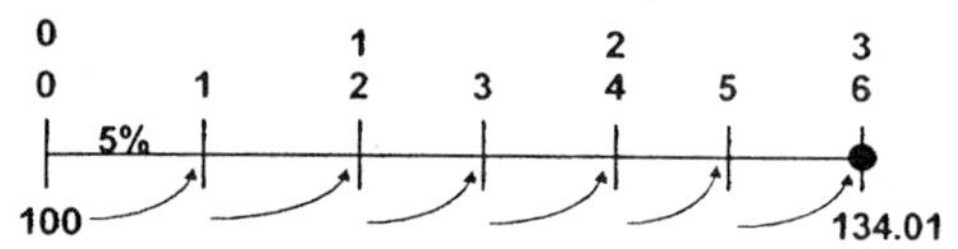

Semiannually: $FV_6 = \$100(1.05)^6 = \$134.01.$

8 - 33

We will deal with 3 different rates:

i_{Nom} = nominal, or stated, or quoted, rate per year.

i_{Per} = periodic rate.

EAR = EFF% = effective annual rate

8 - 34

- i_{Nom} is stated in contracts. Periods per year (m) must also be given.
- Examples:
  - 8%; Quarterly
  - 8%, Daily interest (365 days)

8 - 35

- Periodic rate = $i_{Per} = i_{Nom}/m$, where m is number of compounding periods per year. m = 4 for quarterly, 12 for monthly, and 360 or 365 for daily compounding.
- Examples:

  8% quarterly: i_{Per} = 8%/4 = 2%.

  8% daily (365): i_{Per} = 8%/365 = 0.021918%.

8 - 36

- Effective Annual Rate (EAR = EFF%): The annual rate which causes PV to grow to the same FV as under multi-period compounding.

  Example: EFF% for 10%, semiannual:

  $$FV = (1 + i_{Nom}/m)^m = (1.05)^2 = 1.1025.$$

  EFF% = 10.25% because $(1.1025)^1 = 1.1025$.

  Any PV would grow to same FV at 10.25% annually or 10% semiannually.

8 - 37

- An investment with monthly payments is different from one with quarterly payments. Must put on EFF% basis to compare rates of return. Use EFF% only for comparisons.
- Banks say "interest paid daily." Same as compounded daily.

8 - 38

How do we find EFF% for a nominal rate of 10%, compounded semiannually?

$$EFF\% = \left(1 + \frac{i_{Nom}}{m}\right)^m - 1$$

$$= \left(1 + \frac{0.10}{2}\right)^2 - 1.0$$

$$= (1.05)^2 - 1.0$$

$$= 0.1025 = 10.25\%.$$

Or use a financial calculator.

8 - 39

EAR = EFF% of 10%

EAR_{Annual} = 10%.

$EAR_Q = (1 + 0.10/4)^4 - 1$ = 10.38%.

$EAR_M = (1 + 0.10/12)^{12} - 1$ = 10.47%.

$EAR_{D(360)} = (1 + 0.10/360)^{360} - 1$ = 10.52%.

8 - 40

FV of \$100 after 3 years under 10% semiannual compounding? Quarterly?

$$FV_n = PV\left(1 + \frac{i_{Nom}}{m}\right)^{mn}.$$

$$FV_{3S} = \$100\left(1 + \frac{0.10}{2}\right)^{2x3}$$

$$= \$100(1.05)^6 = \$134.01.$$

$$FV_{3Q} = \$100(1.025)^{12} = \$134.49.$$

8 - 41

Can the effective rate ever be equal to the nominal rate?

- Yes, but only if annual compounding is used, i.e., if m = 1.
- If m > 1, EFF% will always be greater than the nominal rate.

8 - 42

When is each rate used?

i_{Nom}: Written into contracts, quoted by banks and brokers. <u>Not</u> used in calculations or shown on time lines.

8 - 43

i_{Per}: Used in calculations, shown on time lines.

If i_{Nom} has annual compounding, then $i_{Per} = i_{Nom}/1 = i_{Nom}$.

8 - 44

EAR = EFF%: Used to compare returns on investments with different payments per year.

(Used for calculations if and only if dealing with annuities where payments don't match interest compounding periods.)

8 - 45

What's the value at the end of Year 3 of the following CF stream if the quoted interest rate is 10%, compounded semiannually?

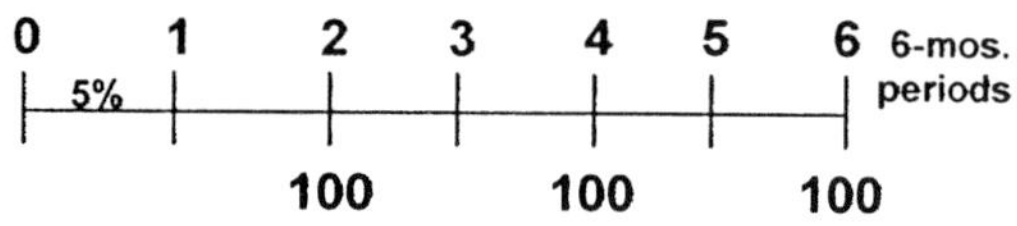

8 - 46

- Payments occur annually, but compounding occurs each 6 months.
- So we can't use normal annuity valuation techniques.

8 - 47

1st Method: Compound Each CF

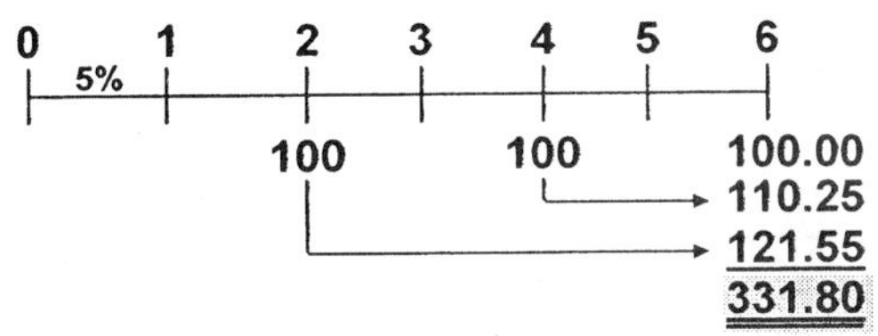

$FVA_3 = \$100(1.05)^4 + \$100(1.05)^2 + \$100$
$= \$331.80.$

8 - 48

2nd Method: Treat as an Annuity

Could you find the FV with a financial calculator?

Yes, by following these steps:

a. Find the EAR for the quoted rate:

$$EAR = \left(1 + \frac{0.10}{2}\right)^2 - 1 = 10.25\%.$$

8 - 49

b. Use EAR = 10.25% as the annual rate in your calculator:

INPUTS	3	10.25	0	-100	
	N	I/YR	PV	PMT	FV
OUTPUT					331.80

8 - 50

What's the PV of this stream?

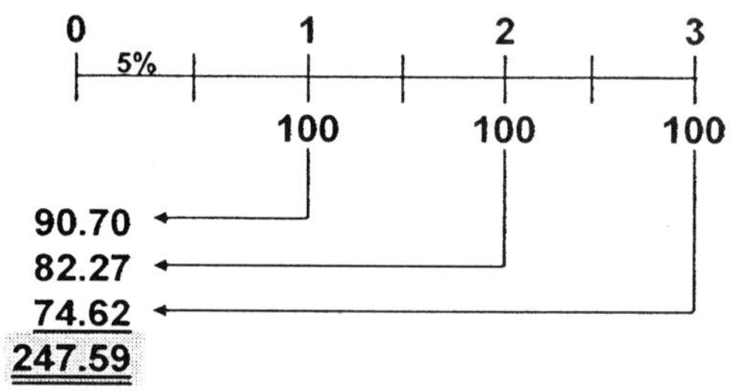

8 - 51

Amortization

Construct an amortization schedule for a $1,000, 10% annual rate loan with 3 equal payments.

8 - 52

Step 1: Find the required payments.

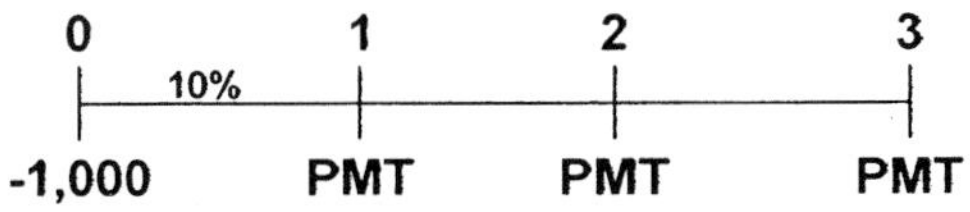

INPUTS	3	10	-1000		0
	N	I/YR	PV	PMT	FV
OUTPUT				402.11	

8 - 53

Step 2: Find interest charge for Year 1.

INT_t = Beg bal_t (i)
INT_1 = \$1,000(0.10) = **\$100.**

Step 3: Find repayment of principal in Year 1.

Repmt = PMT - INT
= \$402.11 - \$100
= **\$302.11.**

8 - 54

Step 4: Find ending balance after Year 1.

End bal = Beg bal - Repmt
= \$1,000 - \$302.11 = \$697.89.

Repeat these steps for Years 2 and 3 to complete the amortization table.

8 - 55

YR	BEG BAL	PMT	INT	PRIN PMT	END BAL
1	$1,000	$402	$100	$302	$698
2	698	402	70	332	366
3	366	402	37	366	0
TOT		1,206.34	206.34	1,000	

Interest declines. Tax implications.

8 - 56

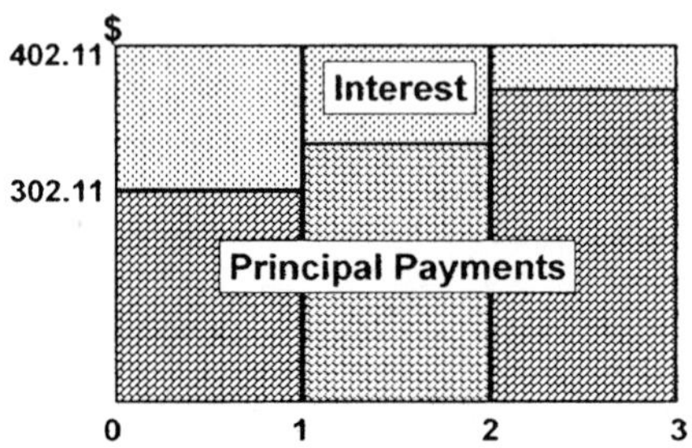

Level payments. Interest declines because outstanding balance declines. Lender earns 10% on loan outstanding, which is falling.

8 - 57

- **Amortization tables are widely used--for home mortgages, auto loans, business loans, retirement plans, and so on. They are very important!**
- **Financial calculators (and spreadsheets) are great for setting up amortization tables.**

8 - 58

On January 1 you deposit $100 in an account that pays a nominal interest rate of 11.33463%, with daily compounding (365 days).

How much will you have on October 1, or after 9 months (273 days)? (Days given.)

8 - 59

i_{Per} = 11.33463%/365
= 0.031054% per day.

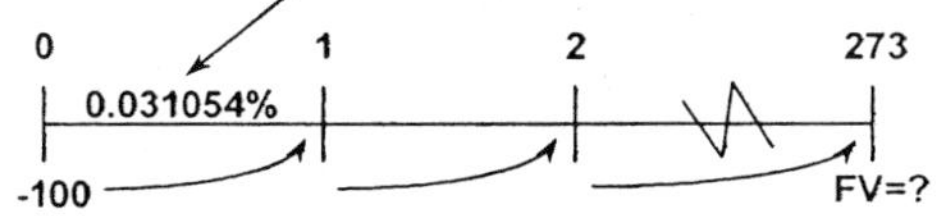

FV_{273} = $100(1.00031054)^{273}
= $100(1.08846) = $108.85.

Note: % in calculator, decimal in equation.

8 - 60

i_{Per} = i_{Nom}/m
= 11.33463/365
= 0.031054% per day.

INPUTS	273		-100	0	
	N	I/YR	PV	PMT	FV
OUTPUT					108.85

Enter i in one step.
Leave data in calculator.

8 - 61

Now suppose you leave your money in the bank for 21 months, which is 1.75 years or 273 + 365 = 638 days.

How much will be in your account at maturity?

Answer: Override N = 273 with N = 638. FV = $121.91.

8 - 62

i_{Per} = 0.031054% per day.

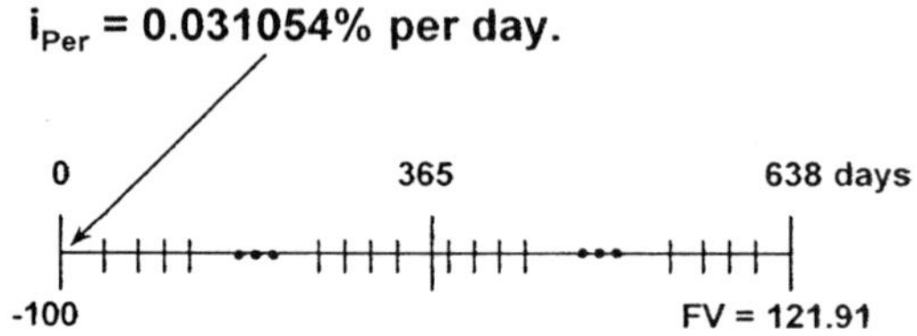

$$\begin{aligned} FV &= \$100(1 + 0.1133463/365)^{638} \\ &= \$100(1.00031054)^{638} \\ &= \$100(1.2191) \\ &= \$121.91. \end{aligned}$$

8 - 63

You are offered a note which pays $1,000 in 15 months (or 456 days) for $850. You have $850 in a bank which pays a 6.76649% nominal rate, with 365 daily compounding, which is a daily rate of 0.018538% and an EAR of 7.0%. You plan to leave the money in the bank if you don't buy the note. The note is riskless.

Should you buy it?

8 - 64

i_{Per} =0.018538% per day.

3 Ways to Solve:

1. Greatest future wealth: FV
2. Greatest wealth today: PV
3. Highest rate of return: Highest EFF%

8 - 65

1. Greatest Future Wealth

Find FV of $850 left in bank for 15 months and compare with note's FV = $1,000.

$$FV_{Bank} = \$850(1.00018538)^{456} = \$924.97 \text{ in bank.}$$

Buy the note: $1,000 > $924.97.

8 - 66

Calculator Solution to FV:

$$i_{Per} = i_{Nom}/m = 6.76649\%/365 = 0.018538\% \text{ per day.}$$

INPUTS	456		-850	0	
	N	I/YR	PV	PMT	FV
OUTPUT					924.97

Enter i_{Per} in one step.

8 - 67

2. Greatest Present Wealth

Find PV of note, and compare with its $850 cost:

$$PV = \$1,000/(1.00018538)^{456} = \$918.95.$$

8 - 68

		6.76649/365 =			
INPUTS	456	.018538		0	1000
	N	I/YR	PV	PMT	FV
OUTPUT			-918.95		

PV of note is greater than its $850 cost, so buy the note. Raises your wealth.

8 - 69

3. Rate of Return

Find the EFF% on note and compare with 7.0% bank pays, which is your opportunity cost of capital:

$$FV_n = PV(1 + i)^n$$

$$\$1,000 = \$850(1 + i)^{456}$$

Now we must solve for i.

8 - 70

INPUTS	456		-850	0	1000
	N	I/YR	PV	PMT	FV
OUTPUT		0.035646% per day			

Convert % to decimal:

Decimal = 0.035646/100 = 0.00035646.

EAR = EFF% = $(1.00035646)^{365} - 1$
= 13.89%.

8 - 71

Using interest conversion:

P/YR = 365
NOM% = 0.035646(365) = 13.01
EFF% = 13.89

Since 13.89% > 7.0% opportunity cost, buy the note.

BLUEPRINTS: CHAPTER 9
BONDS AND THEIR VALUATION

Robert Balik and Carol Kiefer are vice-presidents of Mutual of Chicago Insurance Company and codirectors of the company's pension fund management division. A major new client, the California League of Cities, has requested that Mutual of Chicago present an investment seminar to the mayors of the represented cities, and Balik and Kiefer, who will make the actual presentation, have asked you to help them by answering the following questions. Because the Walt Disney Company operates in one of the league's cities, you are to work Disney into the presentation.

a. What are the key features of a bond?

b. What are call provisions and sinking fund provisions? Do these provisions make bonds more or less risky?

c. How is the value of any asset whose value is based on expected future cash flows determined?

d. How is the value of a bond determined? What is the value of a 10-year, $1,000 par value bond with a 10 percent annual coupon if its required rate of return is 10 percent?

e. (1) What would be the value of the bond described in Part d if, just after it had been issued, the expected inflation rate rose by 3 percentage points, causing investors to require a 13 percent return? Would we now have a discount or a premium bond? (If you do not have a financial calculator, $PVIF_{13\%,10}$ = 0.2946; $PVIFA_{13\%,10}$ = 5.4262.)

(2) What would happen to the bonds' value if inflation fell, and k_d declined to 7 percent? Would we now have a premium or a discount bond?

(3) What would happen to the value of the 10-year bond over time if the required rate of return remained at 13 percent, or if it remained at 7 percent? (Hint: With a financial calculator, enter N, I, PMT, and FV, and then change (override) N to see what happens to the PV as the bond approaches maturity.)

f. (1) What is the yield to maturity on a 10-year, 9 percent annual coupon, $1,000 par value bond that sells for $887.00? That sells for $1,134.20? What does the fact that a bond sells at a discount or at a premium tell you about the relationship between k_d and the bond's coupon rate?

(2) What are the total return, the current yield, and the capital gains yield for the discount bond? (Assume the bond is held to maturity and the company does not default on the bond.)

g. What is *interest rate (or price) risk*? Which bond has more interest rate risk, an annual payment 1-year bond or a 30-year bond? Why?

h. What is *reinvestment rate risk*? Which has more reinvestment rate risk, a 1-year bond or a 10-year bond?

i. How does the equation for valuing a bond change if semiannual payments are made? Find the value of a 10-year, semiannual payment, 10 percent coupon bond if nominal k_d = 13%. (Hint: $PVIF_{6.5\%,20} = 0.2838$ and $PVIFA_{6.5\%,20} = 11.0185$.)

j. Suppose you could buy, for $1,000, either a 10 percent, 10-year, annual payment bond or a 10 percent, 10-year, semiannual payment bond. They are equally risky. Which would you prefer? If $1,000 is the proper price for the semiannual bond, what is the equilibrium price for the annual payment bond?

k. Suppose a 10-year, 10 percent, semiannual coupon bond with a par value of $1,000 is currently selling for $1,135.90, producing a nominal yield to maturity of 8 percent. However, the bond can be called after 5 years for a price of $1,050.

(1) What is the bond's *nominal yield to call (YTC)*?

(2) If you bought this bond, do you think you would be more likely to earn the YTM or the YTC? Why?

l. Disney's bonds were issued with a yield to maturity of 7.5 percent. Does the yield to maturity represent the promised or expected return on the bond?

m. Disney's bonds were rated AA- by S&P. Would you consider these bonds investment grade or junk bonds?

n. What factors determine a company's bond rating?

o. If this compan were to default on the bonds, would the company be immediately liquidated? Would the bondholders be assured of receiving all of their promised payments?

CHAPTER 9
Bonds and Their Valuation

- Key features of bonds
- Bond valuation
- Measuring yield
- Assessing risk

Key Features of a Bond

1. **Par value:** Face amount; paid at maturity. Assume $1,000.

2. **Coupon interest rate:** Stated interest rate. Multiply by par value to get dollars of interest. Generally fixed.

(More...)

3. **Maturity:** Years until bond must be repaid. Declines.

4. **Issue date:** Date when bond was issued.

5. **Default risk:** Risk that issuer will not make interest or principal payments.

9 - 4

How does adding a call provision affect a bond?

- Issuer can refund if rates decline. That helps the issuer but hurts the investor.
- Therefore, borrowers are willing to pay more, and lenders require more, on callable bonds.
- Most bonds have a deferred call and a declining call premium.

9 - 5

What's a sinking fund?

- Provision to pay off a loan over its life rather than all at maturity.
- Similar to amortization on a term loan.
- Reduces risk to investor, shortens average maturity.
- But not good for investors if rates decline after issuance.

9 - 6

Sinking funds are generally handled in 2 ways

1. Call x% at par per year for sinking fund purposes.
2. Buy bonds on open market.

Company would call if k_d is below the coupon rate and bond sells at a premium. Use open market purchase if k_d is above coupon rate and bond sells at a discount.

9 - 7

Financial Asset Valuation

0	1	2		n
k			...	
Value	CF_1	CF_2		CF_n

$$PV = \frac{CF_1}{(1+k)^1} + \frac{CF_2}{(1+k)^2} + \ldots + \frac{CF_n}{(1+k)^n}.$$

9 - 8

- The discount rate (k_i) is the <u>opportunity cost of capital</u>, i.e., the rate that could be earned on alternative investments of equal risk.

$$k_i = k^* + IP + LP + MRP + DRP$$

for debt securities.

9 - 9

What's the value of a 10-year, 10% coupon bond if k_d = 10%?

0	1	2		10
10%			...	
V = ?	100	100		100 + 1,000

$$V_B = \frac{\$100}{(1+k_d)^1} + \ldots + \frac{\$100}{(1+k_d)^{10}} + \frac{\$1,000}{(1+k_d)^{10}}$$

$= \$90.91 + \ldots + \$38.55 + \$385.54$

$= \$1,000.$

9 - 10

The bond consists of a 10-year, 10% annuity of $100/year plus a $1,000 lump sum at t = 10:

PV annuity	=	$ 614.46
PV maturity value	=	385.54
Value of bond	=	$1,000.00

	N	I/YR	PV	PMT	FV
INPUTS	10	10		100	1000
OUTPUT			-1,000		

9 - 11

What would happen if expected inflation rose by 3%, causing k = 13%?

	N	I/YR	PV	PMT	FV
INPUTS	10	13		100	1000
OUTPUT			-837.21		

When k_d rises, above the coupon rate, the bond's value falls below par, so it sells at a discount.

9 - 12

What would happen if inflation fell, and k_d declined to 7%?

	N	I/YR	PV	PMT	FV
INPUTS	10	7		100	1000
OUTPUT			-1,210.71		

If coupon rate > k_d, price rises above par, and bond sells at a premium.

9 - 13

Suppose the bond was issued 20 years ago and now has 10 years to maturity. What would happen to its value over time if the required rate of return remained at 10%, or at 13%, or at 7%?

9 - 14

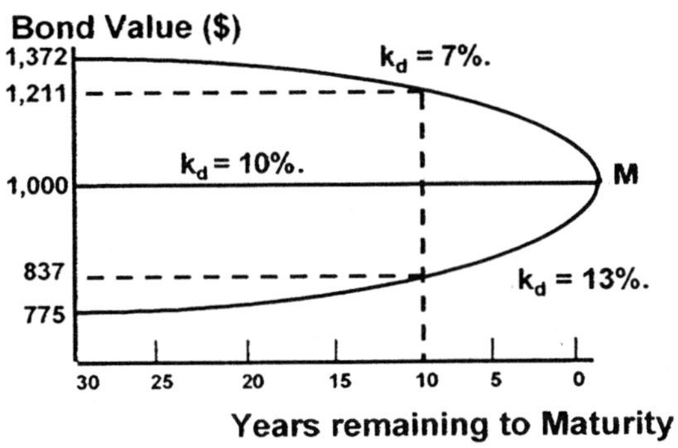

9 - 15

- **At maturity, the value of any bond must equal its par value.**
- **The value of a premium bond would decrease to $1,000.**
- **The value of a discount bond would increase to $1,000.**
- **A par bond stays at $1,000 if k_d remains constant.**

9 - 16

What's "yield to maturity"?

- YTM is the rate of return earned on a bond held to maturity. Also called "promised yield."

9 - 17

What's the YTM on a 10-year, 9% annual coupon, $1,000 par value bond that sells for $887?

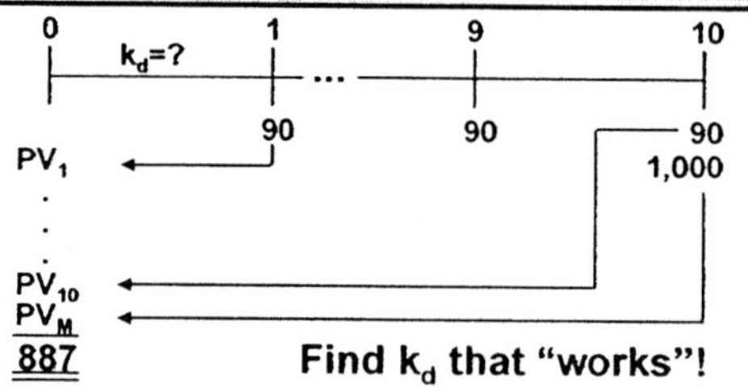

Find k_d that "works"!

9 - 18

Find k_d

$$V_B = \frac{INT}{(1+k_d)^1} + \cdots + \frac{INT}{(1+k_d)^N} + \frac{M}{(1+k_d)^N}$$

$$887 = \frac{90}{(1+k_d)^1} + \cdots + \frac{90}{(1+k_d)^{10}} + \frac{1{,}000}{(1+k_d)^{10}}$$

	N	I/YR	PV	PMT	FV
INPUTS	10		-887	90	1000
OUTPUT		10.91			

9 - 19

- If coupon rate < k_d, bond sells at a discount.
- If coupon rate = k_d, bond sells at its par value.
- If coupon rate > k_d, bond sells at a premium.
- If k_d rises, price falls.
- Price = par at maturity.

9 - 20

Find YTM if price were $1,134.20.

	N	I/YR	PV	PMT	FV
INPUTS	10		-1134.2	90	1000
OUTPUT		7.08			

Sells at a premium. Because coupon = 9% > k_d = 7.08%, bond's value > par.

9 - 21

Definitions

$$\text{Current yield} = \frac{\text{Annual coupon pmt}}{\text{Current price}}$$

$$\text{Capital gains yield} = \frac{\text{Change in price}}{\text{Beginning price}}$$

$$\text{Exp total return} = \text{YTM} = \text{Exp Curr yld} + \text{Exp cap gains yld}$$

9 - 22

Find current yield and capital gains yield for a 9%, 10-year bond when the bond sells for $887 and YTM = 10.91%.

$$\text{Current yield} = \frac{\$90}{\$887}$$

$$= 0.1015 = \boxed{10.15\%.}$$

9 - 23

YTM = Current yield + Capital gains yield.

Cap gains yield = YTM - Current yield
= 10.91% - 10.15%
= 0.76%.

Could also find values in Years 1 and 2, get difference, and divide by value in Year 1. Same answer.

9 - 24

What's interest rate (or price) risk? Does a 1-year or 10-year 10% bond have more risk?

Interest rate risk: Rising k_d causes bond's price to fall.

k_d	1-year	Change	10-year	Change
5%	$1,048		$1,386	
		4.8%		38.6%
10%	1,000		1,000	
		4.4%		25.1%
15%	956		749	

9 - 25

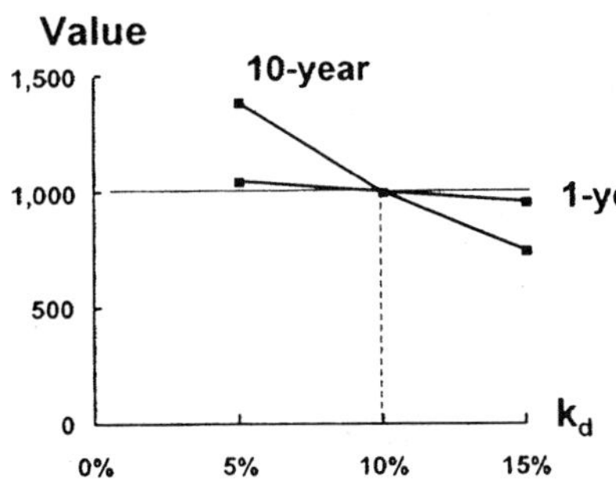

9 - 26

What is reinvestment rate risk?

The risk that CFs will have to be reinvested in the future at lower rates, reducing income.

Illustration: Suppose you just won $500,000 playing the lottery. You'll invest the money and live off the interest. You buy a 1-year bond with a YTM of 10%.

9 - 27

Year 1 income = $50,000. At year-end get back $500,000 to reinvest.

If rates fall to 3%, income will drop from $50,000 to $15,000. Had you bought 30-year bonds, income would have remained constant.

9 - 28

- Long-term bonds: High interest rate risk, low reinvestment rate risk.
- Short-term bonds: Low interest rate risk, high reinvestment rate risk.
- Nothing is riskless!

9 - 29

True or False: "All 10-year bonds have the same price and reinvestment rate risk."

False! Low coupon bonds have less reinvestment rate risk but more price risk than high coupon bonds.

9 - 30

Semiannual Bonds

1. Multiply years by 2 to get periods = 2n.
2. Divide nominal rate by 2 to get periodic rate = $k_d/2$.
3. Divide annual INT by 2 to get PMT = INT/2.

INPUTS	2n	$k_d/2$	OK	INT/2	OK
	N	I/YR	PV	PMT	FV
OUTPUT					

9 - 31

Find the value of 10-year, 10% coupon, semiannual bond if k_d = 13%.

	N	I/YR	PV	PMT	FV
	2(10)	13/2		100/2	
INPUTS	20	6.5		50	1000
OUTPUT			-834.72		

9 - 32

You could buy, for $1,000, either a 10%, 10-year, annual payment bond or an equally risky 10%, 10-year semiannual bond. Which would you prefer?

The semiannual bond's EFF% is:

$$EFF\% = \left(1 + \frac{i_{Nom}}{m}\right)^m - 1 = \left(1 + \frac{0.10}{2}\right)^2 - 1 = 10.25\%.$$

10.25% > 10% EFF% on annual bond, so buy semiannual bond.

9 - 33

If $1,000 is the proper price for the semiannual bond, what is the proper price for the annual payment bond?

- Semiannual bond has k_{Nom} = 10%, with EFF% = 10.25%. Should earn same EFF% on annual payment bond, so:

	N	I/YR	PV	PMT	FV
INPUTS	10	10.25		100	1000
OUTPUT			-984.80		

9 - 34

- At a price of $984.80, the annual and semiannual bonds would be in equilibrium, because investors would earn EFF% = 10.25% on either bond.

9 - 35

A 10-year, 10% semiannual coupon, $1,000 par value bond is selling for $1,135.90 with an 8% yield to maturity. It can be called after 5 years at $1,050.

What's the bond's nominal yield to call (YTC)?

	N	I/YR	PV	PMT	FV
INPUTS	10		-1135.9	50	1050
OUTPUT		3.765 x 2 = 7.53%			

9 - 36

k_{Nom} = 7.53% is the rate brokers would quote. Could also calculate EFF% to call:

EFF% = $(1.03765)^2 - 1$ = 7.672%.

This rate could be compared to monthly mortgages, and so on.

9 - 37

If you bought bonds, would you be more likely to earn YTM or YTC?

- Coupon rate = 10% vs. YTC = k_d = 7.53%. Could raise money by selling new bonds which pay 7.53%.
- Could thus replace bonds which pay $100/year with bonds that pay only $75.30/year.
- Investors should expect a call, hence YTC = 7.5%, not YTM = 8%.

9 - 38

- In general, if a bond sells at a premium, then (1) coupon > k_d, so (2) a call is likely.
- So, expect to earn:
  - YTC on premium bonds.
  - YTM on par & discount bonds.

9 - 39

- Disney recently issued 100-year bonds with a YTM of 7.5%--this represents the promised return. The expected return was less than 7.5% when the bonds were issued.
- If issuer defaults, investors receive less than the promised return. Therefore, the expected return on corporate and municipal bonds is less than the promised return.

9 - 40

Bond Ratings Provide One Measure of Default Risk

	Investment Grade				Junk Bonds			
Moody's	Aaa	Aa	A	Baa	Ba	B	Caa	C
S&P	AAA	AA	A	BBB	BB	B	CCC	D

9 - 41

What factors affect default risk and bond ratings?

- Financial performance
  - Debt ratio
  - TIE, FCC ratios
  - Current ratios

(More...)

9 - 42

- Provisions in the bond contract
  - Secured versus unsecured debt
  - Senior versus subordinated debt
  - Guarantee provisions
  - Sinking fund provisions
  - Debt maturity

(More...)

9 - 43

- Other factors
  - Earnings stability
  - Regulatory environment
  - Potential product liability
  - Accounting policies

9 - 44

Top Ten Largest U.S. Corporate Bond Financings, as of July 1999

Issuer	Date	Amount
Ford Motor Co.	July 1999	$8.6 billion
AT&T	Mar 1999	$8.0 billion
RJR Holdings	May 1989	$6.1 billion
WorldCom	Aug 1998	$6.1 billion
Sprint	Nov 1998	$5.0 billion

9 - 45

Bankruptcy

- Two main chapters of Federal Bankruptcy Act:
  - Chapter 11, Reorganization
  - Chapter 7, Liquidation
- Typically, company wants Chapter 11, creditors may prefer Chapter 7.

9 - 46

- If company can't meet its obligations, it files under Chapter 11. That stops creditors from foreclosing, taking assets, and shutting down the business.
- Company has 120 days to file a reorganization plan.
  - Court appoints a "trustee" to supervise reorganization.
  - Management usually stays in control.

9 - 47

- Company must demonstrate in its reorganization plan that it is "worth more alive than dead."

Otherwise, judge will order liquidation under Chapter 7.

9 - 48

- If the company is liquidated, here's the payment priority:
  1. Secured creditors from sales of secured assets.
  2. Trustee's costs
  3. Wages, subject to limits
  4. Taxes
  5. Unfunded pension liabilities
  6. Unsecured creditors
  7. Preferred stock
  8. Common stock

9 - 49

- In a liquidation, unsecured creditors generally get zero. This makes them more willing to participate in reorganization even though their claims are greatly scaled back.
- Various groups of creditors vote on the reorganization plan. If both the majority of the creditors and the judge approve, company "emerges" from bankruptcy with lower debts, reduced interest charges, and a chance for success.

BLUEPRINTS: CHAPTER 10
STOCKS AND THEIR VALUATION

Robert Balik and Carol Kiefer are senior vice-presidents of the Mutual of Chicago Insurance Company. They are co-directors of the company's pension fund management division, with Balik having responsibility for fixed income securities (primarily bonds) and Kiefer being responsible for equity investments. A major new client, the California League of Cities, has requested that Mutual of Chicago present an investment seminar to the mayors of the represented cities, and Balik and Kiefer, who will make the actual presentation, have asked you to help them.

To illustrate the common stock valuation process, Balik and Kiefer have asked you to analyze the Bon Temps Company, an employment agency that supplies word processor operators and computer programmers to businesses with temporarily heavy workloads. You are to answer the following questions.

a. Describe briefly the legal rights and privileges of common stockholders.

b. (1) Write out a formula that can be used to value any stock, regardless of its dividend pattern.

(2) What is a constant growth stock? How are constant growth stocks valued?

(3) What happens if a company has a constant g which exceeds k_s? Will many stocks have expected $g > k_s$ in the short run (i.e., for the next few years)? In the long run (i.e., forever)?

c. Assume that Bon Temps has a beta coefficient of 1.2, that the risk-free rate (the yield on T-bonds) is 7 percent, and that the required rate of return on the market is 12 percent. What is the required rate of return on the firm's stock?

d. Assume that Bon Temps is a constant growth company whose last dividend (D_0, which was paid yesterday) was $2.00, and whose dividend is expected to grow indefinitely at a 6 percent rate.

(1) What is the firm's expected dividend stream over the next 3 years?

(2) What is the firm's current stock price?

(3) What is the stock's expected value 1 year from now?

(4) What are the expected dividend yield, the capital gains yield, and the total return during the first year?

e. Now assume that the stock is currently selling at $30.29. What is the expected rate of return on the stock?

f. What would the stock price be if its dividends were expected to have zero growth?

g. Now assume that Bon Temps is expected to experience supernormal growth of 30 percent for the next 3 years, then to return to its long-run constant growth rate of 6 percent. What is the stock's value under these conditions? What is its expected dividend yield and capital gains yield in Year 1? In Year 4?

h. Is the stock price based more on long-term or short-term expectations? Answer this by finding the percentage of Bon Temps current stock price based on dividends expected more than 3 years in the future.

i. Suppose Bon Temps is expected to experience zero growth during the first 3 years and then to resume its steady-state growth of 6 percent in the fourth year. What is the stock's value now? What is its expected dividend yield and its capital gains yield in Year 1? In Year 4?

j. Finally, assume that Bon Temps' earnings and dividends are expected to decline by a constant 6 percent per year, that is, $g = -6\%$. Why would anyone be willing to buy such a stock and at what price should it sell? What would be the dividend yield and capital gains yield in each year?

k. What does market equilibrium mean?

l. If equilibrium does not exist, how will it be established?

m. What is the Efficient Markets Hypothesis, what are its three forms, and what are its implications?

n. Phyfe Company recently issued preferred stock. It pays an annual dividend of $5, and the issue price was $50 per share. What is the expected return to an investor on this preferred stock?

10 - 1

CHAPTER 10
Stocks and Their Valuation

- Features of common stock
- Determining common stock values
- Efficient markets
- Preferred stock

10 - 2

Facts about Common Stock

- Represents ownership.
- Ownership implies control.
- Stockholders elect directors.
- Directors hire management.
- Management's goal: Maximize stock price.

10 - 3

What's classified stock? How might classified stock be used?

- Classified stock has special provisions.
- Could classify existing stock as founders' shares, with voting rights but dividend restrictions.
- New shares might be called "Class A" shares, with voting restrictions but full dividend rights.

10 - 4

When is a stock sale an initial public offering (IPO)?

- A firm "goes public" through an IPO when the stock is first offered to the public.
- Prior to an IPO, shares are typically owned by the firm's managers, key employees, and, in many situations, venture capital providers.

10 - 5

Average Initial Returns on IPOs in Various Countries

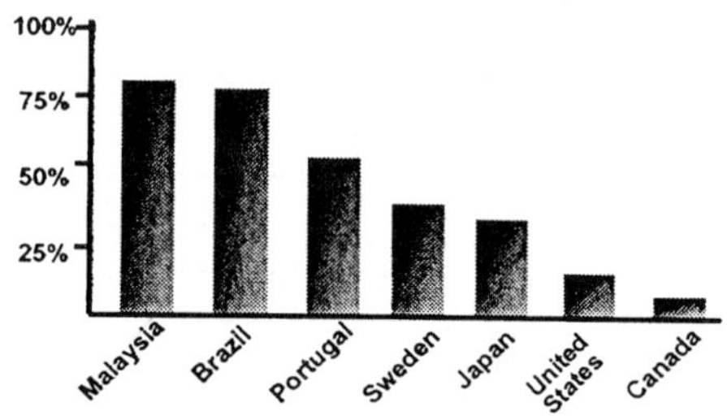

10 - 6

Different Approaches for Valuing Common Stock

- Dividend growth model
- Using the multiples of comparable firms
- Free cash flow method (covered in Chapter 12)

10 - 7

Stock Value = PV of Dividends

$$\hat{P}_0 = \frac{D_1}{(1+k_s)^1} + \frac{D_2}{(1+k_s)^2} + \frac{D_3}{(1+k_s)^3} + \ldots + \frac{D_\infty}{(1+k_s)^\infty}$$

What is a constant growth stock?

One whose dividends are expected to grow forever at a constant rate, g.

10 - 8

For a constant growth stock,

$$D_1 = D_0(1+g)^1$$
$$D_2 = D_0(1+g)^2$$
$$D_t = D_t(1+g)^t$$

If g is constant, then:

$$\hat{P}_0 = \frac{D_0(1+g)}{k_s - g} = \frac{D_1}{k_s -}$$

10 - 9

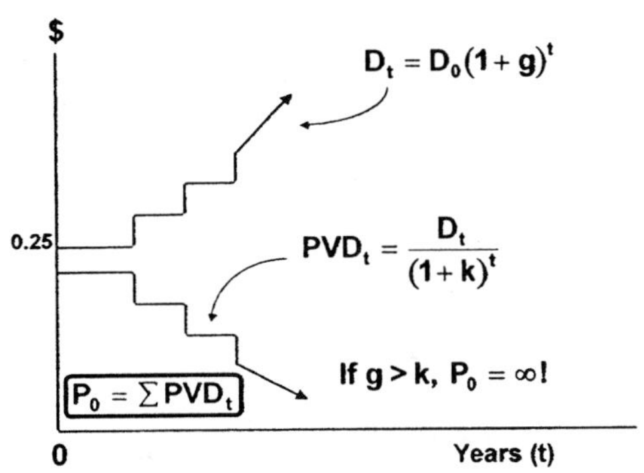

10 - 10

What happens if $g > k_s$?

$$\hat{P}_0 = \frac{D_1}{k_s - g} \text{ requires } k_s > g.$$

- If $k_s < g$, get negative stock price, which is nonsense.
- We can't use model unless (1) $g < k_s$ and (2) g is expected to be constant forever. Because g must be a long-term growth rate, it cannot be $> k_s$.

10 - 11

Assume beta = 1.2, k_{RF} = 7%, and k_M = 12%. What is the required rate of return on the firm's stock?

Use the SML to calculate k_s:

$$k_s = k_{RF} + (k_M - k_{RF})b_{Firm}$$
$$= 7\% + (12\% - 7\%)(1.2)$$
$$= 13\%.$$

10 - 12

D_0 was \$2.00 and g is a constant 6%. Find the expected dividends for the next 3 years, and their PVs. k_s = 13%.

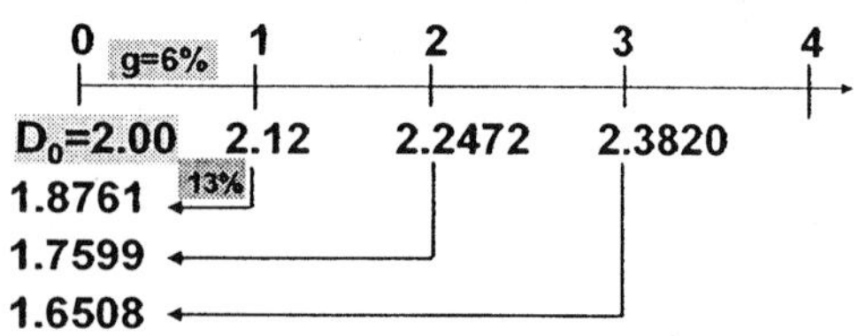

10 - 13

What's the stock's market value? D_0 = 2.00, k_s = 13%, g = 6%.

Constant growth model:

$$\hat{P}_0 = \frac{D_0(1+g)}{k_s - g} = \frac{D_1}{k_s -}$$

$$= \frac{\$2.12}{0.13 - 0.06} = \frac{\$2.12}{0.07} \$30.29.$$

10 - 14

What is the stock's market value one year from now, $\hat{P}_1$?

- D_1 will have been paid, so expected dividends are D_2, D_3, D_4 and so on. Thus,

$$\hat{P}_1 = \frac{D_2}{k_s - g}$$

$$= \frac{\$2.2472}{0.07} = \$32.10.$$

10 - 15

Find the expected dividend yield and capital gains yield during the first year.

$$\text{Dividend yield} = \frac{D_1}{P_0} = \frac{\$2.12}{\$30.29} = 7.0\%.$$

$$\text{CG Yield} = \frac{\hat{P}_1 - P_0}{P_0} = \frac{\$32.10 - \$30.29}{\$30.29}$$

$$= 6.0\%.$$

10 - 16

Find the total return during the first year.

- Total return = Dividend yield + Capital gains yield.
- Total return = 7% + 6% = 13%.
- Total return = 13% = k_s.
- For constant growth stock:

  Capital gains yield = 6% = g.

10 - 17

Rearrange model to rate of return form:

$$\hat{P}_0 = \frac{D_1}{k_s - g} \text{ to } \hat{k}_s = \frac{D_1}{P_0} + g.$$

Then, $\hat{k}_s$ = \$2.12/\$30.29 + 0.06
= 0.07 + 0.06 = 13%.

10 - 18

What would P_0 be if g = 0?

The dividend stream would be a perpetuity.

0	1	2	3
k_s=13%	2.00	2.00	2.00

$$\hat{P}_0 = \frac{PMT}{k} = \frac{\$2.00}{0.13} = \$15.38.$$

10 - 19

If we have supernormal growth of 30% for 3 years, then a long-run constant g = 6%, what is $\hat{P}_0$? k is still 13%.

- Can no longer use constant growth model.
- However, growth becomes constant after 3 years.

10 - 20

Nonconstant growth followed by constant growth:

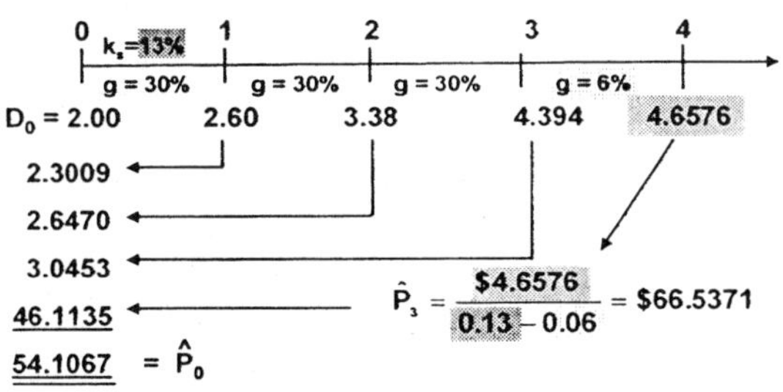

10 - 21

What is the expected dividend yield and capital gains yield at t = 0? At t = 4?

At t = 0:

$$\text{Dividend yield} = \frac{D_1}{P_0} = \frac{\$2.60}{\$54.11} = 4.8\%.$$

CG Yield = 13.0% - 4.8% = 8.2%.

(More...)

10 - 22

- During nonconstant growth, dividend yield and capital gains yield are not constant.
- If current growth is greater than g, current capital gains yield is greater than g.
- After t = 3, g = constant = 6%, so the t t = 4 capital gains gains yield = 6%.
- Because k_s = 13%, the t = 4 dividend yield = 13% - 6% = 7%.

10 - 23

Is the stock price based on short-term growth?

- The current stock price is $54.11.
- The PV of dividends beyond year 3 is $46.11 ($\hat{P}_3$ discounted back to t = 0).
- The percentage of stock price due to "long-term" dividends is:

$$\frac{\$46.11}{\$54.11} = 85.2\%.$$

10 - 24

If most of a stock's value is due to long-term cash flows, why do so many managers focus on quarterly earnings?

- Sometimes changes in quarterly earnings are a signal of future changes in cash flows. This would affect the current stock price.
- Sometimes managers have bonuses tied to quarterly earnings.

10 - 25

Suppose g = 0 for t = 1 to 3, and then g is a constant 6%. What is $\hat{P}_0$?

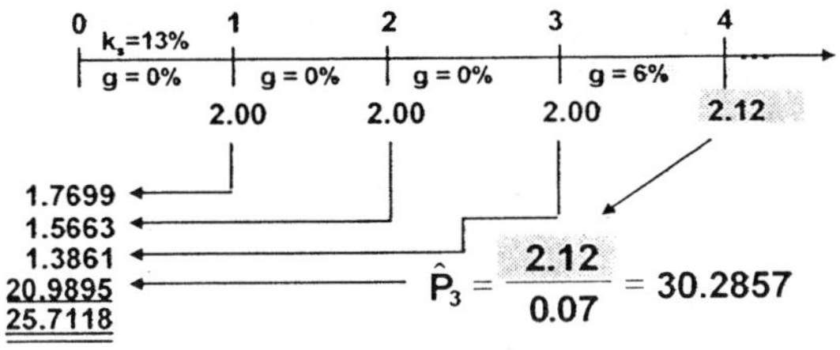

10 - 26

What is dividend yield and capital gains yield at t = 0 and at t = 3?

t = 0: $\frac{D_1}{P_0} = \frac{2.00}{\$25.72} = 7.8\%.$

CGY = 13.0% - 7.8% = 5.2%.

t = 3: Now have constant growth with g = capital gains yield = 6% and dividend yield = 7%.

10 - 27

If g = -6%, would anyone buy the stock? If so, at what price?

Firm still has earnings and still pays dividends, so $\hat{P}_0 > 0$:

$$\hat{}_0 = \frac{D_0(1+g)}{k_s - g} = \frac{D_1}{k_s - }$$

$$= \frac{\$2.00(0.94)}{0.13 - (-0.06)} = \frac{\$1.88}{0.19} = \$9.89.$$

10 - 28

What are the annual dividend and capital gains yield?

Capital gains yield = g = -6.0%.

Dividend yield = 13.0% - (-6.0%)
= 19.0%.

Both yields are constant over time, with the high dividend yield (19%) offsetting the negative capital gains yield.

10 - 29

Using the Multiples of Comparable Firms to Estimate Stock Price

- Analysts often use the following multiples to value stocks:
  - P/E
  - P/CF or P/EBITDA
  - P/Sales
  - P/Customer
- Example: Based on comparable firms, estimate the appropriate P/E. Multiply this by expected earnings to back out an estimate of the stock price.

10 - 30

What is market equilibrium?

In equilibrium, stock prices are stable. There is no general tendency for people to buy versus to sell.

The expected price, $\hat{P}$, must equal the actual price, P. In other words, the fundamental value must be the same as the price.

(More...)

10 - 31

In equilibrium, expected returns must equal required returns:

$$\hat{k}_s = D_1/P_0 + g = k_s = k_{RF} + (k_M - k_{RF})b.$$

10 - 32

How is equilibrium established?

If $\hat{k}_s = \frac{\hat{D}_1}{P_0} + g > k_s$, then P_0 is "too low."

If the price is lower than the fundamental value, then the stock is a "bargain."

Buy orders will exceed sell orders, the price will be bid up, and D_1/P_0 falls until

$$D_1/P_0 + g = \hat{k}_s = k_s.$$

10 - 33

Why do stock prices change?

$$\hat{P}_0 = \frac{D_1}{k_i - g}$$

- $k_i = k_{RF} + (k_M - k_{RF})b_i$ could change.
  - Inflation expectations
  - Risk aversion
  - Company risk
- g could change.

10 - 34

What's the Efficient Market Hypothesis (EMH)?

Securities are normally in equilibrium and are "fairly priced." One cannot "beat the market" except through good luck or inside information.

(More...)

10 - 35

1. Weak-form EMH:

Can't profit by looking at past trends. A recent decline is no reason to think stocks will go up (or down) in the future. Evidence supports weak-form EMH, but "technical analysis" is still used.

10 - 36

2. Semistrong-form EMH:

All publicly available information is reflected in stock prices, so it doesn't pay to pore over annual reports looking for undervalued stocks. Largely true.

10 - 37

3. **Strong-form EMH:**
All information, even inside information, is embedded in stock prices. Not true--insiders can gain by trading on the basis of insider information, but that's illegal.

10 - 38

Markets are generally efficient because:

1. 100,000 or so trained analysts--MBAs, CFAs, and PhDs--work for firms like Fidelity, Merrill, Morgan, and Prudential.
2. These analysts have similar access to data and megabucks to invest.
3. Thus, news is reflected in P_0 almost instantaneously.

10 - 39

Preferred Stock

- Hybrid security.
- Similar to bonds in that preferred stockholders receive a fixed dividend which must be paid before dividends can be paid on common stock.
- However, unlike bonds, preferred stock dividends can be omitted without fear of pushing the firm into bankruptcy.

10 - 40

What's the expected return on preferred stock with V_{ps} = \$50 and annual dividend = \$5?

$$V_{ps} = \$50 = \frac{\$5}{\hat{k}_{ps}}$$

$$\hat{k}_{ps} = \frac{\$5}{\$50} = 0.10 = 10.0\%.$$

BLUEPRINTS: CHAPTER 11
THE COST OF CAPITAL

During the last few years, Cox Technologies has been too constrained by the high cost of capital to make many capital investments. Recently, though, capital costs have been declining, and the company has decided to look seriously at a major expansion program that had been proposed by the marketing department. Assume that you are an assistant to Jerry Lee, the financial vice-president. Your first task is to estimate Cox's cost of capital. Lee has provided you with the following data, which he believes may be relevant to your task:

1. The firm's tax rate is 40 percent.
2. The current price of Cox's 12 percent coupon, semiannual payment, noncallable bonds with 15 years remaining to maturity is $1,153.72. Cox does not use short-term interest-bearing debt on a permanent basis. New bonds would be privately placed with no flotation cost.
3. The current price of the firm's 10 percent, $100 par value, quarterly dividend, perpetual preferred stock is $113.10. Cox would incur flotation costs of $2.00 per share on a new issue.
4. Cox's common stock is currently selling at $50 per share. Its last dividend (D_0) was $4.19, and dividends are expected to grow at a constant rate of 5 percent in the foreseeable future. Cox's beta is 1.2, the yield on T-bonds is 7 percent, and the market risk premium is estimated to be 6 percent. For the bond-yield-plus-risk-premium approach, the firm uses a 4 percentage point risk premium.
5. Cox's target capital structure is 30 percent long-term debt, 10 percent preferred stock, and 60 percent common equity.

To structure the task somewhat, Lee has asked you to answer the following questions.

a. (1) What sources of capital should be included when you estimate Cox's weighted average cost of capital (WACC)?

(2) Should the component costs be figured on a before-tax or an after-tax basis?

(3) Should the costs be historical (embedded) costs or new (marginal) costs?

b. What is the market interest rate on Cox's debt and its component cost of debt?

c. (1) What is the firm's cost of preferred stock?

(2) Cox's preferred stock is riskier to investors than its debt, yet the preferred's yield to investors is lower than the yield to maturity on the debt. Does this suggest that

you have made a mistake? (Hint: Think about taxes.)

d. (1) What are the two primary ways companies raise common equity?

(2) Why is there a cost associated with reinvested earnings?

(3) Cox doesn't plan to issue new shares of common stock. Using the CAPM approach, what is Cox's estimated cost of equity?

e. (1) What is the estimated cost of equity using the discounted cash flow (DCF) approach?

(2) Suppose the firm has historically earned 15 percent on equity (ROE) and retained 35 percent of earnings, and investors expect this situation to continue in the future. How could you use this information to estimate the future dividend growth rate, and what growth rate would you get? Is this consistent with the 5 percent growth rate given earlier?

(3) Could the DCF method be applied if the growth rate was not constant? How?

f. What is the cost of equity based on the bond-yield-plus-risk-premium method?

g. What is your final estimate for the cost of equity, k_s?

h. What is Cox's weighted average cost of capital (WACC)?

i. What factors influence a company's WACC?

j. Should the company use the composite WACC as the hurdle rate for each of its projects?

k. What are three types of project risk How is each type of risk used?

l. What procedures are usd to determine the risk-adjusted cost of capital for a particular project or division? What approaches are used to measure a project's beta?

m. Cox is interested in establishing a new division, which will focus primarily on developing new Internet-based projects. In trying to determine the cost of capital for this new division, you discover that stand-alone firms involved in similar projects have on average the following characteristics:

- Their capital structure is 10 percent debt and 90 percent common equity.
- Their cost of debt is typically 12 percent.
- The beta is 1.7.

Given this information, what would your estimate be for the division's cost of capital?

n. Explain in words why new common stock that is raised externally has a higher percentage cost than equity that is raised internally by reinvesting earnings.

o. (1) Cox estimates that if it issues new common stock, the flotation cost will be 15 percent. Coleman incorporates the flotation costs into the DCF approach. What is the estimated cost of newly issued stock, taking into account the flotation cost?

(2) Suppose Cox issues 30-year debt with a par value of $1,000 and a coupon rate of 10 percent, paid annually. If flotation costs are 2 percent, what is the after-tax cost of debt for the new bond issue?

p. What four common mistakes in estimating the WACC should Cox avoid?

11 - 1

CHAPTER 11
The Cost of Capital

- Cost of Capital Components
  - Debt
  - Preferred
  - Common Equity
- WACC

11 - 2

What types of long-term capital do firms use?

- Long-term debt
- Preferred stock
- Common equity

11 - 3

Should we focus on before-tax or after-tax capital costs?

- Tax effects associated with financing can be incorporated either in capital budgeting cash flows or in cost of capital.
- Most firms incorporate tax effects in the cost of capital. Therefore, focus on after-tax costs.
- Only cost of debt is affected.

11 - 4

Should we focus on historical (embedded) costs or new (marginal) costs?

The cost of capital is used primarily to make decisions which involve raising and investing new capital. So, we should focus on marginal costs.

11 - 5

A 15-year, 12% semiannual bond sells for $1,153.72. What's k_d?

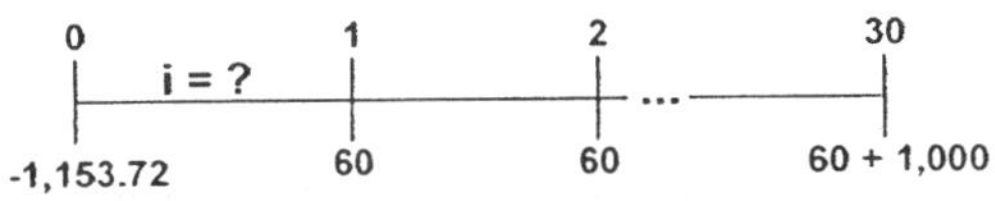

INPUTS	30		-1153.72	60	1000
	N	I/YR	PV	PMT	FV
OUTPUT		5.0% x 2 = k_d = 10%			

11 - 6

Component Cost of Debt

- Interest is tax deductible, so

  $k_{d\,AT} = k_{d\,BT}(1 - T)$

  $= 10\%(1 - 0.40) = 6\%.$

- Use nominal rate.
- Flotation costs small, so ignore.

11 - 7

What's the cost of preferred stock?
P_P = \$113.10; 10%Q; Par = \$100; F = \$2.

Use this formula:

$$k_{ps} = \frac{D_{ps}}{P_n} = \frac{0.1(\$100)}{\$113.10 - \$2.00}$$

$$= \frac{\$10}{\$111.10} = 0.090 = 9.0\%.$$

11 - 8

Picture of Preferred

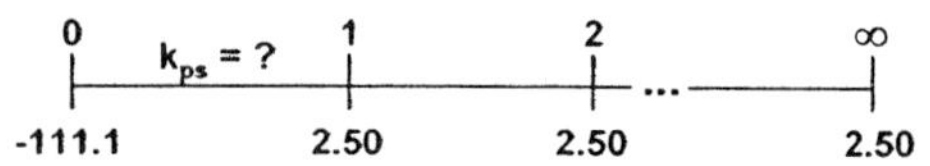

$$\$111.10 = \frac{D_Q}{k_{Per}} = \frac{\$2.50}{k_{Per}}.$$

$$k_{Per} = \frac{\$2.50}{\$111.10} = 2.25\%; k_{ps(Nom)} = 2.25\%(4) = 9\%.$$

11 - 9

Note:

- **Flotation costs for preferred are significant, so are reflected. Use net price.**
- **Preferred dividends are not deductible, so no tax adjustment. Just k_{ps}.**
- **Nominal k_{ps} is used.**

11 - 10

Is preferred stock more or less risky to investors than debt?

- More risky; company not required to pay preferred dividend.
- However, firms want to pay preferred dividend. Otherwise, (1) cannot pay common dividend, (2) difficult to raise additional funds, and (3) preferred stockholders may gain control of firm.

11 - 11

Why is yield on preferred lower than k_d?

- Corporations own most preferred stock, because 70% of preferred dividends are nontaxable to corporations.
- Therefore, preferred often has a lower B-T yield than the B-T yield on debt.
- The A-T yield to investors and A-T cost to the issuer are higher on preferred than on debt, which is consistent with the higher risk of preferred.

11 - 12

Example:

k_{ps} = 9% k_d = 10% T = 40%

$k_{ps, AT} = k_{ps} - k_{ps}(1 - 0.7)(T)$

$= 9\% - 9\%(0.3)(0.4) = 7.92\%$

$k_{d, AT} = 10\% - 10\%(0.4) = \underline{6.00\%}$

A-T Risk Premium on Preferred = $\underline{\underline{1.92\%}}$

11 - 13

What are the two ways that companies can raise common equity?

- Companies can issue new shares of common stock.
- Companies can reinvest earnings.

11 - 14

Why is there a cost for reinvested earnings?

- Earnings can be reinvested or paid out as dividends.
- Investors could buy other securities, earn a return.
- Thus, there is an opportunity cost if earnings are reinvested.

11 - 15

- Opportunity cost: The return stockholders could earn on alternative investments of equal risk.
- They could buy similar stocks and earn k_s, or company could repurchase its own stock and earn k_s. So, k_s, is the cost of reinvested earnings and it is the cost of equity.

11 - 16

Three ways to determine the cost of equity, k_s:

1. CAPM: $k_s = k_{RF} + (k_M - k_{RF})b$
   $= k_{RF} + (RP_M)b.$
2. DCF: $k_s = D_1/P_0 + g.$
3. Own-Bond-Yield-Plus-Risk Premium:

   $k_s = k_d + RP.$

11 - 17

What's the cost of equity based on the CAPM? $k_{RF} = 7\%$, $RP_M = 6\%$, $b = 1.2$.

$k_s = k_{RF} + (k_M - k_{RF})b.$

$= 7.0\% + (6.0\%)1.2 = 14.2\%.$

11 - 18

What's the DCF cost of equity, k_s? Given: $D_0 = \$4.19$; $P_0 = \$50$; $g = 5\%$.

$$k_s = \frac{D_1}{P_0} + g = \frac{D_0(1+g)}{P_0} + g$$

$$= \frac{\$4.19(1.05)}{\$50} + 0.05$$

$$= 0.088 + 0.05$$

$$= 13.8\%.$$

11 - 19

Suppose the company has been earning 15% on equity (ROE = 15%) and retaining 35% (dividend payout = 65%), and this situation is expected to continue.

What's the expected future g?

11 - 20

Retention growth rate:

g = b(ROE) = 0.35(15%) = 5.25%.

Here b = Fraction retained.

Close to g = 5% given earlier. Think of bank account paying 10% with b = 0, b = 1.0, and b = 0.5. What's g?

11 - 21

Could DCF methodology be applied if g is not constant?

- YES, nonconstant g stocks are expected to have constant g at some point, generally in 5 to 10 years.
- But calculations get complicated. See "Ch 11 Tool Kit.xls".

11 - 22

Find k_s using the own-bond-yield-plus-risk-premium method. (k_d = 10%, RP = 4%.)

$k_s = k_d + RP$
$= 10.0\% + 4.0\% = 14.0\%$

- This RP $\neq$ CAPM RP_M.
- Produces ballpark estimate of k_s. Useful check.

11 - 23

What's a reasonable final estimate of k_s?

Method	Estimate
CAPM	14.2%
DCF	13.8%
k_d + RP	14.0%
Average	14.0%

11 - 24

What's the WACC?

$$WACC = w_d k_d(1 - T) + w_{ps}k_{ps} + w_{ce}k_s$$

$$= 0.3(10\%)(0.6) + 0.1(9\%) + 0.6(14\%)$$

$$= 1.8\% + 0.9\% + 8.4\% = 11.1\%.$$

11 - 25

WACC Estimates for Some Large U. S. Corporations

Company	WACC
Intel	12.9%
General Electric	11.9
Motorola	11.3
Coca-Cola	11.2
Walt Disney	10.0
AT&T	9.8
Wal-Mart	9.8
Exxon	8.8
H. J. Heinz	8.5
BellSouth	8.2

11 - 26

What factors influence a company's WACC?

- Market conditions, especially interest rates and tax rates.
- The firm's capital structure and dividend policy.
- The firm's investment policy. Firms with riskier projects generally have a higher WACC.

11 - 27

Should the company use the composite WACC as the hurdle rate for each of its projects?

- NO! The composite WACC reflects the risk of an average project undertaken by the firm. Therefore, the WACC only represents the "hurdle rate" for a typical project with average risk.
- Different projects have different risks. The project's WACC should be adjusted to reflect the project's risk.

11 - 28

Risk and the Cost of Capital

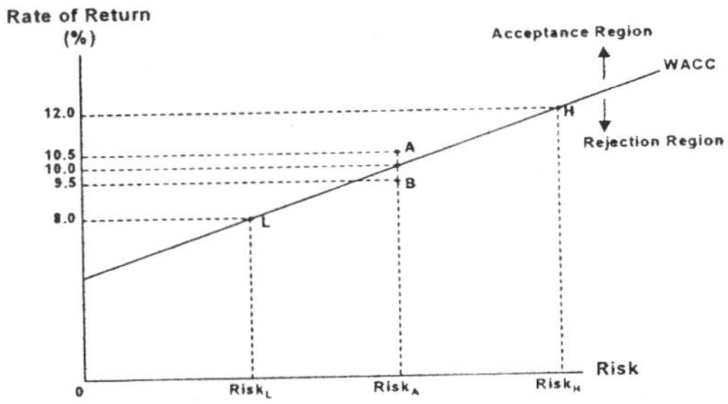

11 - 29

Divisional Cost of Capital

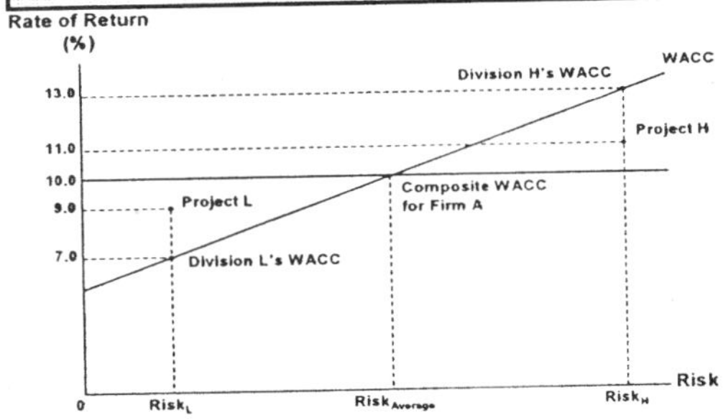

11 - 30

What are the three types of project risk?

- Stand-alone risk
- Corporate risk
- Market risk

11 - 31

How is each type of risk used?

- Market risk is theoretically best in most situations.
- However, creditors, customers, suppliers, and employees are more affected by corporate risk.
- Therefore, corporate risk is also relevant.

11 - 32

What procedures are used to determine the risk-adjusted cost of capital for a particular project or division?

- Subjective adjustments to the firm's composite WACC.
- Estimate what the cost of capital would be if the project/division were a stand-alone firm. This requires estimating the project's beta.

11 - 33

Methods for Estimating Beta for a Division or a Project

1. Pure play. Find several publicly traded companies exclusively in project's business.

   Use average of their betas as proxy for project's beta.

   Hard to find such companies.

11 - 34

2. Accounting beta. Run regression between project's ROA and S&P index ROA.

   Accounting betas are correlated (0.5 – 0.6) with market betas.

   But normally can't get data on new projects' ROAs before the capital budgeting decision has been made.

11 - 35

Find the division's market risk and cost of capital based on the CAPM, given these inputs:

- Target debt ratio = 10%.
- k_d = 12%.
- k_{RF} = 7%.
- Tax rate = 40%.
- $beta_{Division}$ = 1.7.
- Market risk premium = 6%.

11 - 36

- Beta = 1.7, so division has more market risk than average.
- Division's required return on equity:

$$k_s = k_{RF} + (k_M - k_{RF})b_{Div.}$$
$$= 7\% + (6\%)1.7 = 17.2\%.$$

$$WACC_{Div.} = w_d k_d(1 - T) + w_c k_s$$
$$= 0.1(12\%)(0.6) + 0.9(17.2\%)$$
$$= 16.2\%.$$

11 - 37

How does the division's WACC compare with the firm's overall WACC?

- Division WACC = 16.2% versus company WACC = 11.1%.
- Indicates that the division's market risk is greater than firm's average project.
- "Typical" projects within this division would be accepted if their returns are above 16.2%.

11 - 38

Why is the cost of internal equity from reinvested earnings cheaper than the cost of issuing new common stock?

1. When a company issues new common stock they also have to pay flotation costs to the underwriter.
2. Issuing new common stock may send a negative signal to the capital markets, which may depress stock price.

11 - 39

Estimate the cost of new common equity: P_0=\$50, D_0=\$4.19, g=5%, and F=15%.

$$k_e = \frac{D_0(1+g)}{\text{[illegible]}} + g$$

$$= \frac{\$4.19(1.05)}{\$50(1-0.15)} + 5.0\%$$

$$= \$4.40 + 5.0\% = 15.4\%.$$

11 - 40

Estimate the cost of new 30-year debt: Par=$1,000, Coupon=10%paid annually, and F=15%.

- Using a financial calculator:
  - N = 30
  - PV = 1000(1-.02) = 980
  - PMT = -(.10)(1000)(1-.4) = -60
  - FV = -1000
- Solving for I: 6.15%

11 - 41

Comments about flotation costs:

- Flotation costs depend on the risk of the firm and the type of capital being raised.
- The flotation costs are highest for common equity. However, since most firms issue equity infrequently, the per-project cost is fairly small.
- We will frequently ignore flotation costs when calculating the WACC.

11 - 42

Four Mistakes to Avoid

1. When estimating the cost of debt, use the current interest rate on new debt, not the coupon rate on existing debt.
2. When estimating the risk premium for the CAPM approach, don't subtract the *current* long-term T-bond rate from the *historical* average return on common stocks.

(More ...)

11 - 43

For example, if the historical k_M has been about 12.7% and inflation drives the current k_{RF} up to 10%, the current market risk premium is not 12.7% - 10% = 2.7%!

(More ...)

11 - 44

3. Use the target capital structure to determine the weights.

   If you don't know the target weights, then use the current market value of equity, and never the book value of equity.

   If you don't know the market value of debt, then the book value of debt often is a reasonable approximation, especially for short-term debt.

(More...)

11 - 45

4. Capital components are sources of funding that come from investors.

   Accounts payable, accruals, and deferred taxes are not sources of funding that come from investors, so they are not included in the calculation of the WACC.

   We do adjust for these items when calculating the cash flows of the project, but not when calculating the WACC.

BLUEPRINTS: CHAPTER 12

PUTTING THE PIECES TOGETHER: CORPORATE VALUATION AND VALUE-BASED MANAGEMENT

You have been hired as a consultant to Kulpa Fishing Supplies (KFS), a company that is seeking to increase its value. KFS has asked you to estimate the value of two privately held companies that KFS is considering acquiring. But first, the senior management of KFS would like for you to explain how to value companies that don't pay any dividends. You have structured your presentation around the following questions.

a. List the two types of assets that companies own.

b. What are assets-in-place? How can their value be estimated?

c. What are non-operating assets? How can their value be estimated?

d. What is the total value of a corporation? Who has claims on this value?

e. The first acquisition target is a privately held company in a mature industry. The company currently has free cash flow of $20 million. Its WACC is 10% and it is expected to grow at a constant rate of 5%. The company has marketable securities of $100 million. It is financed with $200 million of debt, $50 million of preferred stock, and $210 million of book equity.

   (1) What is its value of operations?

   (2) What is its total corporate value? What is its value of equity?

   (3) What is its MVA (MVA = Total corporate value – total book value)?

f. The second acquisition target is a privately held company in a growing industry. The target has recently borrowed $40 million to finance its expansion; it has no other debt or preferred stock. It pays no dividends and currently has no marketable securities. KFS expects the company to produce free cash flows of -$5 million in one year, $10 million in two years, and $20 million in three years. After three years, free cash flow will grow at a rate of 6%. Its WACC is 10% and it currently has 10 million shares of stock.

   (1) What is its horizon value (i.e., its value of operations at year three)? What is its current value of operations (i.e., at time zero)?

(2) What is its value of equity on a price per share basis?

g. KFS is also interested in applying value-based management to its own divisions. Explain what value-based management is.

h. What are the four value drivers? How does each of them affect value?

i. What is expected return on invested capital (EROIC)? Why is the spread between EROIC and WACC so important?

j. KFS has two divisions. Both have current sales of $1,000, current expected growth of 5%, and a WACC of 10%. Division A has high profitability (OP=6%) but high capital requirements (CR=78%). Division B has low profitability (OP=4%) but low capital requirements (CR=27%). What is the MVA of each division, based on the current growth of 5%? What is the MVA of each division if growth is 6%?

k. What is the EROIC of each division for 5% growth and for 6% growth? How is this related to MVA?

l. The managers at KFS have heard that corporate governance can affect shareholder value. List for them the two primary mechanisms of corporate governance.

m. Why is entrenched management potentially harmful to shareholders?

n. List three provisions in the corporate charter that affect takeovers.

o. Explain the difference between insiders and outsiders on the board of directors. What are interlocking boards?

p. What is a stock option in a compensation plan?

12 - 1

CHAPTER 12
Corporate Valuation and Value-Based Management

- Corporate Valuation
- Value-Based Management
- Corporate Governance

12 - 2

Corporate Valuation: List the two types of assets that a company owns.

- Assets-in-place
- Financial, or nonoperating, assets

12 - 3

Assets-in-Place

- Assets-in-place are tangible, such as buildings, machines, inventory.
- Usually they are expected to grow.
- They generate free cash flows.
- The PV of their expected future free cash flows, discounted at the WACC, is the value of operations.

12 - 4

Value of Operations

$$V_{Op} = \sum_{t=1}^{\infty} \frac{FCF_t}{(1+WACC)^t}$$

12 - 5

Nonoperating Assets

- Marketable securities
- Ownership of non-controlling interest in another company
- Value of nonoperating assets usually is very close to figure that is reported on balance sheets.

12 - 6

Total Corporate Value

- Total corporate value is sum of:
  - Value of operations
  - Value of nonoperating assets

12 - 7

Claims on Corporate Value

- Debtholders have first claim.
- Preferred stockholders have the next claim.
- Any remaining value belongs to stockholders.

12 - 8

Applying the Corporate Valuation Model

- Forecast the financial statements, as shown in Chapter 4.
- Calculate the projected free cash flows.
- Model can be applied to a company that does not pay dividends, a privately held company, or a division of a company, since FCF can be calculated for each of these situations.

12 - 9

Data for Valuation

- FCF_0 = \$20 million
- WACC = 10%
- g = 5%
- Marketable securities = \$100 million
- Debt = \$200 million
- Preferred stock = \$50 million
- Book value of equity = \$210 million

12 - 10

Value of Operations: Constant Growth

Suppose FCF grows at constant rate g.

$$V_{Op} = \sum_{t=1}^{\infty} \frac{FCF_t}{(1+WACC)^t}$$

$$= \sum_{t=1}^{\infty} \frac{FCF_0 (1+g)^t}{(1+WACC)^t}$$

12 - 11

Constant Growth Formula

- Notice that the term in parentheses is less than one and gets smaller as t gets larger. As t gets very large, term approaches zero.

$$V_{Op} = \sum_{t=1}^{\infty} FCF_0 \left(\frac{1+g}{1+WACC} \right)^t$$

12 - 12

Constant Growth Formula (Cont.)

- The summation can be replaced by a single formula:

$$V_{Op} = \frac{FCF_1}{(WACC-g)}$$

$$= \frac{FCF_0 (1+g)}{(WACC-g)}$$

12 - 13

Find Value of Operations

$$V_{Op} = \frac{FCF_0(1+g)}{(WACC-g)}$$

$$V_{Op} = \frac{20(1+0.05)}{(0.10-0.05)} = 420$$

12 - 14

Value of Equity

- Sources of Corporate Value
  - Value of operations = $420
  - Value of non-operating assets = $100
- Claims on Corporate Value
  - Value of Debt = $200
  - Value of Preferred Stock = $50
  - Value of Equity = ?

12 - 15

Value of Equity

Total corporate value = V_{Op} + Mkt. Sec.
= $420 + $100
= $520 million

Value of equity = Total - Debt - Pref.
= $520 - $200 - $50
= $270 million

12 - 16

Market Value Added (MVA)

- MVA = Total corporate value of firm minus total book value of firm
- Total book value of firm = book value of equity + book value of debt + book value of preferred stock
- MVA = $520 - ($210 + $200 + $50)

  = $60 million

12 - 17

Breakdown of Corporate Value

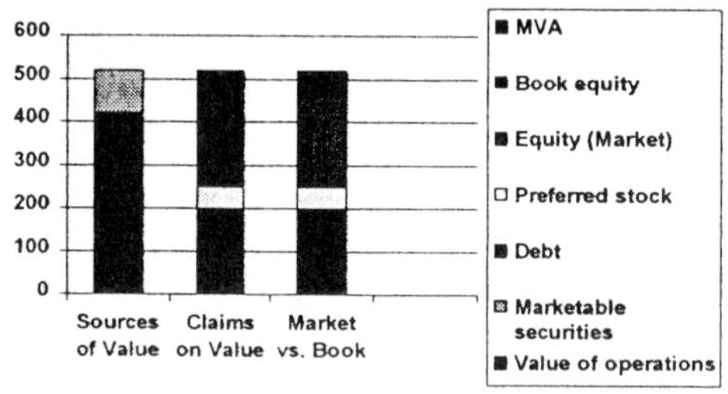

12 - 18

Expansion Plan: Nonconstant Growth

- Finance expansion by borrowing $40 million and halting dividends.
- Projected free cash flows (FCF):
  - Year 1 FCF = -$5 million.
  - Year 2 FCF = $10 million.
  - Year 3 FCF = $20 million
  - FCF grows at constant rate of 6% after year 3.

(More...)

12 - 19

- The weighted average cost of capital, k_c, is 10%.
- The company has 10 million shares of stock.

12 - 20

Horizon Value

- Free cash flows are forecast for three years in this example, so the forecast horizon is three years.
- Growth in free cash flows is not constant during the forecast,so we can't use the constant growth formula to find the value of operations at time 0.

12 - 21

Horizon Value (Cont.)

- Growth is constant after the horizon (3 years), so we can modify the constant growth formula to find the value of all free cash flows beyond the horizon, discounted back to the horizon.

12 - 22

Horizon Value Formula

$$HV = V_{Op\ at\ time\ t} = \frac{FCF_t(1+g)}{(WACC-g)}$$

- Horizon value is also called terminal value, or continuing value.

12 - 23

Find the value of operations by discounting the free cash flows at the cost of capital.

0 k_c=10% 1 2 3 4 (g = 6%)

FCF= -5.00 10.00 20.00 21.2

-4.545 ←
8.264 ←
15.026 ←
398.197 ← $V_{op\ at\ 3} = \frac{\$21.2}{0.10 - 0.06} = \$530.$

416.942 = V_{op}

12 - 24

Find the price per share of common stock.

Value of equity = Value of operations - Value of debt
= $416.94 - $40
= $376.94 million.

Price per share = $376.94 /10 = $37.69.

12 - 25

Value-Based Management (VBM)

- VBM is the systematic application of the corporate valuation model to all corporate decisions and strategic initiatives.
- The objective of VBM is to increase Market Value Added (MVA)

12 - 26

MVA and the Four Value Drivers

- MVA is determined by four drivers:
  - Sales growth
  - Operating profitability (OP=NOPAT/Sales)
  - Capital requirements (CR=Operating capital / Sales)
  - Weighted average cost of capital

12 - 27

MVA for a Constant Growth Firm

$$MVA_t = \left[\frac{Sales_t(1+g)}{WACC-g}\right]\left[OP - WACC\left(\frac{CR}{(1+g)}\right)\right]$$

12 - 28

Insights from the Constant Growth Model

- The first bracket is the MVA of a firm that gets to keep all of its sales revenues (i.e., its operating profit margin is 100%) and that never has to make additional investments in operating capital.

$$\left[\frac{\text{Sales}_t(1+g)}{\text{WACC}-g}\right]$$

12 - 29

Insights (Cont.)

- The second bracket is the operating profit (as a %) the firm gets to keep, less the return that investors require for having tied up their capital in the firm.

$$\left[\text{OP} - \text{WACC}\left(\frac{\text{CR}}{(1+g)}\right)\right]$$

12 - 30

Improvements in MVA due to the Value Drivers

- MVA will improve if:
  - WACC is reduced
  - operating profitability (OP) increases
  - the capital requirement (CR) decreases

12 - 31

The Impact of Growth

- The second term in brackets can be either positive or negative, depending on the relative size of profitability, capital requirements, and required return by investors.

$$\left[\mathrm{OP} - \mathrm{WACC}\left(\frac{\mathrm{CR}}{(1+g)}\right)\right]$$

12 - 32

The Impact of Growth (Cont.)

- If the second term in brackets is negative, then growth decreases MVA. In other words, profits are not enough to offset the return on capital required by investors.
- If the second term in brackets is positive, then growth increases MVA.

12 - 33

Expected Return on Invested Capital (EROIC)

- The expected return on invested capital is the NOPAT expected next period divided by the amount of capital that is currently invested:

$$\mathrm{EROIC}_t = \frac{\mathrm{NOPAT}_{t+1}}{\mathrm{Capital}_t}$$

12 - 34

MVA in Terms of Expected ROIC

$$MVA_t = \frac{Capital_t\left[EROIC_t - WACC\right]}{WACC - g}$$

If the spread between the expected return, $EROIC_t$, and the required return, WACC, is positive, then MVA is positive and growth makes MVA larger. The opposite is true if the spread is negative.

12 - 35

The Impact of Growth on MVA

- A company has two divisions. Both have current sales of $1,000, current expected growth of 5%, and a WACC of 10%.
- Division A has high profitability (OP=6%) but high capital requirements (CR=78%).
- Division B has low profitability (OP=4%) but low capital requirements (CR=27%).

12 - 36

What is the impact on MVA if growth goes from 5% to 6%?

	Division A		Division B	
OP	6%	6%	4%	4%
CR	78%	78%	27%	27%
Growth	5%	6%	5%	6%
MVA	(300.0)	(360.0)	300.0	385.0

Note: MVA is calculated using the formula on slide 12-27.

12 - 37

Expected ROIC and MVA

	Division A		Division B	
$Capital_0$	$780	$780	$270	$270
Growth	5%	6%	5%	6%
$Sales_1$	$1,050	$1,060	$1,050	$1,060
$NOPAT_1$	$63	$63.6	$42	$42.4
$EROIC_0$	8.1%	8.2%	15.6%	15.7%
MVA	(300.0)	(360.0)	300.0	385.0

12 - 38

Analysis of Growth Strategies

- The expected ROIC of Division A is less than the WACC, so the division should postpone growth efforts until it improves EROIC by reducing capital requirements (e.g., reducing inventory) and/or improving profitability.
- The expected ROIC of Division B is greater than the WACC, so the division should continue with its growth plans.

12 - 39

Two Primary Mechanisms of Corporate Governance

- "Stick"
  - Provisions in the charter that affect takeovers.
  - Composition of the board of directors.
- "Carrot: Compensation plans.

12 - 40

Entrenched Management

- Occurs when there is little chance that poorly performing managers will be replaced.
- Two causes:
  - Anti-takeover provisions in the charter
  - Weak board of directors

12 - 41

How are entrenched managers harmful to shareholders?

- Management consumes perks:
  - Lavish offices and corporate jets
  - Excessively large staffs
  - Memberships at country clubs
- Management accepts projects (or acquisitions) to make firm larger, even if MVA goes down.

12 - 42

Anti-Takeover Provisions

- Targeted share repurchases (i.e., greenmail)
- Shareholder rights provisions (i.e., poison pills)
- Restricted voting rights plans

12 - 43

Board of Directors

- Weak boards have many insiders (i.e., those who also have another position in the company) compared with outsiders.
- Interlocking boards are weaker (CEO of company A sits on board of company B, CEO of B sits on board of A).

12 - 44

Stock Options in Compensation Plans

- Gives owner of option the right to buy a share of the company's stock at a specified price (called the exercise price) even if the actual stock price is higher.
- Usually can't exercise the option for several years (called the vesting period).

12 - 45

Stock Options (Cont.)

- Can't exercise the option after a certain number of years (called the expiration, or maturity, date).

BLUEPRINTS: CHAPTER 13

THE BASICS OF CAPITAL BUDGETING: EVALUATING CASH FLOWS

Assume that you recently went to work for Axis Components Company, a supplier of auto repair parts used in the after-market with products from Chrysler, Ford, and other auto makers. Your boss, the chief financial officer (CFO), has just handed you the estimated cash flows for two proposed projects. Project L involves adding a new item to the firm's ignition system line; it would take some time to build up the market for this product, so the cash inflows would increase over time. Project S involves an add-on to an existing line, and its cash flows would decrease over time. Both projects have 3-year lives, because Axis is planning to introduce entirely new models after 3 years.

Here are the projects' net cash flows (in thousands of dollars):

	Expected Net Cash Flow	
Year	Project L	Project S
0	($100)	($100)
1	10	70
2	60	50
3	80	20

Depreciation, salvage values, net working capital requirements, and tax effects are all included in these cash flows.

The CFO also made subjective risk assessments of each project, and he concluded that both projects have risk characteristics which are similar to the firm's average project. Axis's weighted average cost of capital is 10 percent. You must now determine whether one or both of the projects should be accepted.

a. What is capital budgeting? Are there any similarities between a firm's capital budgeting decisions and an individual's investment decisions?

b. What is the difference between independent and mutually exclusive projects? Between projects with normal and nonnormal cash flows?

c. (1) What is the payback period? Find the paybacks for Projects L and S.

(2) What is the rationale for the payback method? According to the payback criterion, which project or projects should be accepted if the firm's maximum acceptable payback is 2 years, and if Projects L and S are independent? If they are mutually exclusive?

(3) What is the difference between the regular and discounted payback periods?

(4) What is the main disadvantage of discounted payback? Is the payback method of any real usefulness in capital budgeting decisions?

d. (1) Define the term *net present value (NPV)*. What is each project's NPV?

(2) What is the rationale behind the NPV method? According to NPV, which project or projects should be accepted if they are independent? Mutually exclusive?

(3) Would the NPVs change if the cost of capital changed?

e. (1) Define the term *internal rate of return (IRR)*. What is each project's IRR?

(2) How is the IRR on a project related to the YTM on a bond?

(3) What is the logic behind the IRR method? According to IRR, which projects should be accepted if they are independent? Mutually exclusive?

(4) Would the projects' IRRs change if the cost of capital changed?

f. (1) Draw NPV profiles for Projects L and S. At what discount rate do the profiles cross?

(2) Look at your NPV profile graph without referring to the actual NPVs and IRRs. Which project or projects should be accepted if they are independent? Mutually exclusive? Explain. Are your answers correct at any cost of capital less than 23.6 percent?

g. (1) What is the underlying cause of ranking conflicts between NPV and IRR?

(2) What is the "reinvestment rate assumption," and how does it affect the NPV versus IRR conflict?

(3) Which method is the best? Why?

h. (1) Define the term *modified IRR (MIRR)*. Find the MIRRs for Projects L and S.

(2) What are the MIRR's advantages and disadvantages vis-a-vis the regular IRR? What are the MIRR's advantages and disadvantages vis-a-vis the NPV?

i. As a separate project (Project P), the firm is considering sponsoring a pavilion at the upcoming World's Fair. The pavilion would cost $800,000, and it is expected to result in $5 million of incremental cash inflows during its 1 year of operation. However, it would then take another year, and $5 million of costs, to demolish the site and return it to its original condition. Thus, Project P's expected net cash flows look like this (in millions of dollars):

Year	Net Cash Flows
0	($0.8)
1	5.0
2	(5.0)

The project is estimated to be of average risk, so its cost of capital is 10 percent.

(1) What is Project P's NPV? What is its IRR? Its MIRR?

(2) Draw Project P's NPV profile. Does Project P have normal or nonnormal cash flows? Should this project be accepted?

j. In an unrelated analysis, Axis must choose between the following two mutually exclusive projects:

	Expected Net Cash Flow	
Year	Project S	Project L
0	($100,000)	($100,000)
1	60,000	33,500
2	60,000	33,500
3	--	33,500
4	--	33,500

The projects provide a necessary service, so whichever one is selected is expected to be repeated into the foreseeable future. Both projects have a 10 percent cost of capital.

(1) What is each project's initial NPV without replication?

(2) Now apply the replacement chain approach to determine the projects' extended NPVs. Which project should be chosen?

(3) Repeat the analysis using the equivalent annual annuity approach.

(4) Now assume that the cost to replicate Project S in 2 years will increase to $105,000 because of inflationary pressures. How should the analysis be handled now, and which project should be chosen?

k. Axis is also considering another project which has a physical life of 3 years; that is, the machinery will be totally worn out after 3 years. However, if the project were terminated prior to the end of 3 years, the machinery would have a positive salvage value. Here are the project's estimated cash flows:

Year	Initial Investment and Operating Cash Flows	End-of-Year Net Salvage Value
0	($5,000)	$5,000
1	2,100	3,100
2	2,000	2,000
3	1,750	0

Using the 10 percent cost of capital, what is the project's NPV if it is operated for the full 3 years? Would the NPV change if the company planned to terminate the project at the end of Year 2? At the end of Year 1? What is the project's optimal (economic) life?

l. After examining all the potential projects, the CFO discovers that there are many more projects this year with positive NPVs than in a normal year. What two problems might this extra large capital budget cause?

13 - 1

CHAPTER 13

The Basics of Capital Budgeting: Evaluating Cash Flows

13 - 2

What is capital budgeting?

- Analysis of potential additions to fixed assets.
- Long-term decisions; involve large expenditures.
- Very important to firm's future.

13 - 3

Steps

1. Estimate CFs (inflows & outflows).
2. Assess riskiness of CFs.
3. Determine k = WACC for project.
4. Find NPV and/or IRR.
5. Accept if NPV > 0 and/or IRR > WACC.

13 - 4

What is the difference between independent and mutually exclusive projects?

Projects are:

independent, if the cash flows of one are unaffected by the acceptance of the other.

mutually exclusive, if the cash flows of one can be adversely impacted by the acceptance of the other.

13 - 5

An Example of Mutually Exclusive Projects

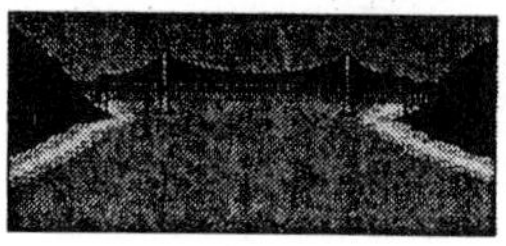

BRIDGE vs. BOAT to get products across a river.

13 - 6

Normal Cash Flow Project:

Cost (negative CF) followed by a series of positive cash inflows. One change of signs.

Nonnormal Cash Flow Project:

Two or more changes of signs. Most common: Cost (negative CF), then string of positive CFs, then cost to close project. Nuclear power plant, strip mine.

13 - 7

Inflow (+) or Outflow (-) in Year

0	1	2	3	4	5	N	NN
-	+	+	+	+	+	N	
-	+	+	+	+	-		NN
-	-	-	+	+	+	N	
+	+	+	-	-	-	N	
-	+	+	-	+	-		NN

13 - 8

What is the payback period?

The number of years required to recover a project's cost,

or how long does it take to get the business's money back?

13 - 9

Payback for Project L (Long: Most CFs in out years)

	0	1	2	2.4	3
CF_t	-100	10	60	100	80
Cumulative	-100	-90	-30	0	50

Payback_L = 2 + 30/80 = 2.375 years

13 - 10

Project S (Short: CFs come quickly)

	0	1	1.6	2	3
CF_t	-100	70	100	50	20
Cumulative	-100	-30	0	20	40

$Payback_S = 1 + 30/50 = 1.6$ years

13 - 11

Strengths of Payback:

1. Provides an indication of a project's risk and liquidity.
2. Easy to calculate and understand.

Weaknesses of Payback:

1. Ignores the TVM.
2. Ignores CFs occurring after the payback period.

13 - 12

Discounted Payback: Uses discounted rather than raw CFs.

10%	0	1	2	3
CF_t	-100	10	60	80
$PVCF_t$	-100	9.09	49.59	60.11
Cumulative	-100	-90.91	-41.32	18.79

Discounted payback $= 2 + 41.32/60.11 = 2.7$ yrs

Recover invest. + cap. costs in 2.7 yrs.

13 - 13

NPV: Sum of the PVs of inflows and outflows.

$$NPV = \sum_{t=0}^{n} \frac{CF_t}{(1+k)^t}$$

Cost often is CF_0 and is negative.

$$NPV = \sum_{t=1}^{n} \frac{CF_t}{(1+k)^t} + CF_0$$

13 - 14

What's Project L's NPV?

Project L:

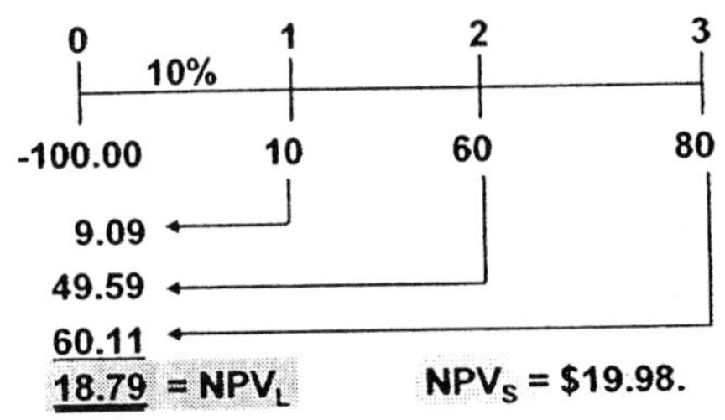

NPV_S = $19.98.

13 - 15

Calculator Solution

Enter in CFLO for L:

-100 CF_0

10 CF_1

60 CF_2

80 CF_3

10 I NPV = 18.78 = NPV_L

13 - 16

Rationale for the NPV Method

NPV = PV inflows - Cost
= Net gain in wealth.

Accept project if NPV > 0.

Choose between mutually exclusive projects on basis of higher NPV. Adds most value.

13 - 17

Using NPV method, which project(s) should be accepted?

- If Projects S and L are mutually exclusive, accept S because $NPV_S > NPV_L$.
- If S & L are independent, accept both; NPV > 0.

13 - 18

Internal Rate of Return: IRR

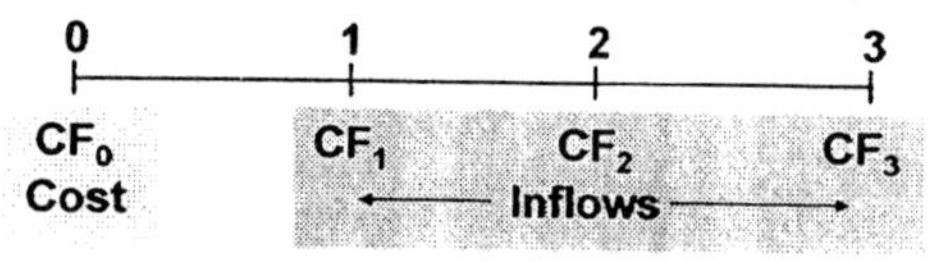

IRR is the discount rate that forces PV inflows = cost. This is the same as forcing NPV = 0.

13 - 19

NPV: Enter k, solve for NPV.

$$\sum_{t=0}^{n} \frac{CF_t}{(1+k)^t} = NPV.$$

IRR: Enter NPV = 0, solve for IRR.

$$\sum_{t=0}^{n} \frac{CF_t}{(1+IRR)^t} = 0.$$

13 - 20

What's Project L's IRR?

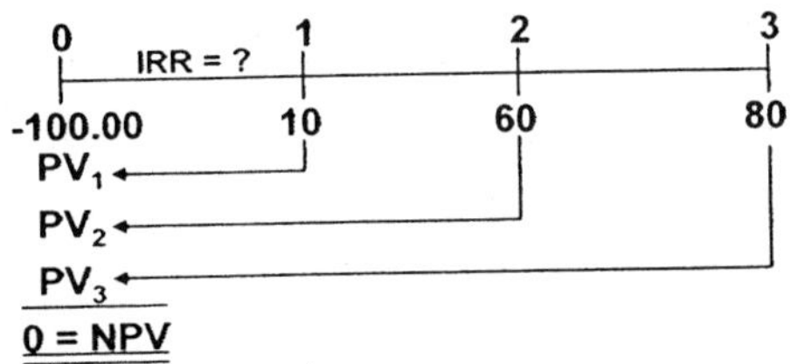

Enter CFs in CFLO, then press IRR:

IRR_L = 18.13%. IRR_S = 23.56%.

13 - 21

Find IRR if CFs are constant:

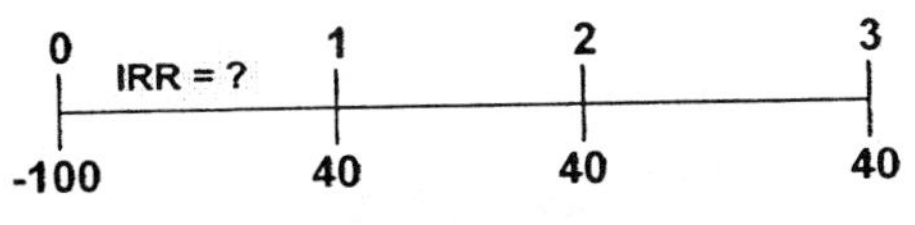

	N	I/YR	PV	PMT	FV
INPUTS	3		-100	40	0
OUTPUT		9.70%			

Or, with CFLO, enter CFs and press IRR = 9.70%.

13 - 22

Q. How is a project's IRR related to a bond's YTM?

A. They are the same thing. A bond's YTM is the IRR if you invest in the bond.

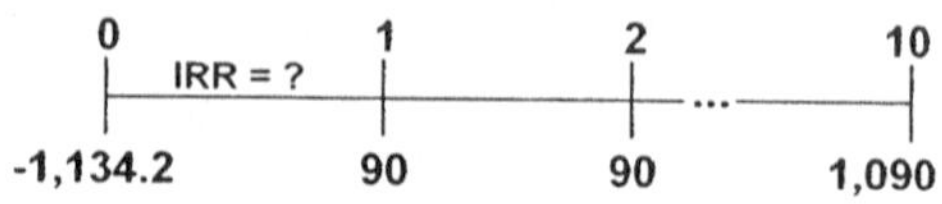

IRR = 7.08% (use TVM or CFLO).

13 - 23

Rationale for the IRR Method

If IRR > WACC, then the project's rate of return is greater than its cost-- some return is left over to boost stockholders' returns.

<u>Example</u>: WACC = 10%, IRR = 15%.
Profitable.

13 - 24

IRR Acceptance Criteria

- If IRR > k, accept project.
- If IRR < k, reject project.

13 - 25

Decisions on Projects S and L per IRR

- If S and L are independent, accept both. IRRs > k = 10%.
- If S and L are **mutually exclusive**, accept S because $IRR_S > IRR_L$.

13 - 26

Construct NPV Profiles

Enter CFs in CFLO and find NPV_L and NPV_S at different discount rates:

k	NPV_L	NPV_S
0	50	40
5	33	29
10	19	20
15	7	12
20	(4)	5

13 - 27

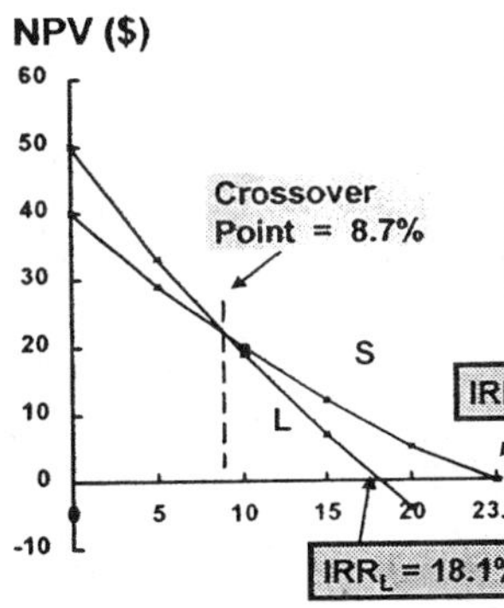

k	NPV_L	NPV_S
0	50	40
5	33	29
10	19	20
15	7	12
20	(4)	5

13 - 28

NPV and IRR always lead to the same accept/reject decision for independent projects:

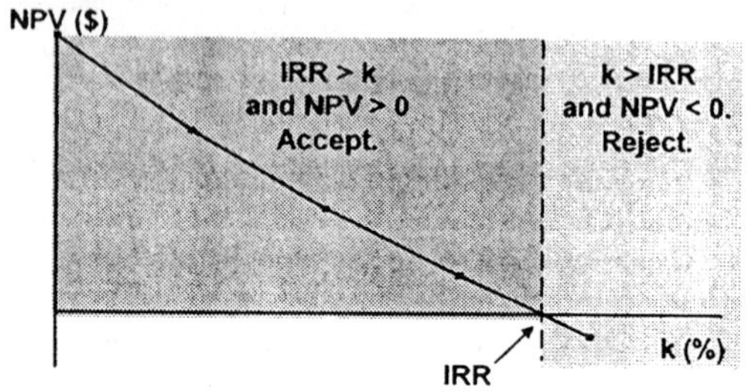

13 - 29

Mutually Exclusive Projects

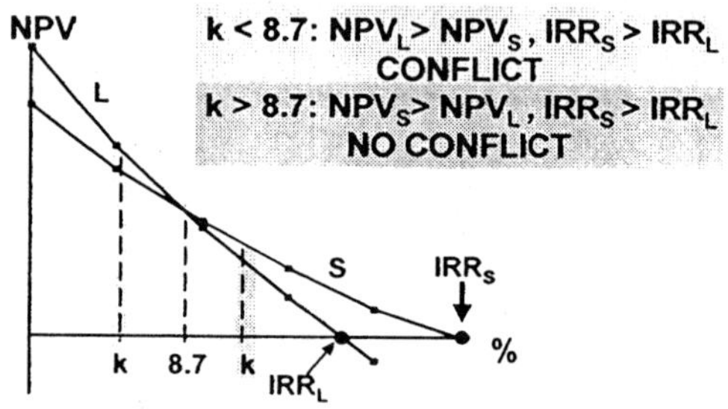

13 - 30

To Find the Crossover Rate

1. **Find cash flow differences between the projects. See data at beginning of the case.**
2. **Enter these differences in CFLO register, then press IRR. Crossover rate = 8.68%, rounded to 8.7%.**
3. **Can subtract S from L or vice versa, but better to have first CF negative.**
4. **If profiles don't cross, one project dominates the other.**

13 - 31

Two Reasons NPV Profiles Cross

1. **Size (scale) differences.** Smaller project frees up funds at t = 0 for investment. The higher the opportunity cost, the more valuable these funds, so high k favors small projects.
2. **Timing differences.** Project with faster payback provides more CF in early years for reinvestment. If k is high, early CF especially good, $NPV_S > NPV_L$.

13 - 32

Reinvestment Rate Assumptions

- NPV assumes reinvest at k (opportunity cost of capital).
- IRR assumes reinvest at IRR.
- Reinvest at opportunity cost, k, is more realistic, so NPV method is best. NPV should be used to choose between mutually exclusive projects.

13 - 33

Managers like rates--prefer IRR to NPV comparisons. Can we give them a better IRR?

Yes, MIRR is the discount rate which causes the PV of a project's terminal value (TV) to equal the PV of costs. TV is found by compounding inflows at WACC.

Thus, MIRR assumes cash inflows are reinvested at WACC.

13 - 34

MIRR for Project L (k = 10%)

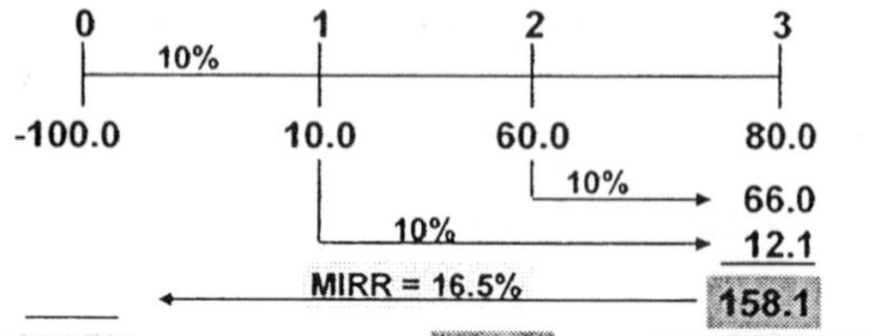

-100.0 — PV outflows

$$\$100 = \frac{\$158.1}{(1+MIRR_L)^3}$$

TV inflows

$MIRR_L$ = 16.5%

13 - 35

To find TV with 10B, enter in CFLO:

CF_0 = 0, CF_1 = 10, CF_2 = 60, CF_3 = 80
I = 10

NPV = 118.78 = PV of inflows.

Enter PV = -118.78, N = 3, I = 10, PMT = 0.
Press FV = 158.10 = FV of inflows.

Enter FV = 158.10, PV = -100, PMT = 0, N = 3.
Press I = 16.50% = MIRR.

13 - 36

Why use MIRR versus IRR?

MIRR correctly assumes reinvestment at opportunity cost = WACC. MIRR also avoids the problem of multiple IRRs.

Managers like rate of return comparisons, and MIRR is better for this than IRR.

13 - 37

Pavilion Project: NPV and IRR?

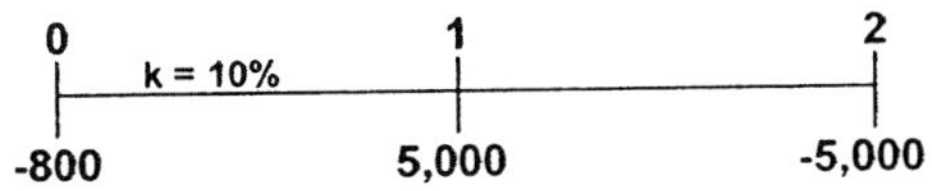

Enter CFs in CFLO, enter I = 10.

NPV = -386.78

IRR = ERROR. Why?

13 - 38

We got IRR = ERROR because there are 2 IRRs. Nonnormal CFs--two sign changes. Here's a picture:

NPV Profile

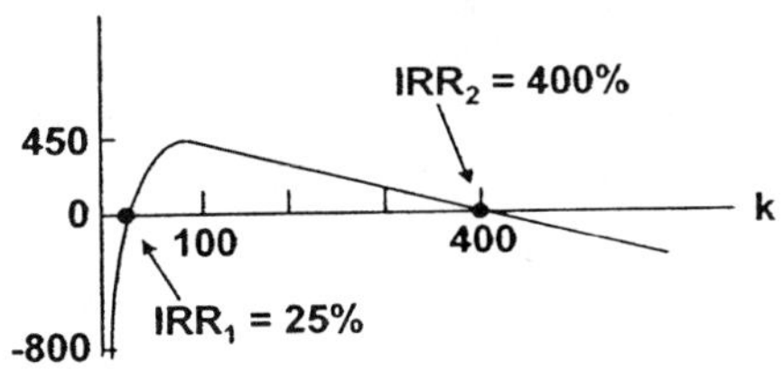

13 - 39

Logic of Multiple IRRs

1. At very low discount rates, the PV of CF_2 is large & negative, so NPV < 0.
2. At very high discount rates, the PV of both CF_1 and CF_2 are low, so CF_0 dominates and again NPV < 0.
3. In between, the discount rate hits CF_2 harder than CF_1, so NPV > 0.
4. Result: 2 IRRs.

13 - 40

Could find IRR with calculator:

1. Enter CFs as before.
2. Enter a "guess" as to IRR by storing the guess. Try 10%:

   10 ▬ STO

   ▬ IRR = 25% = lower IRR

   Now guess large IRR, say, 200:

   200 ▬ STO

   ▬ IRR = 400% = upper IRR

13 - 41

When there are nonnormal CFs and more than one IRR, use MIRR:

0	1	2
-800,000	5,000,000	-5,000,000

PV outflows @ 10% = -4,932,231.40.

TV inflows @ 10% = 5,500,000.00.

MIRR = 5.6%

13 - 42

Accept Project P?

NO. Reject because MIRR = 5.6% < k = 10%.

Also, if MIRR < k, NPV will be negative: NPV = -$386,777.

13 - 43

S and L are mutually exclusive and will be repeated. k = 10%. Which is better? (000s)

0	1	2	3	4
Project S:				
(100)	60	60		
Project L:				
(100)	33.5	33.5	33.5	33.5

13 - 44

	S	L
CF_0	-100,000	-100,000
CF_1	60,000	33,500
N_j	2	4
I	10	10
NPV	4,132	6,190

$NPV_L > NPV_S$. But is L better? Can't say yet. Need to perform common life analysis.

13 - 45

- **Note that Project S could be repeated after 2 years to generate additional profits.**
- **Can use either <u>replacement chain</u> or <u>equivalent annual annuity</u> analysis to make decision.**

13 - 46

Replacement Chain Approach (000s)

Project S with Replication:

	0	1	2	3	4
Project S:	(100)	60	60		
			(100)	60	60
	(100)	60	(40)	60	60

NPV = $7,547.

13 - 47

Or, use NPVs:

	0	1	2	3	4
	4,132		4,132		
	3,415 ← 10% ← 4,132				
	7,547				

Compare to Project L NPV = $6,190.

13 - 48

If the cost to repeat S in two years rises to $105,000, which is best? (000s)

	0	1	2	3	4
Project S:	(100)	60	60		
			(105)	60	60
			(45)		

NPV_S = $3,415 < NPV_L = $6,190.
Now choose L.

13 - 49

Consider another project with a 3-year life. If terminated prior to Year 3, the machinery will have positive salvage value.

Year	CF	Salvage Value
0	($5,000)	$5,000
1	2,100	3,100
2	2,000	2,000
3	1,750	0

13 - 50

CFs Under Each Alternative (000s)

	0	1	2	3
1. No termination	(5)	2.1	2	1.75
2. Terminate 2 years	(5)	2.1	4	
3. Terminate 1 year	(5)	5.2		

13 - 51

Assuming a 10% cost of capital, what is the project's optimal, or economic life?

$NPV_{(no)}$ = -$123.
$NPV_{(2)}$ = $215.
$NPV_{(1)}$ = -$273.

13 - 52

Conclusions

- The project is acceptable only if operated for 2 years.
- A project's engineering life does not always equal its economic life.

13 - 53

Choosing the Optimal Capital Budget

- Finance theory says to accept all positive NPV projects.
- Two problems can occur when there is not enough internally generated cash to fund all positive NPV projects:
  - An increasing marginal cost of capital.
  - Capital rationing

13 - 54

Increasing Marginal Cost of Capital

- Externally raised capital can have large flotation costs, which increase the cost of capital.
- Investors often perceive large capital budgets as being risky, which drives up the cost of capital.

(More...)

13 - 55

- If external funds will be raised, then the NPV of all projects should be estimated using this higher marginal cost of capital.

13 - 56

Capital Rationing

- Capital rationing occurs when a company chooses not to fund all positive NPV projects.
- The company typically sets an upper limit on the total amount of capital expenditures that it will make in the upcoming year.

(More...)

13 - 57

Reason: Companies want to avoid the direct costs (i.e., flotation costs) and the indirect costs of issuing new capital.

Solution: Increase the cost of capital by enough to reflect all of these costs, and then accept all projects that still have a positive NPV with the higher cost of capital.

(More...)

13 - 58

Reason: Companies don't have enough managerial, marketing, or engineering staff to implement all positive NPV projects.

Solution: Use linear programming to maximize NPV subject to not exceeding the constraints on staffing.

(More...)

13 - 59

Reason: Companies believe that the project's managers forecast unreasonably high cash flow estimates, so companies "filter" out the worst projects by limiting the total amount of projects that can be accepted.

Solution: Implement a post-audit process and tie the managers' compensation to the subsequent performance of the project.

BLUEPRINTS: CHAPTER 14

CASH FLOW ESTIMATION AND RISK ANALYSIS

John Crockett Furniture Company is considering adding a new line to its product mix, and the capital budgeting analysis is being conducted by Joan Samuels, a recently graduated finance MBA. The production line would be set up in unused space in Crockett's main plant. The machinery's invoice price would be approximately $200,000; another $10,000 in shipping charges would be required; and it would cost an additional $30,000 to install the equipment. Further, the firm's inventories would have to be increased by $25,000 to handle the new line, but its accounts payable would rise by $5,000. The machinery has an economic life of 4 years, and Crockett has obtained a special tax ruling which places the equipment in the MACRS 3-year class. The machinery is expected to have a salvage value of $25,000 after 4 years of use.

The new line would generate $125,000 in incremental net revenues (before taxes and excluding depreciation) in each of the next 4 years. The firm's tax rate is 40 percent, and its overall weighted average cost of capital is 10 percent.

a. Set up, without numbers, a time line for the project's cash flows.

b. (1) Construct incremental operating cash flow statements for the project's 4 years of operations.

   (2) Does your cash flow statement include any financial flows such as interest expense or dividends? Why or why not?

c. (1) Suppose the firm had spent $100,000 last year to rehabilitate the production line site. Should this be included in the analysis? Explain.

   (2) Now assume that the plant space could be leased out to another firm at $25,000 a year. Should this be included in the analysis? If so, how?

   (3) Finally, assume that the new product line is expected to decrease sales of the firm's other lines by $50,000 per year. Should this be considered in the analysis? If so, how?

d. Disregard the assumptions in Part c. What is Crockett's net investment outlay on this project? What is the net nonoperating cash flow at the time the project is terminated? Based on these cash flows, what are the project's NPV, IRR, MIRR, and payback? Do these indicators suggest that the project should be undertaken?

e. Assume that inflation is expected to average 5 percent over the next 4 years. Does it appear that Crockett's cash flow estimates are real or nominal? That is, are all the cash flows stated in the Time 0 dollars or have the cash flows been increased to account for expected inflation? Further, would it appear that the 10 percent cost of capital is a nominal or real interest rate? Does it appear that the current NPV is biased because of inflation effects? If so, in what direction, and how could any bias be removed?

f. What does the term "risk" mean in the context of capital budgeting, to what extent can risk be quantified, and when risk is quantified, is the quantification based primarily on statistical analysis of historical data or on subjective, judgmental estimates?

g. (1) What are the three types of risk that are relevant in capital budgeting?

(2) How is each of these risk types measured, and how do they relate to one another?

(3) How is each type of risk used in the capital budgeting process?

h. (1) What is sensitivity analysis?

(2) Perform a sensitivity analysis on the unit sales, salvage value, and cost of capital for the project. Assume that each of these variables can vary from its base case, or expected, value by plus and minus 10, 20, and 30 percent. Include a sensitivity diagram, and discuss the results.

(3) What is the primary weakness of sensitivity analysis? What is its primary usefulness?

i. Assume that Joan Samuels is confident of her estimates of all the variables that affect the project's cash flows except unit sales: If product acceptance is poor, unit sales would be only 900 units a year, while a strong consumer response would produce sales of 1,600 units. In either case, cash costs would still amount to 50 percent of revenues. Joan believes that there is a 25 percent chance of poor acceptance, a 25 percent chance of excellent acceptance, and a 50 percent chance of average acceptance (the base case).

(1) What is scenario analysis?

(2) What is the worst-case NPV? The best-case NPV?

(3) Use the worst-, most likely, and best-case NPVs and probabilities of occurrence to find the project's expected NPV, standard deviation, and coefficient of variation.

j. (1) Assume that Crockett's average project has a coefficient of variation in the range of 0.2 – 0.4. Would the new furniture line be classified as high risk, average risk, or low risk? What type of risk is being measured here?

(2) Based on common sense, how highly correlated do you think the project would be to the firm's other assets? (Give a correlation coefficient, or range of coefficients, based on your judgment.)

(3) How would this correlation coefficient and the previously calculated σ combine to affect the project's contribution to corporate, or within-firm, risk? Explain.

k. (1) Based on your judgment, what do you think the project's correlation coefficient would be with the general economy and thus with returns on "the market"?

(2) How would this correlation affect the project's market risk?

l. (1) Crockett typically adds or subtracts 3 percentage points to the overall cost of capital to adjust for risk. Should the new furniture line be accepted?

(2) Are there any subjective risk factors that should be considered before the final decision is made?

h. Are there problems with scenario analysis? Define simulation analysis, and discuss its principal advantages and disadvantages.

14 - 1

CHAPTER 14
Cash Flow Estimation and Risk Analysis

- Relevant cash flows
- Working capital treatment
- Inflation
- Risk Analysis: Sensitivity Analysis, Scenario Analysis, and Simulation Analysis

14 - 2

Proposed Project

- Cost: $200,000 + $10,000 shipping + $30,000 installation.
- Depreciable cost $240,000.
- Inventories will rise by $25,000 and payables will rise by $5,000.
- Economic life = 4 years.
- Salvage value = $25,000.
- MACRS 3-year class.

14 - 3

- Incremental gross sales = $250,000.
- Incremental cash operating costs = $125,000.
- Tax rate = 40%.
- Overall cost of capital = 10%.

14 - 4

Set up without numbers a time line for the project CFs.

0	1	2	3	4
Initial Outlay	OCF_1	OCF_2	OCF_3	OCF_4 + Terminal CF
NCF_0	NCF_1	NCF_2	NCF_3	NCF_4

14 - 5

Incremental Cash Flow

= Corporate cash flow with project

minus

Corporate cash flow without project

14 - 6

Should CFs include interest expense? Dividends?

- NO. The costs of capital are already incorporated in the analysis since we use them in discounting.
- If we included them as cash flows, we would be double counting capital costs.

14 - 7

Suppose $100,000 had been spent last year to improve the production line site. Should this cost be included in the analysis?

- **NO. This is a <u>sunk cost</u>. Focus on incremental investment and operating cash flows.**

14 - 8

Suppose the plant space could be leased out for $25,000 a year. Would this affect the analysis?

- **Yes. Accepting the project means we will not receive the $25,000. This is an <u>opportunity cost</u> and it should be charged to the project.**
- **A.T. opportunity cost = $25,000 (1 - T) = $15,000 annual cost.**

14 - 9

If the new product line would decrease sales of the firm's other products by $50,000 per year, would this affect the analysis?

- **Yes. The effects on the other projects' CFs are "externalities".**
- **Net CF loss per year on other lines would be a cost to this project.**
- **Externalities will be positive if new projects are complements to existing assets, negative if substitutes.**

14 - 10

Net Investment Outlay at t = 0 (000s)

Equipment	(\$200)
Freight + Inst.	(40)
Change in NWC	(20)
Net CF_0	(\$260)

ΔNWC = \$25,000 - \$5,000
= \$20,000.

14 - 11

Depreciation Basics

Basis = Cost
+ Shipping
+ Installation
\$240,000

14 - 12

Annual Depreciation Expense (000s)

Year	%	x Basis	= Depr.
1	0.33	\$240	\$ 79
2	0.45		108
3	0.15		36
4	0.07		17

14 - 13

Year 1 Operating Cash Flows (000s)

	Year 1
Net revenue	$125
Depreciation	(79)
Before-tax income	$ 46
Taxes (40%)	(18)
Net income	$ 28
Depreciation	79
Net operating CF	$107

14 - 14

Year 4 Operating Cash Flows (000s)

	Year 1	Year 4
Net revenue	$125	$125
Depreciation	(79)	(17)
Before-tax income	$ 46	$108
Taxes (40%)	(18)	(43)
Net income	$ 28	$ 65
Depreciation	79	17
Net operating CF	$107	$ 82

14 - 15

Net Terminal Cash Flow at t = 4 (000s)

Salvage value	$25
Tax on SV	(10)
Recovery on NWC	20
Net terminal CF	$35

14 - 16

What if you terminate a project before the asset is fully depreciated?

Cash flow from sale = Sale proceeds
- taxes paid.

Taxes are based on difference between sales price and tax basis, where:

Basis = Original basis - Accum. deprec.

14 - 17

Example: If Sold After 3 Years (000s)

- Original basis = $240.
- After 3 years = $17 remaining.
- Sales price = $25.
- Tax on sale = 0.4($25-$17)
  = $3.2.
- Cash flow = $25-$3.2=$21.7.

14 - 18

Project Net CFs on a Time Line

0	1	2	3	4
(260)*	107	118	89	117

Enter CFs in CFLO register and I = 10.
NPV = $81,573.
IRR = 23.8%.

*In thousands.

14 - 19

What is the project's MIRR? (000s)

0	1	2	3	4
(260)*	107	118	89	117.0
			→	97.9
		→		142.8
	→			142.4
(260) ←		MIRR = ?		500.1

14 - 20

Calculator Solution

1. Enter positive CFs in CFLO:
   I = 10; Solve for NPV = $341.60.
2. Use TVM keys: PV = 341.60, N = 4
   I = 10; PMT = 0; Solve for FV = 500.10.
   (TV of inflows)
3. Use TVM keys: N = 4; FV = 500.10;
   PV = -260; PMT= 0; Solve for I = 17.8.

MIRR = 17.8%.

14 - 21

What is the project's payback? (000s)

0	1	2	3	4
(260)*	107	118	89	117
Cumulative:				
(260)	(153)	(35)	54	171

Payback = 2 + 35/89 = 2.4 years.

14 - 22

If 5% inflation is expected over the next 5 years, are the firm's cash flow estimates accurate?

- No. Net revenues are assumed to be constant over the 4-year project life, so inflation effects have not been incorporated into the cash flows.

14 - 23

Real vs. Nominal Cash flows

- In DCF analysis, k includes an estimate of inflation.
- If cash flow estimates are not adjusted for inflation (i.e., are in today's dollars), this will bias the NPV downward.
- This bias may offset the optimistic bias of management.

14 - 24

What does "risk" mean in capital budgeting?

- Uncertainty about a project's future profitability.
- Measured by σ_{NPV}, σ_{IRR}, beta.
- Will taking on the project increase the firm's and stockholders' risk?

14 - 25

Is risk analysis based on historical data or subjective judgment?

- Can sometimes use historical data, but generally cannot.
- So risk analysis in capital budgeting is usually based on subjective judgments.

14 - 26

What three types of risk are relevant in capital budgeting?

- Stand-alone risk
- Corporate risk
- Market (or beta) risk

14 - 27

How is each type of risk measured, and how do they relate to one another?

1. Stand-Alone Risk:
   - The project's risk if it were the firm's only asset and there were no shareholders.
   - Ignores both firm and shareholder diversification.
   - Measured by the σ or CV of NPV, IRR, or MIRR.

14 - 28

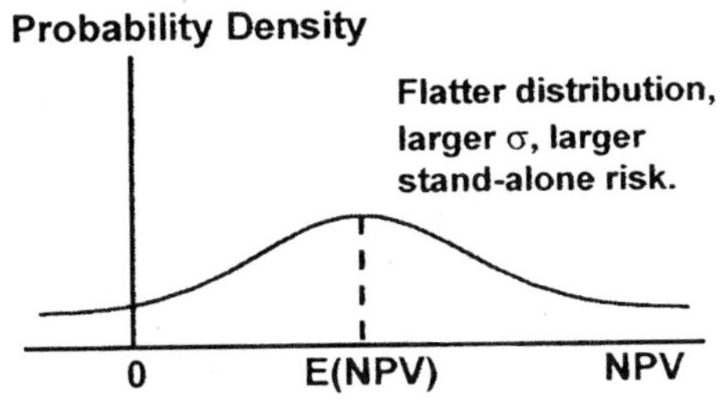

Such graphics are increasingly used by corporations.

14 - 29

2. Corporate Risk:
- Reflects the project's effect on corporate earnings stability.
- Considers firm's other assets (diversification within firm).
- Depends on:
  - project's σ, and
  - its correlation with returns on firm's other assets.
- Measured by the project's corporate beta.

14 - 30

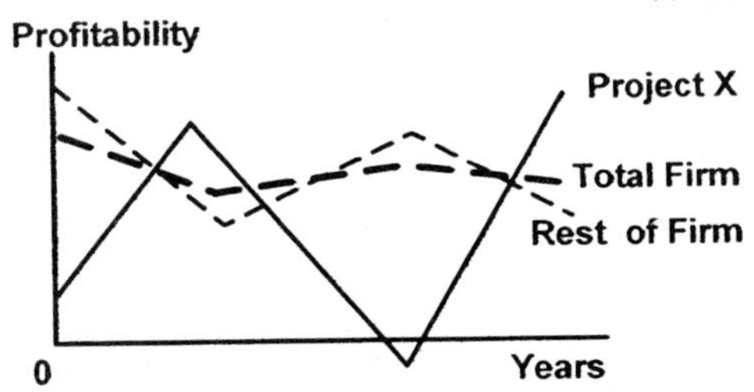

1. Project X is negatively correlated to firm's other assets.
2. If r < 1.0, some diversification benefits.
3. If r = 1.0, no diversification effects.

14 - 31

3. Market Risk:

- Reflects the project's effect on a well-diversified stock portfolio.
- Takes account of stockholders' other assets.
- Depends on project's σ and correlation with the stock market.

14 - 32

How is each type of risk used?

- Market risk is theoretically best in most situations.
- However, creditors, customers, suppliers, and employees are more affected by corporate risk.
- Therefore, corporate risk is also relevant.

14 - 33

- Stand-alone risk is easiest to measure, more intuitive.
- Core projects are highly correlated with other assets, so stand-alone risk generally reflects corporate risk.
- If the project is highly correlated with the economy, stand-alone risk also reflects market risk.

14 - 34

What is sensitivity analysis?

- Shows how changes in a variable such as unit sales affect NPV or IRR.
- Each variable is fixed except one. Change this one variable to see the effect on NPV or IRR.
- Answers "what if" questions, e.g. "What if sales decline by 30%?"

14 - 35

Illustration

Change from	Resulting NPV (000s)		
Base Level	Unit Sales	Salvage	k
-30%	$ 10	$78	$105
-20	35	80	97
-10	58	81	89
0	82	82	82
+10	105	83	74
+20	129	84	67
+30	153	85	61

14 - 36

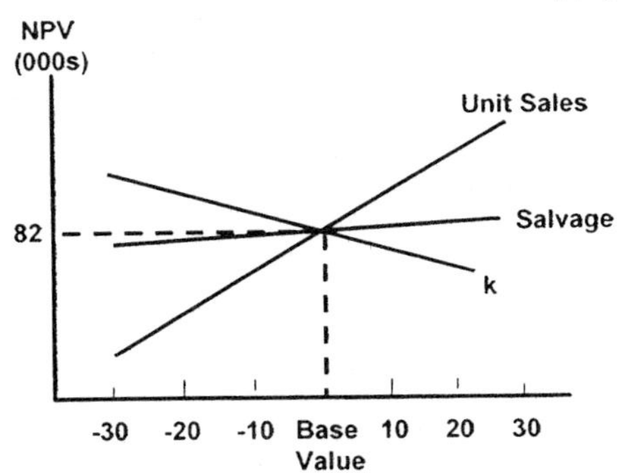

14 - 37

Results of Sensitivity Analysis

- Steeper sensitivity lines show greater risk. Small changes result in large declines in NPV.
- Unit sales line is steeper than salvage value or k, so for this project, should worry most about accuracy of sales forecast.

14 - 38

What are the weaknesses of sensitivity analysis?

- Does not reflect diversification.
- Says nothing about the likelihood of change in a variable, i.e. a steep sales line is not a problem if sales won't fall.
- Ignores relationships among variables.

14 - 39

Why is sensitivity analysis useful?

- Gives some idea of stand-alone risk.
- Identifies dangerous variables.
- Gives some breakeven information.

14 - 40

What is scenario analysis?

- Examines several possible situations, usually worst case, most likely case, and best case.
- Provides a range of possible outcomes.

14 - 41

Assume we know with certainty all variables except unit sales, which could range from 900 to 1,600.

Scenario	Probability	NPV(000)
Worst	0.25	$ 15
Base	0.50	82
Best	0.25	148

E(NPV) = $ 82

σ(NPV) = 47

CV(NPV) = σ(NPV)/E(NPV) = 0.57

14 - 42

If the firm's average project has a CV of 0.2 to 0.4, is this a high-risk project? What type of risk is being measured?

- Since CV = 0.57 > 0.4, this project has high risk.
- CV measures a project's stand-alone risk. It does not reflect firm or stockholder diversification.

14 - 43

Would a project in a firm's core business likely be highly correlated with the firm's other assets?

- Yes. Economy and customer demand would affect all core products.
- But each product would be more or less successful, so correlation < +1.0.
- Core projects probably have correlations within a range of +0.5 to +0.9.

14 - 44

How do correlation and σ affect a project's contribution to corporate risk?

- If σ_P is relatively high, then project's corporate risk will be high unless diversification benefits are significant.
- If project cash flows are highly correlated with the firm's aggregate cash flows, then the project's corporate risk will be high if σ_P is high.

14 - 45

Would a core project in the furniture business be highly correlated with the general economy and thus with the "market"?

- Probably. Furniture is a deferrable luxury good, so sales are probably correlated with but more volatile than the general economy.

14 - 46

Would correlation with the economy affect market risk?

- Yes.
  - High correlation increases market risk (beta).
  - Low correlation lowers it.

14 - 47

With a 3% risk adjustment, should our project be accepted?

- Project k = 10% + 3% = 13%.
- That's 30% above base k.
- NPV = $60,541.
- Project remains acceptable after accounting for differential (higher) risk.

14 - 48

Should subjective risk factors be considered?

- Yes. A numerical analysis may not capture all of the risk factors inherent in the project.
- For example, if the project has the potential for bringing on harmful lawsuits, then it might be riskier than a standard analysis would indicate.

14 - 49

Are there any problems with scenario analysis?

- Only considers a few possible outcomes.
- Assumes that inputs are perfectly correlated--all "bad" values occur together and all "good" values occur together.
- Focuses on stand-alone risk, although subjective adjustments can be made.

14 - 50

What is a simulation analysis?

- A computerized version of scenario analysis which uses continuous probability distributions.
- Computer selects values for each variable based on given probability distributions.

(More...)

14 - 51

- NPV and IRR are calculated.
- Process is repeated many times (1,000 or more).
- End result: Probability distribution of NPV and IRR based on sample of simulated values.
- Generally shown graphically.

14 - 52

Probability Density

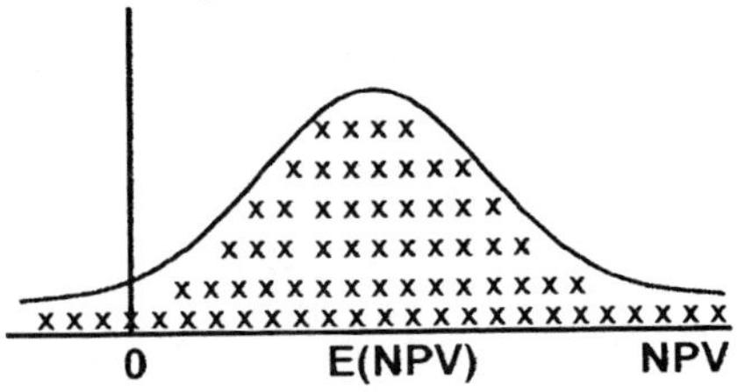

Also gives σ_{NPV}, CV_{NPV}, probability of NPV > 0.

14 - 53

What are the advantages of simulation analysis?

- Reflects the probability distributions of each input.
- Shows range of NPVs, the expected NPV, σ_{NPV}, and CV_{NPV}.
- Gives an intuitive graph of the risk situation.

14 - 54

What are the disadvantages of simulation?

- Difficult to specify probability distributions and correlations.
- If inputs are bad, output will be bad: "Garbage in, garbage out."

(More...)

14 - 55

- Sensitivity, scenario, and simulation analyses do not provide a decision rule. They do not indicate whether a project's expected return is sufficient to compensate for its risk.
- Sensitivity, scenario, and simulation analyses all ignore diversification. Thus they measure only stand-alone risk, which may not be the most relevant risk in capital budgeting.

BLUEPRINTS: CHAPTER 15

FINANCIAL OPTIONS WITH APPLICATIONS TO REAL OPTIONS

Assume that you have just been hired as a financial analyst by Tropical Sweets Inc., a mid-sized California company that specializes in creating exotic candies from tropical fruits such as mangoes, papayas, and dates. The firm's CEO, George Yamaguchi, recently returned from an industry corporate executive conference in San Francisco, and one of the sessions he attended was on real options. Since no one at Tropical Sweets is familiar with the basics of either financial or real options, Yamaguchi has asked you to prepare a brief report that the firm's executives could use to gain at least a cursory understanding of the topics.

To begin, you gathered some outside materials on the subject and used these materials to draft a list of pertinent questions that need to be answered. In fact, one possible approach to the paper is to use a question-and-answer format. Now that the questions have been drafted, you have to develop the answers.

a. What is a real option? What is a financial option? What is the single most important characteristic of an option?

b. Options have a unique set of terminology. Define the following terms: (1) call option; (2) put option; (3) exercise price; (4) striking, or strike, price; (5) option price; (6) expiration date; (7) exercise value; (8) covered option; (9) naked option; (10) in-the-money call; (11) out-of-the-money call; and (12) LEAP.

c. Consider Tropical Sweets' call option with a $25 strike price. The following table contains historical values for this option at different stock prices:

Stock Price	Call Option Price
$25	$ 3.00
30	7.50
35	12.00
40	16.50
45	21.00
50	25.50

(1) Create a table which shows (a) stock price, (b) strike price, (c) exercise value, (d) option price, and (e) the premium of option price over exercise value.

(2) What happens to the premium of option price over exercise value as the stock price rises? Why?

d. In 1973, Fischer Black and Myron Scholes developed the Black-Scholes Option Pricing Model (OPM).

(1) What assumptions underlie the OPM?

(2) Write out the three equations that constitute the model.

(3) What is the value of the following call option according to the OPM?

Stock price = $27.00
Exercise price = $25.00
Time to expiration = 6 months
Risk-free rate = 6.0%
Stock return variance = 0.11

e. What impact does each of the following call option parameters have on the value of a call option?

(1) Current stock price

(2) Exercise price

(3) Option's term to maturity

(4) Risk-free rate

(5) Variability of the stock price

f. What are some types of real options?

g. What are the five steps for analyzing a real option?

h. Tropical Sweets is considering a project that will cost $70 million and will generate expected cash flows of $30 per year for three years. The cost of capital for this type of project is 10 percent and the risk-free rate is 6 percent. After discussions with the marketing department, you learn that there is a 30 percent chance of high demand, with future cash flows of $45 million per year. There is a 40 percent chance of average demand, with cash flows of $30 million per year. If demand is low (a 30 percent chance), cash flows will be only $15 per year. What is the expected NPV?

i. Now suppose this project has an investment timing option, since it can be delayed for a year. The cost will still be $70 million at the end of the year, and the cash flows for the scenarios will still last three years. However, Tropical Sweets will know the level of demand, and will implement the project only if it adds value to the company. Perform a qualitative assessment of the investment timing option's value.

j. Use decision tree analysis to calculate the NPV of the project with the investment timing option.

k. Use a financial option pricing model to estimate the value of the investment timing option.

l. Now suppose the cost of the project is $75 million and the project cannot be delayed. But if Tropical Sweets implements the project, then Tropical Sweets will have a growth option. It will have the opportunity to replicate the original project at the end of its life. What is total expected NPV of the two projects if both are implemented?

m. Tropical Sweets will replicate the original project only if demand is high. Using decision tree analysis, estimate the value of the project with the growth option.

n. Use a financial option model to estimate the value of the growth option.

o. What happens to the value of the growth option if the variance of the project's return is 14.2 percent? What if it is 50 percent? How might this explain the high valuations of many dot.com companies?

15 - 1

CHAPTER 15
Financial Options with Applications to Real Options

- Financial options
- Black-Scholes Option Pricing Model
- Real options
- Decision trees
- Application of financial options to real options

15 - 2

What is a real option?

- Real options exist when managers can influence the size and risk of a project's cash flows by taking different actions during the project's life in response to changing market conditions.
- Alert managers always look for real options in projects.
- Smarter managers try to create real options.

15 - 3

What is a financial option?

An option is a contract which gives its holder the right, but not the obligation, to buy (or sell) an asset at some predetermined price within a specified period of time.

15 - 4

What is the single most important characteristic of an option?

- It does not obligate its owner to take any action. It merely gives the owner the right to buy or sell an asset.

15 - 5

Option Terminology

- Call option: An option to buy a specified number of shares of a security within some future period.
- Put option: An option to sell a specified number of shares of a security within some future period.
- Exercise (or strike) price: The price stated in the option contract at which the security can be bought or sold.

15 - 6

- Option price: The market price of the option contract.
- Expiration date: The date the option matures.
- Exercise value: The value of a call option if it were exercised today = Current stock price - Strike price.

  Note: The exercise value is zero if the stock price is less than the strike price.

15 - 7

- Covered option: A call option written against stock held in an investor's portfolio.
- Naked (uncovered) option: An option sold without the stock to back it up.
- In-the-money call: A call whose exercise price is less than the current price of the underlying stock.

15 - 8

- Out-of-the-money call: A call option whose exercise price exceeds the current stock price.
- LEAPs: Long-term Equity AnticiPation securities that are similar to conventional options except that they are long-term options with maturities of up to 2 1/2 years.

15 - 9

Consider the following data:

Exercise price = $25.

Stock Price	Call Option Price
$25	$ 3.00
30	7.50
35	12.00
40	16.50
45	21.00
50	25.50

15 - 10

Create a table which shows (a) stock price, (b) strike price, (c) exercise value, (d) option price, and (e) premium of option price over the exercise value.

Price of Stock (a)	Strike Price (b)	Exercise Value of Option (a) - (b)
$25.00	$25.00	$0.00
30.00	25.00	5.00
35.00	25.00	10.00
40.00	25.00	15.00
45.00	25.00	20.00
50.00	25.00	25.00

15 - 11

Table (Continued)

Exercise Value of Option (c)	Mkt. Price of Option (d)	Premium (d) - (c)
$ 0.00	$ 3.00	$ 3.00
5.00	7.50	2.50
10.00	12.00	2.00
15.00	16.50	1.50
20.00	21.00	1.00
25.00	25.50	0.50

15 - 12

Call Premium Diagram

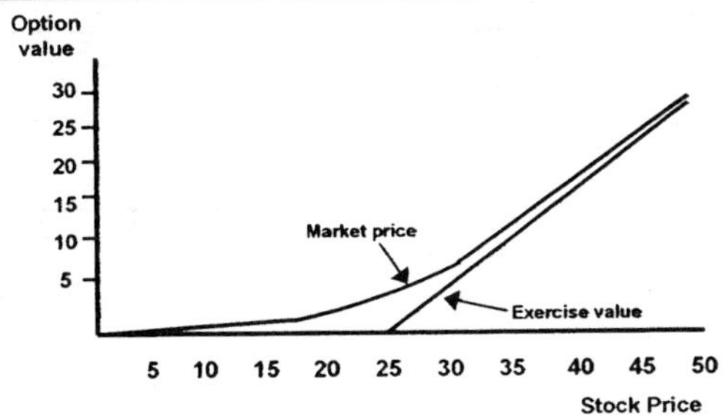

15 - 13

What happens to the premium of the option price over the exercise value as the stock price rises?

- The premium of the option price over the exercise value declines as the stock price increases.
- This is due to the declining degree of leverage provided by options as the underlying stock price increases, and the greater loss potential of options at higher option prices.

15 - 14

What are the assumptions of the Black-Scholes Option Pricing Model?

- The stock underlying the call option provides no dividends during the call option's life.
- There are no transactions costs for the sale/purchase of either the stock or the option.
- k_{RF} is known and constant during the option's life.

(More...)

15 - 15

- Security buyers may borrow any fraction of the purchase price at the short-term risk-free rate.
- No penalty for short selling and sellers receive immediately full cash proceeds at today's price.
- Call option can be exercised only on its expiration date.
- Security trading takes place in continuous time, and stock prices move randomly in continuous time.

15 - 16

What are the three equations that make up the OPM?

$$V = P[N(d_1)] - Xe^{-k_{RF}t}[N(d_2)].$$

$$d_1 = \frac{\ln(P/X) + [k_{RF} + (\sigma^2/2)]t}{\sigma\sqrt{t}}$$

$$d_2 = d_1 - \sigma\sqrt{t}.$$

15 - 17

What is the value of the following call option according to the OPM? Assume: P = \$27; X = \$25; k_{RF} = 6%; t = 0.5 years: σ^2 = 0.11

$$V = \$27[N(d_1)] - \$25e^{-(0.06)(0.5)}[N(d_2)].$$

$$d_1 = \frac{\ln(\$27/\$25) + [(0.06 + 0.11/2)](0.5)}{(0.3317)(0.7071)}$$

$$= 0.5736.$$

$$d_2 = d_1 - (0.3317)(0.7071) = d_1 - 0.2345$$

$$= 0.5736 - 0.2345 = 0.3391.$$

15 - 18

$$N(d_1) = N(0.5736) = 0.5000 + 0.2168$$

$$= 0.7168.$$

$$N(d_2) = N(0.3391) = 0.5000 + 0.1327$$

$$= 0.6327.$$

Note: Values obtained from Excel using NORMSDIST function.

$$V = \$27(0.7168) - \$25e^{-0.03}(0.6327)$$

$$= \$19.3536 - \$25(0.97045)(0.6327)$$

$$= \$4.0036.$$

15 - 19

What impact do the following parameters have on a call option's value?

- Current stock price: Call option value increases as the current stock price increases.
- Exercise price: As the exercise price increases, a call option's value decreases.

15 - 20

- Option period: As the expiration date is lengthened, a call option's value increases (more chance of becoming in the money.)
- Risk-free rate: Call option's value tends to increase as k_{RF} increases (reduces the PV of the exercise price).
- Stock return variance: Option value increases with variance of the underlying stock (more chance of becoming in the money).

15 - 21

How are real options different from financial options?

- Financial options have an underlying asset that is traded--usually a security like a stock.
- A real option has an underlying asset that is not a security--for example a project or a growth opportunity, and it isn't traded.

(More...)

15 - 22

How are real options different from financial options?

- The payoffs for financial options are specified in the contract.
- Real options are "found" or created inside of projects. Their payoffs can be varied.

15 - 23

What are some types of real options?

- Investment timing options
- Growth options
    - Expansion of existing product line
    - New products
    - New geographic markets

15 - 24

Types of real options (Continued)

- Abandonment options
    - Contraction
    - Temporary suspension
- Flexibility options

15 - 25

Five Procedures for Valuing Real Options

1. DCF analysis of expected cash flows, ignoring the option.
2. Qualitative assessment of the real option's value.
3. Decision tree analysis.
4. Standard model for a corresponding financial option.
5. Financial engineering techniques.

15 - 26

Analysis of a Real Option: Basic Project

- Initial cost = \$70 million, Cost of Capital = 10%, risk-free rate = 6%, cash flows occur for 3 years.

Demand	Probability	Annual Cash Flow
High	30%	\$45
Average	40%	\$30
Low	30%	\$15

15 - 27

Approach 1: DCF Analysis

- E(CF) =.3(\$45)+.4(\$30)+.3(\$15)
  = \$30.
- PV of expected CFs = (\$30/1.1) + (\$30/1.1^2) + (\$30/1/1^3) = \$74.61 million.
- Expected NPV = \$74.61 - \$70
  = \$4.61 million

15 - 28

Investment Timing Option

- If we immediately proceed with the project, its expected NPV is $4.61 million.
- However, the project is very risky:
  - If demand is high, NPV = $41.91 million.*
  - If demand is low, NPV = -$32.70 million.*

* See *Ch 15 Mini Case.xls* for calculations.

15 - 29

Investment Timing (Continued)

- If we wait one year, we will gain additional information regarding demand.
- If demand is low, we won't implement project.
- If we wait, the up-front cost and cash flows will stay the same, except they will be shifted ahead by a year.

15 - 30

Procedure 2: Qualitative Assessment

- The value of any real option increases if:
  - the underlying project is very risky
  - there is a long time before you must exercise the option
- This project is risky and has one year before we must decide, so the option to wait is probably valuable.

15 - 31

Procedure 3: Decision Tree Analysis (Implement only if demand is not low.)

2001	Prob.	Cost 2002	Future Cash Flows 2003	2004	2005	NPV this Scenario*
	30%	-$70	$45	$45	$45	$35.70
$0	40%	-$70	$30	$30	$30	$1.79
	30%	$0	$0	$0	$0	$0.00

Discount the cost of the project at the risk-free rate, since the cost is known. Discount the operating cash flows at the cost of capital. Example: $35.70 = -$70/1.06 + $45/1.1^2 + $45/1.1^3 + $45/1.1^3$. See *Ch 15 Mini Case.xls* for calculations.

15 - 32

Use these scenarios, with their given probabilities, to find the project's expected NPV if we wait.

E(NPV) = [0.3($35.70)]+[0.4($1.79)]

+ [0.3 ($0)]

E(NPV) = $11.42.

15 - 33

Decision Tree with Option to Wait vs. Original DCF Analysis

- Decision tree NPV is higher ($11.42 million vs. $4.61).
- In other words, the option to wait is worth $11.42 million. If we implement project today, we gain $4.61 million but lose the option worth $11.42 million.
- Therefore, we should wait and decide next year whether to implement project, based on demand.

15 - 34

The Option to Wait Changes Risk

- The cash flows are less risky under the option to wait, since we can avoid the low cash flows. Also, the cost to implement may not be risk-free.
- Given the change in risk, perhaps we should use different rates to discount the cash flows.
- But finance theory doesn't tell us how to estimate the right discount rates, so we normally do sensitivity analysis using a range of different rates.

15 - 35

Procedure 4: Use the existing model of a financial option.

- The option to wait resembles a financial call option-- we get to "buy" the project for \$70 million in one year if value of project in one year is greater than \$70 million.
- This is like a call option with an exercise price of \$70 million and an expiration date of one year.

15 - 36

Inputs to Black-Scholes Model for Option to Wait

- X = exercise price = cost to implement project = \$70 million.
- k_{RF} = risk-free rate = 6%.
- t = time to maturity = 1 year.
- P = current stock price = Estimated on following slides.
- σ^2 = variance of stock return = Estimated on following slides.

15 - 37

Estimate of P

- For a financial option:
  - P = current price of stock = PV of all of stock's expected future cash flows.
  - Current price is unaffected by the exercise cost of the option.
- For a real option:
  - P = PV of all of project's future expected cash flows.
  - P does not include the project's cost.

15 - 38

Step 1: Find the PV of future CFs at option's exercise year.

2001	Prob.	2002	Future Cash Flows 2003	2004	2005	PV at 2002
	30%		$45	$45	$45	$111.91
	40%		$30	$30	$30	$74.61
	30%		$15	$15	$15	$37.30

Example: $111.91 = $45/1.1 + $45/1.1² + $45/1.1³.
See *Ch 15 Mini Case.xls* for calculations.

15 - 39

Step 2: Find the expected PV at the current date, 2001.

PV_{2001}		PV_{2002}
	High	$111.91
$67.82	Average	$74.61
	Low	$37.30

PV_{2001}=PV of Exp. PV_{2002} = [(0.3* $111.91) +(0.4*$74.61) +(0.3*$37.3)]/1.1 = $67.82.
See *Ch 15 Mini Case.xls* for calculations.

15 - 40

The Input for P in the Black-Scholes Model

- The input for price is the present value of the project's expected future cash flows.
- Based on the previous slides,

  P = $67.82.

15 - 41

Estimating σ^2 for the Black-Scholes Model

- For a financial option, σ^2 is the variance of the stock's rate of return.
- For a real option, σ^2 is the variance of the project's rate of return.

15 - 42

Three Ways to Estimate σ^2

- Judgment.
- The direct approach, using the results from the scenarios.
- The indirect approach, using the expected distribution of the project's value.

15 - 43

Estimating σ^2 with Judgment

- The typical stock has σ^2 of about 12%.
- A project should be riskier than the firm as a whole, since the firm is a portfolio of projects.
- The company in this example has σ^2 = 10%, so we might expect the project to have σ^2 between 12% and 19%.

15 - 44

Estimating σ^2 with the Direct Approach

- Use the previous scenario analysis to estimate the return from the present until the option must be exercised. Do this for each scenario
- Find the variance of these returns, given the probability of each scenario.

15 - 45

Find Returns from the Present until the Option Expires

PV_{2001}		PV_{2002}	Return
	High	\$111.91	65.0%
\$67.82	Average	\$74.61	10.0%
	Low	\$37.30	-45.0%

Example: 65.0% = (\$111.91- \$67.82) / \$67.82.
See *Ch 15 Mini Case.xls* for calculations.

15 - 46

Use these scenarios, with their given probabilities, to find the expected return and variance of return.

E(Ret.)=0.3(0.65)+0.4(0.10)+0.3(-0.45)

E(Ret.)= 0.10 = 10%.

$\sigma^2 = 0.3(0.65-0.10)^2 + 0.4(0.10-0.10)^2$
$+ 0.3(-0.45-0.10)^2$

$\sigma^2 =$ 0.182 = 18.2%.

15 - 47

Estimating σ^2 with the Indirect Approach

- From the scenario analysis, we know the project's expected value and the variance of the project's expected value at the time the option expires.
- The questions is: "Given the current value of the project, how risky must its expected return be to generate the observed variance of the project's value at the time the option expires?"

15 - 48

The Indirect Approach (Cont.)

- From option pricing for financial options, we know the probability distribution for returns (it is lognormal).
- This allows us to specify a variance of the rate of return that gives the variance of the project's value at the time the option expires.

15 - 49

Indirect Estimate of σ^2

- Here is a formula for the variance of a stock's return, if you know the coefficient of variation of the expected stock price at some time, t, in the future:

$$\sigma^2 = \frac{\ln[CV^2 + 1]}{t}$$

We can apply this formula to the real option.

15 - 50

From earlier slides, we know the value of the project for each scenario at the expiration date.

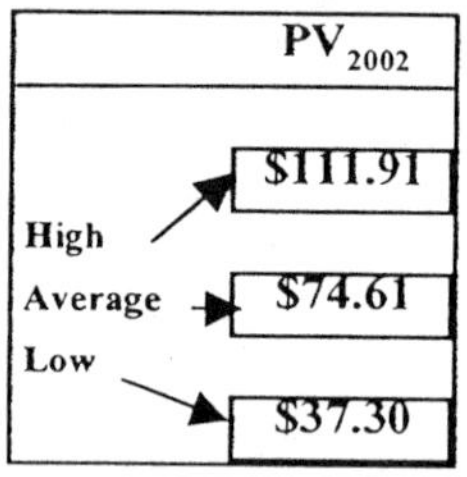

15 - 51

Use these scenarios, with their given probabilities, to find the project's expected PV and σ_{PV}.

E(PV)=.3($111.91)+.4($74.61)+.3($37.3)

E(PV)= **$74.61.**

σ_{PV} = [.3($111.91-$74.61)^2
+ .4($74.61-$74.61)^2
+ .3($37.30-$74.61)^2]$^{1/2}$

σ_{PV} = **$28.90.**

15 - 52

Find the project's expected coefficient of variation, CV_{PV}, at the time the option expires.

CV_{PV} = \$28.90 /\$74.61 = **0.39.**

15 - 53

Now use the formula to estimate σ^2.

- From our previous scenario analysis, we know the project's CV, 0.39, at the time it the option expires (t=1 year).

$$\sigma^2 = \frac{\ln[0.39^2 + 1]}{1} = 14.2\%$$

15 - 54

The Estimate of σ^2

- Subjective estimate:
  - 12% to 19%.
- Direct estimate:
  - 18.2%.
- Indirect estimate:
  - 14.2%
- For this example, we chose 14.2%, but we recommend doing sensitivity analysis over a range of σ^2.

15 - 55

Use the Black-Scholes Model:
P = \$67.83; X = \$70; k_{RF} = 6%;
t = 1 year: $\sigma^2 = 0.142$

$$V = \$67.83[N(d_1)] - \$70e^{-(0.06)(1)}[N(d_2)].$$

$$d_1 = \frac{\ln(\$67.83/\$70)+[(0.06 + 0.142/2)](1)}{(0.142)^{0.5}(1)^{.05}}$$

$$= 0.2641.$$

$$d_2 = d_1 - (0.142)^{0.5}(1)^{.05} = d_1 - 0.3768$$

$$= 0.2641 - 0.3768 = -0.1127.$$

15 - 56

$N(d_1) = N(0.2641) = 0.6041$
$N(d_2) = N(-0.1127) = 0.4551$

$$V = \$67.83(0.6041) - \$70e^{-0.06}(0.4551)$$
$$= \$40.98 - \$70(0.9418)(0.4551)$$
$$= \$10.98.$$

Note: Values of $N(d_i)$ obtained from Excel using NORMSDIST function. See *Ch 15 Mini Case.xls* for details.

15 - 57

Step 5: Use financial engineering techniques.

- **Although there are many existing models for financial options, sometimes none correspond to the project's real option.**
- **In that case, you must use financial engineering techniques, which are covered in later finance courses.**
- **Alternatively, you could simply use decision tree analysis.**

15 - 58

Other Factors to Consider When Deciding When to Invest

- Delaying the project means that cash flows come later rather than sooner.
- It might make sense to proceed today if there are important advantages to being the first competitor to enter a market.
- Waiting may allow you to take advantage of changing conditions.

15 - 59

A New Situation: Cost is $75 Million, No Option to Wait

Cost 2001	Prob.	Future Cash Flows 2002	2003	2004	NPV this Scenario
-$75	30%	$45	$45	$45	$36.91
	40%	$30	$30	$30	-$0.39
	30%	$15	$15	$15	-$37.70

Example: $36.91 = -$75 + $45/1.1 + $45/1.1 + $45/1.1.
See *Ch 15 Mini Case.xls* for calculations.

15 - 60

Expected NPV of New Situation

- E(NPV) = [0.3($36.91)]+[0.4(-$0.39)] + [0.3 (-$37.70)]
- E(NPV) = -$0.39.
- The project now looks like a loser.

15 - 61

Growth Option: You can replicate the original project after it ends in 3 years.

- NPV = NPV Original + NPV Replication

  $= -\$0.39 + -\$0.39/(1+0.10)^3$

  $= -\$0.39 + -\$0.30 = -\$0.69.$

- Still a loser, but you would implement Replication only if demand is high.

Note: the NPV would be even lower if we separately discounted the $75 million cost of Replication at the risk-free rate.

15 - 62

Decision Tree Analysis

Cost		Future Cash Flows						NPV this
2001	Prob.	2002	2003	2004	2005	2006	2007	Scenario
-$75	30%	$45	$45	-$30	$45	$45	$45	$58.02
	40%	$30	$30	$30	$0	$0	$0	-$0.39
	30%	$15	$15	$15	$0	$0	$0	-$37.70

Notes: The 2004 CF includes the cost of the project if it is optimal to replicate. The cost is discounted at the risk-free rate, other cash flows are discounted at the cost of capital. See *Ch 15 Mini Case.xls* for all calculations.

15 - 63

Expected NPV of Decision Tree

- $E(NPV) = [0.3(\$58.02)]+[0.4(-\$0.39)] + [0.3\ (-\$37.70)]$
- $E(NPV) = \$5.94.$

- The growth option has turned a losing project into a winner!

15 - 64

Financial Option Analysis: Inputs

- X = exercise price = cost of implement project = $75 million.
- k_{RF} = risk-free rate = 6%.
- t = time to maturity = 3 years.

15 - 65

Estimating P: First, find the value of future CFs at exercise year.

Cost 2001	Prob.	2002	2003	2004	2005	2006	2007	PV at 2004	Prob. x NPV
	30%				$45	$45	$45	$111.91	$33.57
	40%				$30	$30	$30	$74.61	$29.84
	30%				$15	$15	$15	$37.30	$11.19

Example: $111.91 = $45/1.1 + $45/1.1² + $45/1.1³.
See *Ch 15 Mini Case.xls* for calculations.

15 - 66

Now find the expected PV at the current date, 2001.

PV_{2001}		2002	2003	PV_{2004}
	High			$111.91
$56.05	Average			$74.61
	Low			$37.30

PV_{2001}=PV of Exp. PV_{2004} = [(0.3* $111.91) +(0.4*$74.61) +(0.3*$37.3)]/1.1³ = $56.05.
See *Ch 15 Mini Case.xls* for calculations.

15 - 67

The Input for P in the Black-Scholes Model

- The input for price is the present value of the project's expected future cash flows.
- Based on the previous slides,

  P = \$56.05.

15 - 68

Estimating σ^2: Find Returns from the Present until the Option Expires

PV_{2001}		2002	2003	PV_{2004}	Annual Return
	High			\$111.91	25.9%
\$56.05	Average			\$74.61	10.0%
	Low			\$37.30	-12.7%

Example: 25.9% = $(\$111.91/\$56.05)^{(1/3)} - 1$.
See *Ch 15 Mini Case.xls* for calculations.

15 - 69

Use these scenarios, with their given probabilities, to find the expected return and variance of return.

E(Ret.)=0.3(0.259)+0.4(0.10)+0.3(-0.127)

E(Ret.)= 0.080 = 8.0%.

$$\sigma^2 = 0.3(0.259-0.08)^2 + 0.4(0.10-0.08)^2 + 0.3(-0.1275-0.08)^2$$

$$\sigma^2 = 0.023 = 2.3\%.$$

15 - 70

Why is σ^2 so much lower than in the investment timing example?

- σ^2 has fallen, because the dispersion of cash flows for replication is the same as for the original project, even though it begins three years later. This means the rate of return for the replication is less volatile.
- We will do sensitivity analysis later.

15 - 71

Estimating σ^2 with the Indirect Method

- From earlier slides, we know the value of the project for each scenario at the expiration date.

Scenario	PV_{2004}
High	$111.91
Average	$74.61
Low	$37.30

15 - 72

Use these scenarios, with their given probabilities, to find the project's expected PV and σ_{PV}.

E(PV)=.3($111.91)+.4($74.61)+.3($37.3)

E(PV)= **$74.61.**

σ_{PV} = [.3($111.91-$74.61)^2
+ .4($74.61-$74.61)^2
+ .3($37.30-$74.61)^2]$^{1/2}$

σ_{PV} = **$28.90.**

15 - 73

Now use the indirect formula to estimate σ^2.

- CV_{PV} = \$28.90 /\$74.61 = 0.39.
- The option expires in 3 years, t=3.

$$\sigma^2 = \frac{\ln[0.39^2 + 1]}{3} = 4.7\%$$

15 - 74

Use the Black-Scholes Model:
P = \$56.06; X = \$75; k_{RF} = 6%;
t = 3 years: σ^2 = 0.047

$$V = \$56.06[N(d_1)] - \$75e^{-(0.06)(3)}[N(d_2)].$$

$$d_1 = \frac{\ln(\$56.06/\$75)+[(0.06 + 0.047/2)](3)}{(0.047)^{0.5}(3)^{.05}}$$

= -0.1085.

$d_2 = d_1 - (0.047)^{0.5}(3)^{.05} = d_1 - 0.3755$
= -0.1085 - 0.3755 =- 0.4840.

15 - 75

$N(d_1) = N(0.2641) = 0.4568$
$N(d_2) = N(-0.1127) = 0.3142$

$V = \$56.06(0.4568) - \$75e^{(-0.06)(3)}(0.3142)$
= \$5.92.

Note: Values of $N(d_i)$ obtained from Excel using NORMSDIST function. See *Ch 15 Mini Case.xls* for calculations.

15 - 76

Total Value of Project with Growth Opportunity

Total value = NPV of Original Project + Value of growth option

= -\$0.39 + \$5.92

= \$5.5 million.

15 - 77

Sensitivity Analysis on the Impact of Risk (using the Black-Scholes model)

- If risk, defined by σ^2, goes up, then value of growth option goes up:
  - σ^2 = 4.7%, Option Value = \$5.92
  - σ^2 = 14.2%, Option Value = \$12.10
  - σ^2 = 50%, Option Value = \$24.08
- Does this help explain the high value of many dot.com companies?

BLUEPRINTS: CHAPTER 16
CAPITAL STRUCTURE DECISIONS: THE BASICS

Assume you have just been hired as business manager of PizzaPalace, a pizza restaurant located adjacent to campus. The company's EBIT was $500,000 last year, and since the university's enrollment is capped, EBIT is expected to remain constant (in real terms) over time. Since no expansion capital will be required, PizzaPalace plans to pay out all earnings as dividends. The management group owns about 50 percent of the stock, and the stock is traded in the over-the-counter market.

The firm is currently financed with all equity; it has 100,000 shares outstanding; and P_0 = $20 per share. When you took your MBA corporate finance course, your instructor stated that most firms' owners would be financially better off if the firms used some debt. When you suggested this to your new boss, he encouraged you to pursue the idea. As a first step, assume that you obtained from the firm's investment banker the following estimated costs of debt for the firm at different debt levels (in thousands of dollars):

Amount Borrowed	k_d
$ 0	--
250	10.0%
500	11.0
750	13.0
1,000	16.0

If the company were to recapitalize, debt would be issued, and the funds received would be used to repurchase stock. PizzaPalace is in the 40 percent state-plus-federal corporate tax bracket, the risk-free rate is 6 percent, and the market risk premium is 4 percent.

a. Now, to develop an example which can be presented to PizzaPalace's management to illustrate the effects of financial leverage, consider two hypothetical firms: Firm U, which uses no debt financing, and Firm L, which uses $10,000 of 12 percent debt. Both firms have $20,000 in assets, a 40 percent tax rate, and an expected EBIT of $3,000.

(1) Construct partial income statements, which start with EBIT, for the two firms.

(2) Now calculate ROE for both firms.

(3) What does this example illustrate about the impact of financial leverage on ROE?

b. (1) What is business risk? What factors influence a firm's business risk?

(2) What is operating leverage, and how does it affect a firm's business risk?

c. (1) What is meant by financial leverage and financial risk?

(2) How does financial risk differ from business risk?

d. Now consider the fact that EBIT is not known with certainty, but rather has the following probability distribution:

Economic State	Probability	EBIT
Bad	0.25	$2,000
Average	0.50	3,000
Good	0.25	4,000

Redo the Part a analysis for Firms U and L, but add basic earning power (BEP), return on investment (ROI), [defined as (Net income + Interest)/(Debt + Equity)], and the times-interest-earned (TIE) ratio to the outcome measures. Find the values for each firm in each state of the economy, and then calculate the expected values. Finally, calculate the standard deviation and coefficient of variation of ROE. What does this example illustrate about the impact of debt financing on risk and return?

e. How are financial and business risk measured in a stand-alone risk framework?

f. What does capital structure theory attempt to do? What lessons can be learned from capital structure theory?

g. With the above points in mind, now consider the optimal capital structure for PizzaPalace.

(1) What valuation equations can you use in the analysis?

(2) Could either the MM or the Miller capital structure theories be applied directly in this analysis, and if you presented an analysis based on these theories, how do you think the owners would respond?

h. (1) Describe briefly, without using any numbers, the sequence of events that would take place if PizzaPalace does recapitalize.

(2) What would be the new stock price if PizzaPalace recapitalized and used these amounts of debt: $250,000; $500,000; $750,000?

(3) How many shares would remain outstanding after recapitalization under each debt scenario?

(4) Considering only the levels of debt discussed, what is PizzaPalace's optimal capital structure?

i. It is also useful to determine the effect of any proposed recapitalization on EPS. Calculate the EPS at debt levels of \$0, \$250,000, \$500,000, and \$750,000, assuming that the firm begins at zero debt and recapitalizes to each level in a single step. Is EPS maximized at the same level that maximizes stock price?

j. Calculate the firm's WACC at each debt level. What is the relationship between the WACC and the stock price?

k. Suppose you discovered that PizzaPalace had more business risk than you originally estimated. Describe how this would affect the analysis. What if the firm had less business risk than originally estimated?

l. Is it possible to do an analysis exactly like the PizzaPalace analysis for most firms? Why or why not? What type of analysis do you think a firm should actually use to help set its optimal, or target, capital structure? What other factors should managers consider when setting the target capital structure?

16 - 1

CHAPTER 16
Capital Structure Decisions: The Basics

- Impact of leverage on returns
- Business versus financial risk
- Capital structure theory
- Perpetual cash flow example
- Setting the optimal capital structure in practice

16 - 2

Consider Two Hypothetical Firms

Firm U	Firm L
No debt	$10,000 of 12% debt
$20,000 in assets	$20,000 in assets
40% tax rate	40% tax rate

Both firms have same operating leverage, business risk, and EBIT of $3,000. They differ only with respect to use of debt.

16 - 3

Impact of Leverage on Returns

	Firm U	Firm L
EBIT	$3,000	$3,000
Interest	0	1,200
EBT	$3,000	$1,800
Taxes (40%)	1,200	720
NI	$1,800	$1,080
ROE	9.0%	10.8%

16 - 4

Why does leveraging increase return?

- Total dollar return to investors:
  - U: NI = $1,800.
  - L: NI + Int = $1,080 + $1,200 = $2,280.
  - Difference = $480.
- Taxes paid:
  - U: $1,200; L: $720.
  - Difference = $480.
- More EBIT goes to investors in Firm L.
- Equity $ proportionally lower than NI.

16 - 5

What is business risk?

- Uncertainty about future operating income (EBIT).

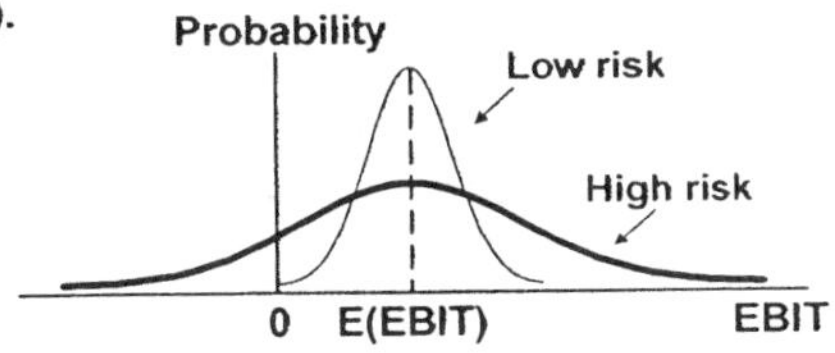

- Note that business risk focuses on operating income, so it ignores financing effects.

16 - 6

Factors That Influence Business Risk

- Uncertainty about demand (unit sales).
- Uncertainty about output prices.
- Uncertainty about input costs.
- Product and other types of liability.
- Degree of operating leverage (DOL).

16 - 7

What is operating leverage, and how does it affect a firm's business risk?

- Operating leverage is the use of fixed costs rather than variable costs.
- The higher the proportion of fixed costs within a firm's overall cost structure, the greater the operating leverage.

(More...)

16 - 8

- Higher operating leverage leads to more business risk, because a small sales decline causes a larger profit decline.

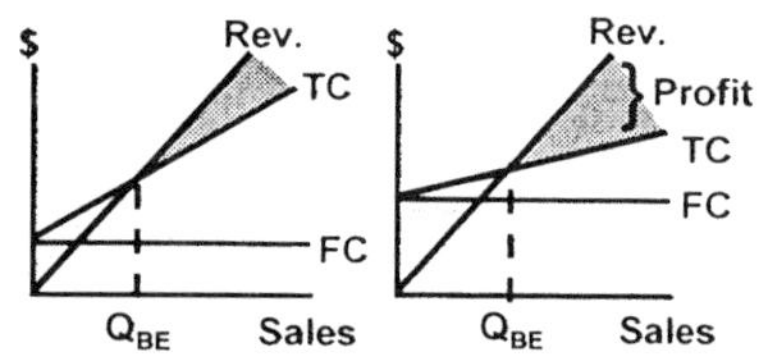

(More...)

16 - 9

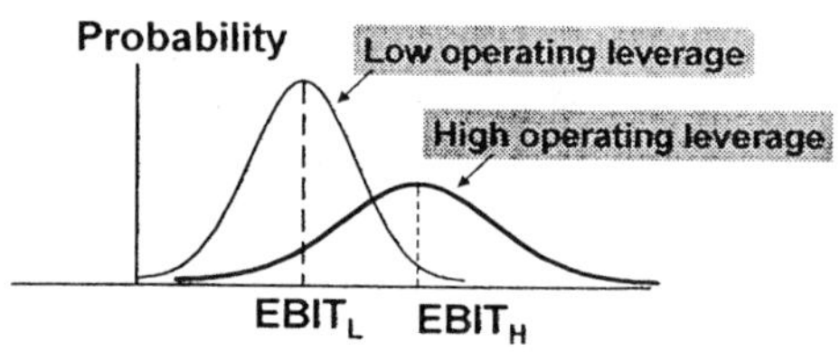

- In the typical situation, higher operating leverage leads to higher expected EBIT, but also increases risk.

16 - 10

Business Risk versus Financial Risk

- Business risk:
  - Uncertainty in future EBIT.
  - Depends on business factors such as competition, operating leverage, etc.
- Financial risk:
  - Additional business risk concentrated on common stockholders when financial leverage is used.
  - Depends on the amount of debt and preferred stock financing.

16 - 11

From a shareholder's perspective, how are financial and business risk measured in the stand-alone sense?

$$\text{Stand-alone risk} = \text{Business risk} + \text{Financial risk}$$

Stand-alone risk = σ_{ROE}.

Business risk = $\sigma_{ROE(U)}$.

Financial risk = $\sigma_{ROE} - \sigma_{ROE(U)}$.

16 - 12

Now consider the fact that EBIT is not known with certainty. What is the impact of uncertainty on stockholder profitability and risk for Firm U and Firm L?

16 - 13

Firm U: Unleveraged

	Economy		
	Bad	Avg.	Good
Prob.	0.25	0.50	0.25
EBIT	$2,000	$3,000	$4,000
Interest	0	0	0
EBT	$2,000	$3,000	$4,000
Taxes (40%)	800	1,200	1,600
NI	$1,200	$1,800	$2,400

16 - 14

Firm L: Leveraged

	Economy		
	Bad	Avg.	Good
Prob.*	0.25	0.50	0.25
EBIT*	$2,000	$3,000	$4,000
Interest	1,200	1,200	1,200
EBT	$ 800	$1,800	$2,800
Taxes (40%)	320	720	1,120
NI	$ 480	$1,080	$1,680

*Same as for Firm U.

16 - 15

Firm U	Bad	Avg.	Good
BEP	10.0%	15.0%	20.0%
ROI*	6.0%	9.0%	12.0%
ROE	6.0%	9.0%	12.0%
TIE	∞	∞	∞

Firm L	Bad	Avg.	Good
BEP	10.0%	15.0%	20.0%
ROI*	8.4%	11.4%	14.4%
ROE	4.8%	10.8%	16.8%
TIE	1.7x	2.5x	3.3x

*ROI = (NI + Interest)/Total financing.

16 - 16

Profitability Measures:

	U	L
E(BEP)	15.0%	15.0%
E(ROI)	9.0%	11.4%
E(ROE)	9.0%	10.8%

Risk Measures:

σ_{ROE}	2.12%	4.24%
CV_{ROE}	0.24	0.39
E(TIE)	∞	2.5x

16 - 17

Conclusions

- Basic earning power = BEP = EBIT/Total assets is unaffected by financial leverage.
- L has higher expected ROI and ROE because of tax savings.
- L has much wider ROE (and EPS) swings because of fixed interest charges. Its higher expected return is accompanied by higher risk. (More...)

16 - 18

- In a stand-alone risk sense, Firm L's stockholders see much more risk than Firm U's.
  - U and L: $\sigma_{ROE(U)}$ = 2.12%.
  - U: σ_{ROE} = 2.12%.
  - L: σ_{ROE} = 4.24%.
- L's financial risk is $\sigma_{ROE} - \sigma_{ROE(U)}$ = 4.24% - 2.12% = 2.12%. (U's is zero.)

(More...)

16 - 19

- For leverage to be positive (increase expected ROE), BEP must be > k_d.
- If k_d > BEP, the cost of leveraging will be higher than the inherent profitability of the assets, so the use of financial leverage will depress net income and ROE.
- In the example, E(BEP) = 15% while interest rate = 12%, so leveraging "works."

16 - 20

Capital Structure Theory

- MM theory
  - Zero taxes
  - Corporate taxes
  - Corporate and personal taxes
- Trade-off theory
- Signaling theory
- Debt financing as a managerial constraint

16 - 21

MM Theory: Zero Taxes

- MM prove, under a very restrictive set of assumptions, that a firm's value is unaffected by its financing mix.
- Therefore, capital structure is irrelevant.
- Any increase in ROE resulting from financial leverage is exactly offset by the increase in risk.

16 - 22

MM Theory: Corporate Taxes

- Corporate tax laws favor debt financing over equity financing.
- With corporate taxes, the benefits of financial leverage exceed the risks: More EBIT goes to investors and less to taxes when leverage is used.
- Firms should use almost 100% debt financing to maximize value.

16 - 23

MM Theory: Corporate and Personal Taxes

- Personal taxes lessen the advantage of corporate debt:
  - Corporate taxes favor debt financing.
  - Personal taxes favor equity financing.
- Use of debt financing remains advantageous, but benefits are less than under only corporate taxes.
- Firms should still use 100% debt.

16 - 24

Hamada's Equation

- MM theory implies that beta changes with leverage.
- b_U is the beta of a firm when it has no debt (the unlevered beta)
- $b_L = b_U(1 + (1 - T)(D/E))$
- In practice, D/E is measured in book values when b_L is calculated.

16 - 25

Trade-off Theory

- MM theory ignores bankruptcy (financial distress) costs, which increase as more leverage is used.
- At low leverage levels, tax benefits outweigh bankruptcy costs.
- At high levels, bankruptcy costs outweigh tax benefits.
- An optimal capital structure exists that balances these costs and benefits.

16 - 26

Signaling Theory

- MM assumed that investors and managers have the same information.
- But, managers often have better information. Thus, they would:
  - Sell stock if stock is overvalued.
  - Sell bonds if stock is undervalued.
- Investors understand this, so view new stock sales as a negative signal.
- Implications for managers?

16 - 27

Debt Financing As a Managerial Constraint

- One agency problem is that managers can use corporate funds for non-value maximizing purposes.
- The use of financial leverage:
  - Bonds "free cash flow."
  - Forces discipline on managers.
- However, it also increases risk of financial distress.

16 - 28

Perpetual Cash Flow Example

Expected EBIT = \$500,000; will remain constant over time.

Firm pays out all earnings as dividends (zero growth).

Currently is all-equity financed. BV of equity = MV of equity

100,000 shares outstanding.

P_0 = \$20; T = 40%; k_{RF} = 6%; RP_M = 4%

16 - 29

Component Cost Estimates

Amount Borrowed (000)	k_d
\$ 0	-
250	10.0%
500	11.0
750	13.0
1,000	16.0

If company recapitalizes, debt would be issued to repurchase stock.

16 - 30

- The MM and Miller models cannot be applied directly because several assumptions are violated.
  - k_d is not a constant.
  - Bankruptcy and agency costs exist.
- In practice, Hamada's equation is used to find k_S for the firm with different levels of debt.

16 - 31

The Optimal Capital Structure

- Calculate the cost of equity at each level of debt.
- Calculate the value of equity at each level of debt.
- Calculate the total value of the firm (value of equity + value of debt) at each level of debt.
- The optimal capital structure maximizes the total value of the firm.

16 - 32

Sequence of Events in a Recapitalization

- Firm announces the recapitalization.
- Investors reassess their views and estimate a new equity value.
- New debt is issued and proceeds are used to repurchase stock at the new equilibrium price.

(More...)

16 - 33

- $\text{Shares Bought} = \dfrac{\text{Debt issued}}{\text{New price/share}}$
- After recapitalization firm would have more debt but fewer common shares outstanding.
- An analysis of several debt levels is given next.

16 - 34

Cost of Equity at Zero Debt

- Since the firm has 0 growth, its current value, \$2,000,000, is given by

  $\text{Dividends}/k_S = (\text{EBIT})(1\text{-T})/k_S$
  $= 500{,}000\ (1 - 0.40)/k_S$

- k_S = 15.0% = unlevered cost of equity.

- $b_U = (k_S - k_{RF})/RP_M = (15 - 6)/4 = 2.25$

16 - 35

Cost of Equity at Each Debt Level

- Hamada's equation says that
  $b_L = b_U\ (1 + (1\text{-T})(D/E))$

Debt(000s)	D/E	b_L	k_S
0	0	2.25	15.00%
250	0.142	2.44	15.77
500	0.333	2.70	16.80
750	0.600	3.06	18.24
1,000	1.000	3.60	20.40

16 - 36

D = \$250, k_d = 10%, k_s = 15.77%.

$$S_1 = \frac{(\text{EBIT} - k_d D)(1 - T)}{k_s}$$

$$= \frac{[\$500 - 0.1(\$250)](0.6)}{0.1577} = \$1{,}807.$$

$$V_1 = S_1 + D_1 = \$1{,}807 + \$250 = \$2{,}057.$$

$$P_1 = \frac{\$2{,}057}{100} = \$20.57.$$

16 - 37

$$\text{Shares repurchased} = \frac{\$250}{\$20.57} = 12.15.$$

$$\text{Shares remaining} = n_1 = 100 - 12.15 = 87.85.$$

Check on stock price:

$$P_1 = \frac{S_1}{n_1} = \frac{\$1,807}{87.85} = \$20.57.$$

Other debt levels treated similarly.

16 - 38

Value of Equity at Each Debt Level

- Equity Value = Dividends/k_S

Debt(000s)	k_D	Divs	k_S	E
0	na	300	15.00%	2,000
250	10%	285	15.77	1,807
500	11%	267	16.80	1,589
750	13%	241.5	18.24	1,324
1,000	16%	204	20.40	1,000

16 - 39

Total Value of Firm

Debt (000s)	E	Total Value	Price per Share
0	2,000	2,000	$20.00
250	1,807	2,057	20.57
500	1,589	2,089	20.89 ←
750	1,324	2,074	20.74
1,000	1,000	2,000	20.00

Total Value is Maximized with 500,000 in debt.

16 - 40

Calculate EPS at debt of $0, $250K, $500K, and $750K, assuming that the firm begins at zero debt and recapitalizes to each level in a single step.

Net income = NI = [EBIT - k_d D](1 - T).
EPS = NI/n.

D	NI	n	EPS
$ 0	$300	100.00	$3.00
250	285	87.85	3.24
500	267	76.07	3.51
750	242	63.84	3.78

16 - 41

- EPS continues to increase beyond the $500,000 optimal debt level.
- Does this mean that the optimal debt level is $750,000, or even higher?

16 - 42

Find the WACC at each debt level.

D	S	V	k_d	k_s	WACC
$ 0	$2,000	$2,000	--	15.00%	15.0%
250	1,807	2,057	10%	15.77	14.6
500	1,589	2,089	11.0	16.80	14.4
750	1,324	2,074	13.0	18.24	14.5
1,000	1,000	2,000	13.0	20.40	15.0

e.g. D = $250:
WACC = ($250/$2,057)(10%)(0.6)
+ ($1,807/$2,057)(15.77%)
= 14.6%.

16 - 43

- The WACC is minimized at D = \$500,000, the same debt level that maximizes stock price.
- Since the value of a firm is the present value of future operating income, the lowest discount rate (WACC) leads to the highest value.

16 - 44

How would higher or lower business risk affect the optimal capital structure?

- At any debt level, the firm's probability of financial distress would be higher. Both k_d and k_s would rise faster than before. The end result would be an optimal capital structure with less debt.
- Lower business risk would have the opposite effect.

16 - 45

Is it possible to do an analysis exactly like the one above for most firms?

- No. The analysis above was based on the assumption of zero growth, and most firms do not fit this category.
- Further, it would be very difficult, if not impossible, to estimate k_s with any confidence.

16 - 46

What type of analysis should firms conduct to help find their optimal, or target, capital structure?

- Financial forecasting models can help show how capital structure changes are likely to affect stock prices, coverage ratios, and so on.

(More...)

16 - 47

- Forecasting models can generate results under various scenarios, but the financial manager must specify appropriate input values, interpret the output, and eventually decide on a target capital structure.
- In the end, capital structure decision will be based on a combination of analysis and judgment.

16 - 48

What other factors would managers consider when setting the target capital structure?

- Debt ratios of other firms in the industry.
- Pro forma coverage ratios at different capital structures under different economic scenarios.
- Lender and rating agency attitudes (impact on bond ratings).

16 - 49

- Reserve borrowing capacity.
- Effects on control.
- Type of assets: Are they tangible, and hence suitable as collateral?
- Tax rates.

BLUEPRINTS: CHAPTER 17

CAPITAL STRUCTURE DECISIONS: EXTENSIONS

Donald Cheney, the CEO of Cheney Electronics, is concerned about his firm's level of debt financing. The company uses short-term debt to finance its temporary working capital needs, but it does not use any permanent (long-term) debt. Other electronics companies average about 30 percent debt, and Mr. Cheney wonders why the difference occurs, and what its effects are on stock prices. To gain some insights into the matter, he poses the following questions to you, his recently hired assistant:

a. *Business Week* recently ran an article on companies' debt policies, and the names Modigliani and Miller (MM) were mentioned several times as leading researchers on the theory of capital structure. Briefly, who are MM, and what assumptions are embedded in the MM and Miller models?

b. Assume that Firms U and L are in the same risk class, and that both have EBIT = \$500,000. Firm U uses no debt financing, and its cost of equity is k_{sU} = 14%. Firm L has \$1 million of debt outstanding at a cost of k_d = 8%. There are no taxes. Assume that the MM assumptions hold, and then:

   (1) Find V, S, k_s, and WACC for Firms U and L.

   (2) Graph (a) the relationships between capital costs and leverage as measured by D/V, and (b) the relationship between value and D.

c. Using the data given in Part b, but now assuming that Firms L and U are both subject to a 40 percent corporate tax rate, repeat the analysis called for in b(1) and b(2) under the MM with-tax model.

d. Now suppose investors are subject to the following tax rates: T_d = 30% and T_s = 12%.

   (1) What is the gain from leverage according to the Miller model?

   (2) How does this gain compare to the gain in the MM model with corporate taxes?

   (3) What does the Miller model imply about the effect of corporate debt on the value of the firm, that is, how do personal taxes affect the situation?

e. What capital structure policy recommendations do the three theories (MM without taxes, MM with corporate taxes, and Miller) suggest to financial managers? Empirically, do firms appear to follow any one of these guidelines?

f. What are financial distress and agency costs? How does the addition of these costs change the MM and Miller models? (Express your answer in words, in equation form, and in graphical form.)

g. How are financial and business risk measured in a market risk framework?

h. What is the asymmetric information, or signaling, theory of capital structure?

i. What is the "pecking order" theory of capital structure?

17 - 1

CHAPTER 17
Capital Structure Decisions: Extensions

- MM and Miller models
- Hamada's equation
- Financial distress and agency costs
- Trade-off models
- Asymmetric information theory

17 - 2

Who are Modigliani and Miller (MM)?

- They published theoretical papers that changed the way people thought about financial leverage.
- They won Nobel prizes in economics because of their work.
- MM's papers were published in 1958 and 1963. Miller had a separate paper in 1977. The papers differed in their assumptions about taxes.

17 - 3

What assumptions underlie the MM and Miller models?

- Firms can be grouped into homogeneous classes based on business risk.
- Investors have identical expectations about firms' future earnings.
- There are no transactions costs.

(More...)

17 - 4

- All debt is riskless, and both individuals and corporations can borrow unlimited amounts of money at the risk-free rate.
- All cash flows are perpetuities. This implies perpetual debt is issued, firms have zero growth, and expected EBIT is constant over time.

(More...)

17 - 5

- MM's first paper (1958) assumed zero taxes. Later papers added taxes.
- No agency or financial distress costs.
- These assumptions were necessary for MM to prove their propositions on the basis of investor arbitrage.

17 - 6

MM with Zero Taxes (1958)

Proposition I:

$$V_L = V_U.$$

Proposition II:

$$k_{sL} = k_{sU} + (k_{sU} - k_d)(D/S).$$

17 - 7

Given the following data, find V, S, k_s, and WACC for Firms U and L.

Firms U and L are in same risk class.

$EBIT_{U,L}$ = \$500,000.

Firm U has no debt; k_{sU} = 14%.

Firm L has \$1,000,000 debt at k_d = 8%.

The basic MM assumptions hold.

There are no corporate or personal taxes.

17 - 8

1. Find V_U and V_L.

$$V_U = \frac{EBIT}{k_{sU}} = \frac{\$500,000}{0.14} = \$3,571,429.$$

$V_L = V_U$ = \$3,571,429.

Questions: What is the derivation of the V_U equation? Are the MM assumptions required?

17 - 9

2. Find the market value of Firm L's debt and equity.

V_L = D + S = \$3,571,429

\$3,571,429 = \$1,000,000 + S

S = \$2,571,429.

17 - 10

3. Find k_{sL}.

$$k_{sL} = k_{sU} + (k_{sU} - k_d)(D/S)$$

$$= 14.0\% + (14.0\% - 8.0\%)\left(\frac{\$1,000,000}{\$2,571,429}\right)$$

$$= 14.0\% + 2.33\% = 16.33\%.$$

17 - 11

4. Proposition I implies WACC = k_{sU}. Verify for L using WACC formula.

$$\text{WACC} = w_d k_d + w_{ce} k_s = (D/V)k_d + (S/V)k_s$$

$$= \left(\frac{\$1,000,000}{\$3,571,429}\right)(8.0\%)$$

$$+\left(\frac{\$2,571,429}{\$3,571,429}\right)(16.33\%)$$

$$= 2.24\% + 11.76\% = 14.00\%.$$

17 - 12

Graph the MM relationships between capital costs and leverage as measured by D/V.

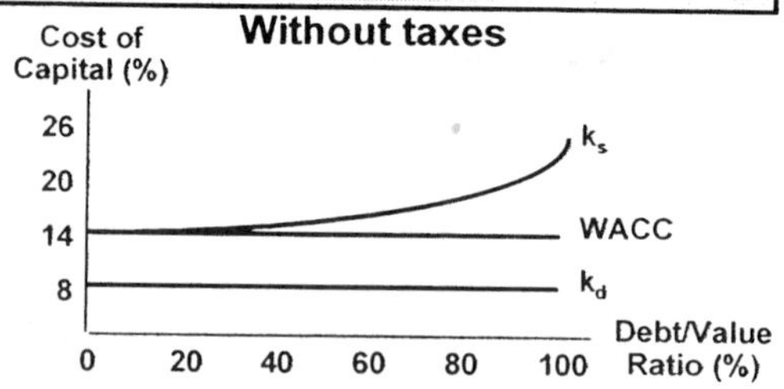

17 - 13

- The more debt the firm adds to its capital structure, the riskier the equity becomes and thus the higher its cost.
- Although k_d remains constant, k_s increases with leverage. The increase in k_s is exactly sufficient to keep the WACC constant.

17 - 14

Graph value versus leverage.

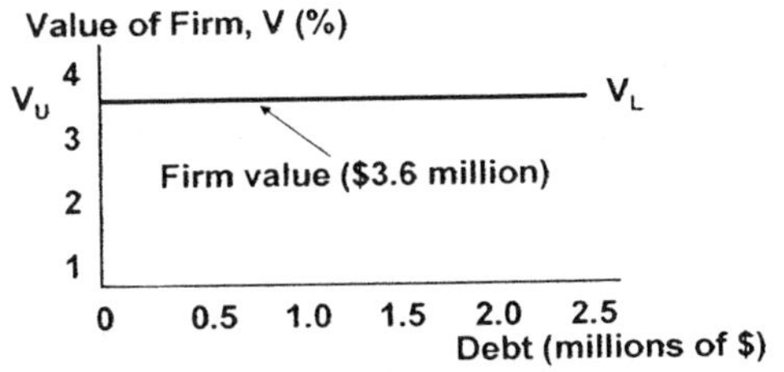

With zero taxes, MM argue that value is unaffected by leverage.

17 - 15

Find V, S, k_s, and WACC for Firms U and L assuming a 40% corporate tax rate.

With corporate taxes added, the MM propositions become:

Proposition I:

$$V_L = V_U + TD.$$

Proposition II:

$$k_{sL} = k_{sU} + (k_{sU} - k_d)(1 - T)(D/S).$$

17 - 16

Notes About the New Propositions

1. When corporate taxes are added, $V_L \neq V_U$. V_L increases as debt is added to the capital structure, and the greater the debt usage, the higher the value of the firm.
2. k_{sL} increases with leverage at a slower rate when corporate taxes are considered.

17 - 17

1. Find V_U and V_L.

$$V_U = \frac{\text{EBIT}(1 - T)}{k_{sU}} = \frac{\$500{,}000(0.6)}{0.14} = \$2{,}142{,}857.$$

Note: Represents a 40% decline from the no taxes situation.

$$V_L = V_U + TD = \$2{,}142{,}857 + 0.4(\$1{,}000{,}000)$$
$$= \$2{,}142{,}857 + \$400{,}000$$
$$= \$2{,}542{,}857.$$

17 - 18

2. Find market value of Firm L's debt and equity.

$$V_L = D + S = \$2{,}542{,}857$$
$$\$2{,}542{,}857 = \$1{,}000{,}000 + S$$
$$S = \$1{,}542{,}857.$$

17 - 19

3. Find k_{sL}.

$$k_{sL} = k_{sU} + (k_{sU} - k_d)(1 - T)(D/S)$$

$$= 14.0\% + (14.0\% - 8.0\%)(0.6)\left(\frac{\$1,000,000}{\$1,542,857}\right)$$

$$= 14.0\% + 2.33\% = 16.33\%.$$

17 - 20

4. Find Firm L's WACC.

$$WACC_L = (D/V)k_d(1 - T) + (S/V)k_s$$

$$= \left(\frac{\$1,000,000}{\$2,542,857}\right)(8.0\%)(0.6)$$

$$+ \left(\frac{\$1,542,857}{\$2,542,857}\right)(16.33\%)$$

$$= 1.89\% + 9.91\% = 11.80\%.$$

When corporate taxes are considered, the WACC is lower for L than for U.

17 - 21

MM relationship between capital costs and leverage when corporate taxes are considered.

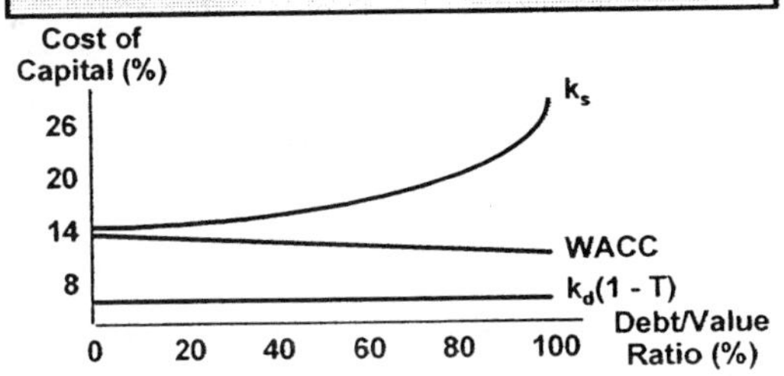

17 - 22

MM relationship between value and debt when corporate taxes are considered.

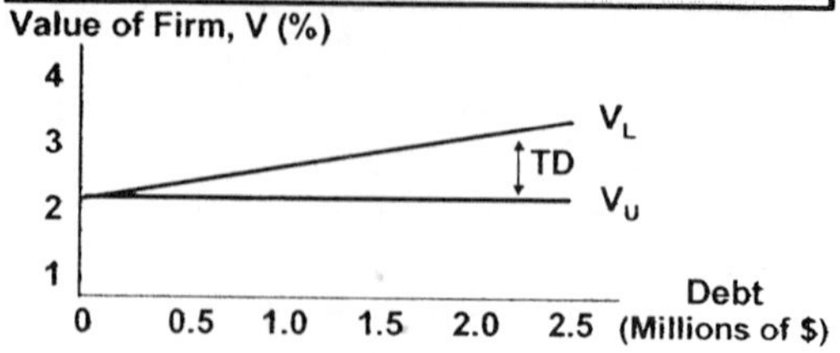

Under MM with corporate taxes, the firm's value increases continuously as more and more debt is used.

17 - 23

Assume investors have the following tax rates: T_d = 30% and T_s = 12%. What is the gain from leverage according to the Miller model?

Miller's Proposition I:

$$V_L = V_U + \left[1 - \frac{(1 - T_c)(1 - T_s)}{(1 - T_d)}\right]D.$$

T_c = corporate tax rate.
T_d = personal tax rate on debt income.
T_s = personal tax rate on stock income.

17 - 24

T_c = 40%, T_d = 30%, and T_s = 12%.

$$V_L = V_U + \left[1 - \frac{(1 - 0.40)(1 - 0.12)}{(1 - 0.30)}\right]D$$

$$= V_U + (1 - 0.75)D$$

$$= V_U + 0.25D.$$

Value rises with debt; each $100 increase in debt raises L's value by $25.

17 - 25

How does this gain compare to the gain in the MM model with corporate taxes?

If only corporate taxes, then

$$V_L = V_U + T_cD = V_U + 0.40D.$$

Here $100 of debt raises value by $40. Thus, personal taxes lowers the gain from leverage, but the net effect depends on tax rates.

(More...)

17 - 26

- If T_s declines, while T_c and T_d remain constant, the slope coefficient (which shows the benefit of debt) is decreased.
- A company with a low payout ratio gets lower benefits under the Miller model than a company with a high payout, because a low payout decreases T_s.

17 - 27

When Miller brought in personal taxes, the value enhancement of debt was lowered. Why?

1. Corporate tax laws favor debt over equity financing because interest expense is tax deductible while dividends are not.

(More...)

17 - 28

2. However, personal tax laws favor equity over debt because stocks provide both tax deferral and a lower capital gains tax rate.
3. This lowers the relative cost of equity vis-a-vis MM's no-personal-tax world and decreases the spread between debt and equity costs.
4. Thus, some of the advantage of debt financing is lost, so debt financing is less valuable to firms.

17 - 29

What does capital structure theory prescribe for corporate managers?

1. MM, No Taxes: Capital structure is irrelevant--no impact on value or WACC.
2. MM, Corporate Taxes: Value increases, so firms should use (almost) 100% debt financing.
3. Miller, Personal Taxes: Value increases, but less than under MM, so again firms should use (almost) 100% debt financing.

17 - 30

Do firms follow the recommendations of capital structure theory?

- Firms don't follow MM/Miller to 100% debt. Debt ratios average about 40%.
- However, debt ratios did increase after MM. Many think debt ratios were too low, and MM led to changes in financial policies.

17 - 31

Define financial distress and agency costs.

Financial distress: As firms use more and more debt financing, they face a higher probability of future financial distress, which brings with it lower sales, EBIT, and bankruptcy costs. Lowers value of stock and bonds.

(More...)

17 - 32

Agency costs: The costs of managers not behaving in the best interests of shareholders and the resulting costs of monitoring managers' actions. Lowers value of stock and bonds.

17 - 33

How do financial distress and agency costs change the MM and Miller models?

- MM/Miller ignored these costs, hence those models show firm value increasing continuously with leverage.
- Since financial distress and agency costs increase with leverage, such costs reduce the value of debt financing.

17 - 34

Here's a valuation model which includes financial distress and agency costs:

$$V_L = V_U + XD - \text{PV of expected fin. distress costs} - \text{PV of agency costs}.$$

- X represents either T_c in the MM model or the more complex Miller term.
- Now, optimal leverage involves a tradeoff between the tax benefits of debt and the costs associated with financial distress and agency.

17 - 35

Relationships between capital costs and leverage when financial distress and agency costs are considered.

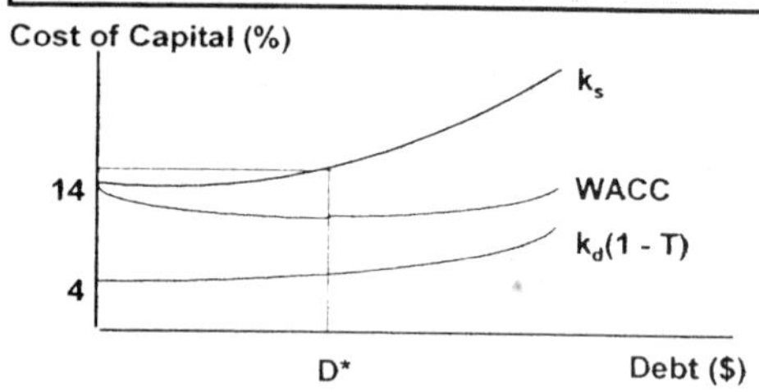

17 - 36

Relationship between value and leverage.

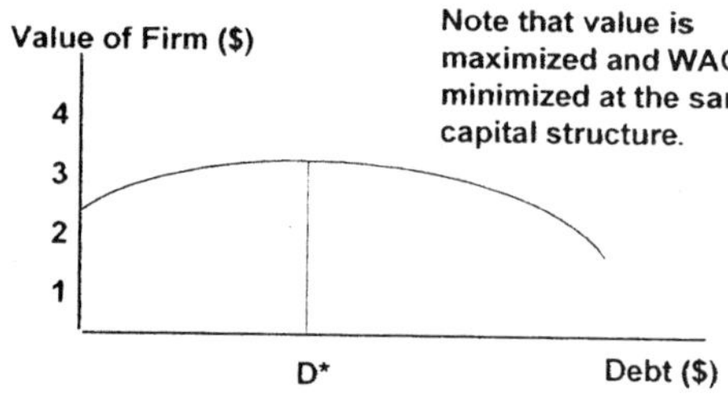

Note that value is maximized and WACC is minimized at the same capital structure.

17 - 37

How are financial and business risk measured in a market risk framework?

$$k_{sL} = k_{RF} + (k_M - k_{RF})b_U + (k_M - k_{RF})b_U(1 - T)(D/S)$$

= Pure time value + Business risk premium + Financial risk premium.

(Hamada's equation)

17 - 38

Hamada's equation for beta:

$$b_L = b_U + b_U(1 - T)(D/S)$$

= Unlevered beta, which reflects the business risk of the firm + Increased volatility of the returns to equity due to the use of debt

= Business risk + Financial risk

17 - 39

What is the "pecking order theory" of capital structure?

- Results of a survey by Donaldson and the asymmetric information theory.
- Firms follow a specific financing order:
  - First use internal funds.
  - Next, draw on marketable securities.
  - Then, issue new debt.
  - Finally, and only as a last resort, issue new common stock.

17 - 40

Does the pecking order theory make sense? Explain.
Is the pecking order theory consistent with the trade-off theory?

- It is consistent with the asymmetric information theory, in which managers avoid issuing equity.
- It is not consistent with trade-off theory.

17 - 41

What is the asymmetric information theory of capital structure?

- Theory recognizes that market participants do not have homogeneous expectations--managers typically have better information than investors.
- Thus, financing actions are interpreted by investors as signals of managerial expectations for the future.

(More...)

17 - 42

- Managers will issue new common stock only when no other alternatives exist or when the stock is overvalued.
- Investors recognize this, so new stock sales are treated as negative signals and stock price falls.
- Managers do not want to trigger a price decline, so firms maintain a reserve borrowing capacity.

BLUEPRINTS: CHAPTER 18
DISTRIBUTIONS TO SHAREHOLDERS: DIVIDENDS AND REPURCHASES

Southeastern Steel Company (SSC) was formed 5 years ago to exploit a new continuous-casting process. SSC's founders, Donald Brown and Margo Valencia, had been employed in the research department of a major integrated-steel company, but when that company decided against using the new process (which Brown and Valencia had developed), they decided to strike out on their own. One advantage of the new process was that it required relatively little capital in comparison with the typical steel company, so Brown and Valencia have been able to avoid issuing new stock, and thus they own all of the shares. However, SCC has now reached the stage where outside equity capital is necessary if the firm is to achieve its growth targets yet still maintain its target capital structure of 60 percent equity and 40 percent debt. Therefore, Brown and Valencia have decided to take the company public. Until now, Brown and Valencia have paid themselves reasonable salaries but routinely reinvested all after-tax earnings in the firm, so dividend policy has not been an issue. However, before talking with potential outside investors, they must decide on a dividend policy.

Assume that you were recently hired by Arthur Adamson & Company (AA), a national consulting firm, which has been asked to help SSC prepare for its public offering. Martha Millon, the senior AA consultant in your group, has asked you to make a presentation to Brown and Valencia in which you review the theory of dividend policy and discuss the following questions.

a. (1) What is meant by the term "dividend policy"?

(2) The terms "irrelevance," "bird-in-the-hand," and "tax preference" have been used to describe three major theories regarding the way dividend policy affects a firm's value. Explain what these terms mean, and briefly describe each theory.

(3) What do the three theories indicate regarding the actions management should take with respect to dividend policy?

(4) Explain the relationships between dividend policy, stock price, and the cost of equity under each dividend policy theory by constructing two graphs such as those shown in Figure 17-1. Dividend payout should be placed on the X axis.

(5) What results have empirical studies of the dividend theories produced? How does all this affect what we can tell managers about dividend policy?

b. Discuss (1) the information content, or signaling, hypothesis, (2) the clientele effect, and (3) their effects on dividend policy.

c. (1) Assume that SSC has an $800,000 capital budget planned for the coming year. You have determined that its present capital structure (60 percent equity and 40 percent debt) is optimal, and its net income is forecasted at $600,000. Use the residual dividend model approach to determine SSC's total dollar dividend and payout ratio. In the process, explain what the residual dividend model is. Then, explain what would happen if net income were forecasted at $400,000, or at $800,000.

(2) In general terms, how would a change in investment opportunities affect the payout ratio under the residual payment policy?

(3) What are the advantages and disadvantages of the residual policy? (Hint: Don't neglect signaling and clientele effects.)

d. What is a dividend reinvestment plan (DRIP), and how does it work?

e. Describe the series of steps that most firms take in setting dividend policy in practice.

f. What are stock repurchases? Discuss the advantages and disadvantages of a firm's repurchasing its own shares.

g. What are stock dividends and stock splits? What are the advantages and disadvantages of stock dividends and stock splits?

18 - 1

CHAPTER 18
Distributions to Shareholders: Dividends and Repurchases

- Theories of investor preferences
- Signaling effects
- Residual model
- Dividend reinvestment plans
- Stock dividends and stock splits
- Stock repurchases

18 - 2

What is "dividend policy"?

- It's the decision to pay out earnings versus retaining and reinvesting them. Includes these elements:
  1. High or low payout?
  2. Stable or irregular dividends?
  3. How frequent?
  4. Do we announce the policy?

18 - 3

Do investors prefer high or low payouts? There are three theories:

- Dividends are irrelevant: Investors don't care about payout.
- Bird-in-the-hand: Investors prefer a high payout.
- Tax preference: Investors prefer a low payout, hence growth.

18 - 4

Dividend Irrelevance Theory

- Investors are indifferent between dividends and retention-generated capital gains. If they want cash, they can sell stock. If they don't want cash, they can use dividends to buy stock.
- Modigliani-Miller support irrelevance.
- Theory is based on unrealistic assumptions (no taxes or brokerage costs), hence may not be true. Need empirical test.

18 - 5

Bird-in-the-Hand Theory

- Investors think dividends are less risky than potential future capital gains, hence they like dividends.
- If so, investors would value high payout firms more highly, i.e., a high payout would result in a high P_0.

18 - 6

Tax Preference Theory

- Retained earnings lead to capital gains, which are taxed at lower rates than dividends: 28% maximum vs. up to 39.6%. Capital gains taxes are also deferred.
- This could cause investors to prefer firms with low payouts, i.e., a high payout results in a low P_0.

18 - 7

Implications of 3 Theories for Managers

Theory	Implication
Irrelevance	Any payout OK
Bird-in-the-hand	Set high payout
Tax preference	Set low payout

But which, if any, is correct???

18 - 8

Possible Stock Price Effects

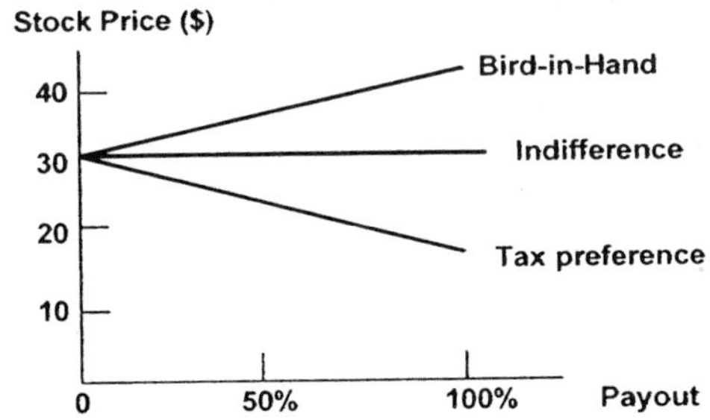

18 - 9

Possible Cost of Equity Effects

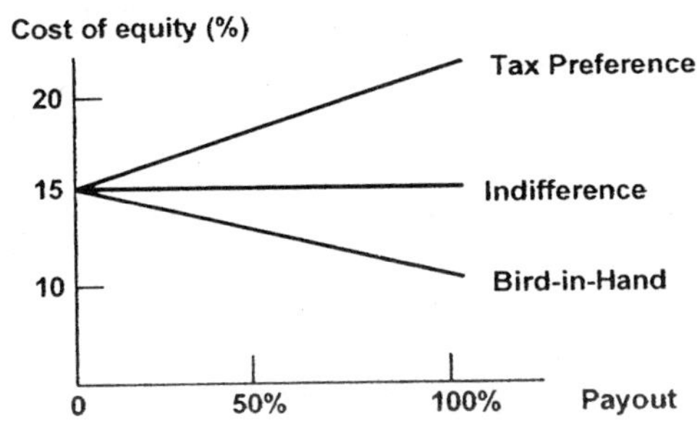

18 - 10

Which theory is most correct?

- Empirical testing has not been able to determine which theory, if any, is correct.
- Thus, managers use judgment when setting policy.
- Analysis is used, but it must be applied with judgment.

18 - 11

What's the "information content," or "signaling," hypothesis?

- Managers hate to cut dividends, so won't raise dividends unless they think raise is sustainable. So, investors view dividend increases as *signals* of management's view of the future.
- Therefore, a stock price increase at time of a dividend increase could reflect higher expectations for future EPS, not a desire for dividends.

18 - 12

What's the "clientele effect"?

- Different groups of investors, or clienteles, prefer different dividend policies.
- Firm's past dividend policy determines its current clientele of investors.
- Clientele effects impede changing dividend policy. Taxes & brokerage costs hurt investors who have to switch companies.

18 - 13

What's the "residual dividend model"?

- Find the retained earnings needed for the capital budget.
- Pay out any leftover earnings (the residual) as dividends.
- This policy minimizes flotation and equity signaling costs, hence minimizes the WACC.

18 - 14

Using the Residual Model to Calculate Dividends Paid

$$\text{Dividends} = \text{Net income} - \left[\left(\begin{array}{c}\text{Target}\\\text{equity}\\\text{ratio}\end{array}\right)\left(\begin{array}{c}\text{Total}\\\text{capital}\\\text{budget}\end{array}\right)\right].$$

18 - 15

Data for SSC

- Capital budget: $800,000. Given.
- Target capital structure: 40% debt, 60% equity. Want to maintain.
- Forecasted net income: $600,000.
- How much of the $600,000 should we pay out as dividends?

18 - 16

Of the $800,000 capital budget, 0.6($800,000) = $480,000 must be equity to keep at target capital structure. [0.4($800,000) = $320,000 will be debt.]

With $600,000 of net income, the residual is $600,000 - $480,000 = $120,000 = dividends paid.

Payout ratio = $120,000/$600,000
= 0.20 = 20%.

18 - 17

How would a drop in NI to $400,000 affect the dividend? A rise to $800,000?

- NI = $400,000: Need $480,000 of equity, so should retain the whole $400,000. Dividends = 0.
- NI = $800,000: Dividends = $800,000 - $480,000 = $320,000. Payout = $320,000/$800,000 = 40%.

18 - 18

How would a change in investment opportunities affect dividend under the residual policy?

- Fewer good investments would lead to smaller capital budget, hence to a higher dividend payout.
- More good investments would lead to a lower dividend payout.

18 - 19

Advantages and Disadvantages of the Residual Dividend Policy

- Advantages: Minimizes new stock issues and flotation costs.
- Disadvantages: Results in variable dividends, sends conflicting signals, increases risk, and doesn't appeal to any specific clientele.
- Conclusion: Consider residual policy when setting target payout, but don't follow it rigidly.

18 - 20

What's a "dividend reinvestment plan (DRIP)"?

- Shareholders can automatically reinvest their dividends in shares of the company's common stock. Get more stock than cash.
- There are two types of plans:
  - Open market
  - New stock

18 - 21

Open Market Purchase Plan

- Dollars to be reinvested are turned over to trustee, who buys shares on the open market.
- Brokerage costs are reduced by volume purchases.
- Convenient, easy way to invest, thus useful for investors.

18 - 22

New Stock Plan

- Firm issues new stock to DRIP enrollees, keeps money and uses it to buy assets.
- No fees are charged, plus sells stock at discount of 5% from market price, which is about equal to flotation costs of underwritten stock offering.

18 - 23

Optional investments sometimes possible, up to $150,000 or so.

Firms that need new equity capital use new stock plans.

Firms with no need for new equity capital use open market purchase plans.

Most NYSE listed companies have a DRIP. Useful for investors.

18 - 24

Setting Dividend Policy

- Forecast capital needs over a planning horizon, often 5 years.
- Set a target capital structure.
- Estimate annual equity needs.
- Set target payout based on the residual model.
- Generally, some dividend growth rate emerges. Maintain target growth rate if possible, varying capital structure somewhat if necessary.

18 - 25

Dividend Payout Ratios for Selected Industries

Industry	Payout ratio
Banking	38.29
Computer Software Services	13.70
Drug	38.06
Electric Utilities (Eastern U. S.)	67.09
Internet	n/a
Semiconductors	24.91
Steel	51.96
Tobacco	55.00
Water utilities	67.35

*None of the internet companies included in the Value Line Investment Survey paid a dividend.

18 - 26

Stock Repurchases

Repurchases: Buying own stock back from stockholders.

Reasons for repurchases:

- As an alternative to distributing cash as dividends.
- To dispose of one-time cash from an asset sale.
- To make a large capital structure change.

18 - 27

Advantages of Repurchases

- Stockholders can tender or not.
- Helps avoid setting a high dividend that cannot be maintained.
- Repurchased stock can be used in takeovers or resold to raise cash as needed.
- Income received is capital gains rather than higher-taxed dividends.
- Stockholders may take as a positive signal--management thinks stock is undervalued.

18 - 28

Disadvantages of Repurchases

- May be viewed as a negative signal (firm has poor investment opportunities).
- IRS could impose penalties if repurchases were primarily to avoid taxes on dividends.
- Selling stockholders may not be well informed, hence be treated unfairly.
- Firm may have to bid up price to complete purchase, thus paying too much for its own stock.

18 - 29

Stock Dividends vs. Stock Splits

- Stock dividend: Firm issues new shares in lieu of paying a cash dividend. If 10%, get 10 shares for each 100 shares owned.
- Stock split: Firm increases the number of shares outstanding, say 2:1. Sends shareholders more shares.

18 - 30

Both stock dividends and stock splits increase the number of shares outstanding, so "the pie is divided into smaller pieces."

Unless the stock dividend or split conveys information, or is accompanied by another event like higher dividends, *the stock price falls so as to keep each investor's wealth unchanged.*

But splits/stock dividends may get us to an "optimal price range."

18 - 31

When should a firm consider splitting its stock?

- There's a widespread belief that the *optimal price range* for stocks is $20 to $80.
- Stock splits can be used to keep the price in the optimal range.
- Stock splits generally occur when management is confident, so are interpreted as *positive signals*.

BLUEPRINTS: CHAPTER 19

INITIAL PUBLIC OFFERINGS, INVESTMENT BANKING, AND FINANCIAL RESTRUCTURING

Randy's, a family-owned restaurant chain operating in Alabama, has grown to the point where expansion throughout the entire Southeast is feasible. The proposed expansion would require the firm to raise about $15 million in new capital. Because Randy's currently has a debt ratio of 50 percent, and also because the family members already have all their personal wealth invested in the company, the family would like to sell common stock to the public to raise the $15 million. However, the family does want to retain voting control. You have been asked to brief the family members on the issues involved by answering the following questions:

a. What agencies regulate securities markets?

b. How are start-up firms usually financed?

c. Differentiate between a private placement and a public offering.

d. Why would a company consider going public? What are some advantages and disadvantages?

e. What are the steps of an initial public offering?

f. What criteria are important in choosing an investment banker?

g. Would companies going public use a negotiated deal or a competitive bid?

h. Would the sale be on an underwritten or best efforts basis?

i. Without actually doing any calculations, describe how the preliminary offering range for the price of an IPO would be determined.

j. What is a roadshow? What is book building?

k. Describe the typical first-day returns of an IPO and the long-term returns to IPO investors.

l. What are the direct and indirect costs of an IPO?

m. What are equity carve-outs?

n. In what other ways are investment banks involved in issuing securities?

o. What is a rights offering?

p. What is meant by going private? What are some advantages and disadvantages?

q. How do companies manage the maturity structure of their debt?

r. What are zero coupon bonds? Briefly describe their tax treatment.

s. Under what conditions would a firm exercise a bond call provision?

t. Explain how firms manage the risk structure of their debt with:
   (1) Project financing.
   (2) Securitization.

19 - 1

CHAPTER 19
Initial Public Offerings, Investment Banking, and Financial Restructuring

- Initial Public Offerings
- Investment Banking and Regulation
- The Maturity Structure of Debt
- Refunding Operations
- The Risk Structure of Debt

19 - 2

What agencies regulate securities markets?

- The Securities and Exchange Commission (SEC) regulates:
  - Interstate public offerings.
  - National stock exchanges.
  - Trading by corporate insiders.
  - The corporate proxy process.
- The Federal Reserve Board controls margin requirements. (More...)

19 - 3

- States control the issuance of securities within their boundaries.
- The securities industry, through the exchanges and the National Association of Securities Dealers (NASD), takes actions to ensure the integrity and credibility of the trading system.
- Why is it important that securities markets be tightly regulated?

19 - 4

How are start-up firms usually financed?

- Founder's resources
- Angels
- Venture capital funds
  - Most capital in fund is provided by institutional investors
  - Managers of fund are called venture capitalists
  - Venture capitalists (VCs) sit on boards of companies they fund

19 - 5

Differentiate between a private placement and a public offering.

- In a private placement, such as to angels or VCs, securities are sold to a few investors rather than to the public at large.
- In a public offering, securities are offered to the public and must be registered with SEC.

(More...)

19 - 6

- Privately placed stock is not registered, so sales must be to "accredited" (high net worth) investors.
  - Send out "offering memorandum" with 20-30 pages of data and information, prepared by securities lawyers.
  - Buyers certify that they meet net worth/income requirements and they will not sell to unqualified investors.

19 - 7

Why would a company consider going public?

- Advantages of going public
  - Current stockholders can diversify.
  - Liquidity is increased.
  - Easier to raise capital in the future.
  - Going public establishes firm value.
  - Makes it more feasible to use stock as employee incentives.
  - Increases customer recognition.

(More...)

19 - 8

- Disadvantages of Going Public
  - Must file numerous reports.
  - Operating data must be disclosed.
  - Officers must disclose holdings.
  - Special "deals" to insiders will be more difficult to undertake.
  - A small new issue may not be actively traded, so market-determined price may not reflect true value.
  - Managing investor relations is time-consuming.

19 - 9

What are the steps of an IPO?

- Select investment banker
- File registration document (S-1) with SEC
- Choose price range for preliminary (or "red herring") prospectus
- Go on roadshow
- Set final offer price in final prospectus

19 - 10

What criteria are important in choosing an investment banker?

- Reputation and experience in this industry
- Existing mix of institutional and retail (i.e., individual) clients
- Support in the post-IPO secondary market
  - Reputation of analyst covering the stock

19 - 11

Would companies going public use a negotiated deal or a competitive bid?

- A negotiated deal.
  - The competitive bid process is only feasible for large issues by major firms. Even here, the use of bids is rare for equity issues.
  - It would cost investment bankers too much to learn enough about the company to make an intelligent bid.

19 - 12

Would the sale be on an underwritten or best efforts basis?

- Most offerings are underwritten.
- In very small, risky deals, the investment banker may insist on a best efforts basis.
- On an underwritten deal, the price is not set until
  - Investor interest is assessed.
  - Oral commitments are obtained.

19 - 13

Describe how an IPO would be priced.

- Since the firm is going public, there is no established price.
- Banker and company project the company's future earnings and free cash flows
- The banker would examine market data on similar companies.

(More...)

19 - 14

- Price set to place the firm's P/E and M/B ratios in line with publicly traded firms in the same industry having similar risk and growth prospects.
- On the basis of all relevant factors, the investment banker would determine a ballpark price, and specify a range (such as $10 to $12) in the preliminary prospectus.

(More...)

19 - 15

What is a roadshow?

- Senior management team, investment banker, and lawyer visit potential institutional investors
- Usually travel to ten to twenty cities in a two-week period, making three to five presentations each day.
- Management can't say anything that is not in prospectus, because company is in "quiet period."

19 - 16

What is "book building?"

- Investment banker asks investors to indicate how many shares they plan to buy, and records this in a "book".
- Investment banker hopes for oversubscribed issue.
- Based on demand, investment banker sets final offer price on evening before IPO.

19 - 17

What are typical first-day returns?

- For 75% of IPOs, price goes up on first day.
- Average first-day return is 14.1%.
- About 10% of IPOs have first-day returns greater than 30%.
- For some companies, the first-day return is well over 100%.

19 - 18

- There is an inherent conflict of interest, because the banker has an incentive to set a low price:
  - to make brokerage customers happy.
  - to make it easy to sell the issue.
- Firm would like price to be high.
- Note that original owners generally sell only a small part of their stock, so if price increases, they benefit.
- Later offerings easier if first goes well.

19 - 19

What are the long-term returns to investors in IPOs?

- Two-year return following IPO is lower than for comparable non-IPO firms.
- On average, the IPO offer price is too low, and the first-day run-up is too high.

19 - 20

What are the direct costs of an IPO?

- Underwriter usually charges a 7% spread between offer price and proceeds to issuer.
- Direct costs to lawyers, printers, accountants, etc. can be over $400,000.

19 - 21

What are the indirect costs of an IPO?

- Money left on the table
  - (End of price on first day - Offer price) x Number of shares
- Typical IPO raises about $70 million, and leaves $9 million on table.
- Preparing for IPO consumes most of management's attention during the pre-IPO months.

19 - 22

If firm issues 7 million shares at $10, what are net proceeds if spread is 7%?

Gross proceeds = 7 x $10 million
= $70 million
Underwriting fee = 7% x $70 million
= $4.9 million
Net proceeds = $70 - $4.9
= $65.1 million

19 - 23

What are equity carve-outs?

- A special IPO in which a parent company creates a new public company by selling stock in a subsidiary to outside investors.
- Parent usually retains controlling interest in new public company.

19 - 24

How are investment banks involved in non-IPO issuances?

- Shelf registration (SEC Rule 415), in which issues are registered but the entire issue is not sold at once, but partial sales occur over a period of time.
- Public and private debt issues
- Seasoned equity offerings (public and private placements)

19 - 25

What is a rights offering?

- A rights offering occurs when current shareholders get the first right to buy new shares.
- Shareholders can either exercise the right and buy new shares, or sell the right to someone else.
- Wealth of shareholders doesn't change whether they exercise right or sell it.

19 - 26

What is meant by going private?

- Going private is the reverse of going public.
- Typically, the firm's managers team up with a small group of outside investors and purchase all of the publicly held shares of the firm.
- The new equity holders usually use a large amount of debt financing, so such transactions are called leveraged buyouts (LBOs).

19 - 27

Advantages of Going Private

- Gives managers greater incentives and more flexibility in running the company.
- Removes pressure to report high earnings in the short run.
- After several years as a private firm, owners typically go public again. Firm is presumably operating more efficiently and sells for more.

19 - 28

Disadvantages of Going Private

- Firms that have recently gone private are normally leveraged to the hilt, so it's difficult to raise new capital.
- A difficult period that normally could be weathered might bankrupt the company.

19 - 29

How do companies manage the maturity structure of their debt?

- Maturity matching
  - Match maturity of assets and debt
- Information asymmetries
  - Firms with strong future prospects will issue short-term debt

19 - 30

Zero Coupon Bonds

- Bonds have no coupon, and pay no interest.
- Only payment is face value at maturity.
- Bonds are sold at discount. If market rates are 9% and firm issues zero coupon bond with 5 years to maturity,
  - $Price_5 = \$1000 / (1.09)^5 = \$649.93$

19 - 31

Tax Treatment of Zero Coupon Bond

- Imputed interest expense is equal to the expected price appreciation, based on initial yield.
- Bond has initial yield of 9%, expected price at end of first year is:
  - $Price_4 = \$1000 / (1.09)^4 = \$708.43$
- Imputed interest = \$708.43 - \$649.93 = \$58.5

19 - 32

Tax Deduction

- Company deducts \$58.5 in the first year, even though it makes no cash payment of interest.
- Imputed interest payment changes each year as price of bond (based on original 9% yield) approaches \$1000.

19 - 33

Under what conditions would a firm exercise a bond call provision?

- If interest rates have fallen since the bond was issued, the firm can replace the current issue with a new, lower coupon rate bond.
- However, there are costs involved in refunding a bond issue. For example,
  - The call premium.
  - Flotation costs on the new issue.

(More...)

19 - 34

- The NPV of refunding compares the interest savings benefit with the costs of the refunding. A positive NPV indicates that refunding today would increase the value of the firm.
- However, it interest rates are expected to fall further, it may be better to delay refunding until some time in the future.

19 - 35

Managing Debt Risk with Project Financing

- Project financings are used to finance a specific large capital project.
- Sponsors provide the equity capital, while the rest of the project's capital is supplied by lenders and/or lessors.
- Interest is paid from project's cash flows, and borrowers don't have recourse.

19 - 36

Managing Debt Risk with Securitization

- Securitization is the process whereby financial instruments that were previously illiquid are converted to a form that creates greater liquidity.
- Examples are bonds backed by mortgages, auto loans, credit card loans (asset-backed), and so on.

BLUEPRINTS: CHAPTER 20
LEASE FINANCING

Lewis Securities Inc. has decided to acquire a new market data and quotation system for its Richmond home office. The system receives current market prices and other information from several on-line data services, then either displays the information on a screen or stores it for later retrieval by the firm's brokers. The system also permits customers to call up current quotes on terminals in the lobby.

The equipment costs $1,000,000, and, if it were purchased, Lewis could obtain a term loan for the full purchase price at a 10 percent interest rate. The equipment is classified as a special-purpose computer, so it falls into the MACRS 3-year class. If the system were purchased, a 4-year maintenance contract could be obtained at a cost of $20,000 per year, payable at the *beginning* of each year. The equipment would be sold after 4 years, and the best estimate of its residual value at that time is $100,000. However, since real-time display system technology is changing rapidly, the actual residual value is uncertain.

As an alternative to the borrow-and-buy plan, the equipment manufacturer informed Lewis that Consolidated Leasing would be willing to write a 4-year guideline lease on the equipment, including maintenance, for payments of $280,000 at the *beginning* of each year. Lewis's marginal federal-plus-state tax rate is 40 percent. You have been asked to analyze the lease-versus-purchase decision, and in the process to answer the following questions:

a. (1) Who are the two parties to a lease transaction?

(2) What are the four primary types of leases, and what are their characteristics?

(3) How are leases classified for tax purposes?

(4) What effect does leasing have on a firm's balance sheet?

(5) What effect does leasing have on a firm's capital structure?

b. (1) What is the present value cost of owning the equipment? (Hint: Set up a time line which shows the net cash flows over the period t = 0 to t = 4, and then find the PV of these net cash flows, or the PV cost of owning.)

(2) Explain the rationale for the discount rate you used to find the PV.

c. What is Lewis's present value cost of leasing the equipment? (Hint: Again, construct a time line.)

d. What is the net advantage to leasing (NAL)? Does your analysis indicate that Lewis should buy or lease the equipment? Explain.

e. Now assume that the equipment's residual value could be as low as $0 or as high as $200,000, but that $100,000 is the expected value. Since the residual value is riskier than the other cash flows in the analysis, this differential risk should be incorporated into the analysis. Describe how this could be accomplished. (No calculations are necessary, but explain how you would modify the analysis if calculations were required.) What effect would increased uncertainty about the residual value have on Lewis's lease-versus-purchase decision?

f. The lessee compares the cost of owning the equipment with the cost of leasing it. Now put yourself in the lessor's shoes. In a few sentences, how should you analyze the decision to write or not write the lease?

g. (1) Assume that the lease payments were actually $300,000 per year, that Consolidated Leasing is also in the 40 percent tax bracket, and that it also forecasts a $100,000 residual value. Also, to furnish the maintenance support, Consolidated would have to purchase a maintenance contract from the manufacturer at the same $20,000 annual cost, again paid in advance. Consolidated Leasing can obtain an expected 10 percent pre-tax return on investments of similar risk. What would Consolidated's NPV and IRR of leasing be under these conditions?

(2) What do you think the lessor's NPV would be if the lease payment were set at $280,000 per year? (Hint: The lessor's cash flows would be a "mirror image" of the lessee's cash flows.)

h. Lewis's management has been considering moving to a new downtown location, and they are concerned that these plans may come to fruition prior to the expiration of the lease. If the move occurs, Lewis would buy or lease an entirely new set of equipment, and hence management would like to include a cancellation clause in the lease contract. What impact would such a clause have on the riskiness of the lease from Lewis's standpoint? From the lessor's standpoint? If you were the lessor, would you insist on changing any of the lease terms if a cancellation clause were added? Should the cancellation clause contain any restrictive covenants and/or penalties of the type contained in bond indentures or provisions similar to call premiums?

20 - 1

CHAPTER 20
Lease Financing

- Types of leases
- Tax treatment of leases
- Effects on financial statements
- Lessee's analysis
- Lessor's analysis
- Other issues in lease analysis

20 - 2

Who are the two parties to a lease transaction?

- The lessee, who uses the asset and makes the lease, or rental, payments.
- The lessor, who owns the asset and receives the rental payments.
- Note that the lease decision is a financing decision for the lessee and an investment decision for the lessor.

20 - 3

What are the four primary lease types?

- Operating lease
  - Short-term and normally cancelable
  - Maintenance usually included
- Financial lease
  - Long-term and normally noncancelable
  - Maintenance usually not included
- Sale and leaseback
- Combination lease

20 - 4

How are leases treated for tax purposes?

- Leases are classified by the IRS as either guideline or nonguideline.
- For a guideline lease, the entire lease payment is deductible to the lessee.
- For a nonguideline lease, only the imputed interest payment is deductible.
- Why should the IRS be concerned about lease provisions?

20 - 5

How does leasing affect a firm's balance sheet?

- For accounting purposes, leases are classified as either capital or operating.
- Capital leases must be shown directly on the lessee's balance sheet.
- Operating leases, sometimes referred to as off-balance sheet financing, must be disclosed in the footnotes.
- Why are these rules in place?

20 - 6

What impact does leasing have on a firm's capital structure?

- Leasing is a substitute for debt.
- As such, leasing uses up a firm's debt capacity.
- Assume a firm has a 50/50 target capital structure. Half of its assets are leased. How should the remaining assets be financed?

20 - 7

Assume that Lewis Securities plans to acquire some new equipment having a 4-year useful life.

- **If the equipment is leased:**
  - **Firm could obtain a 4-year lease which includes maintenance.**
  - **Lease meets IRS guidelines to expense lease payments.**
  - **Rental payment would be $280,000 at the beginning of each year.**

20 - 8

- **Other information:**
  - **Equipment cost: $1,000,000.**
  - **Loan rate on equipment = 10%.**
  - **Marginal tax rate = 40%.**
  - **3-year MACRS life.**
  - **If company borrows and buys, 4 year maintenance contract costs $20,000 at beginning of each year.**
  - **Residual value at t = 4: $100,000.**

20 - 9

Time Line: After-Tax Cost of Owning (In Thousands)

	0	1	2	3	4
AT loan pmt		-60	-60	-60	-1,060
Dep shld		132	180	60	28
Maint	-20	-20	-20	-20	
Tax sav	8	8	8	8	
RV					100
Tax					-40
NCF	-12	60	108	-12	-972

20 - 10

- Note the depreciation shield in each year equals the depreciation expense times the lessee's tax rate. For Year 1, the depreciation shield is

$330,000(0.40) = $132,000.

- The present value of the cost of owning cash flows, when discounted at 6%, is -$639,267.

20 - 11

Why use 6% as the discount rate?

- Leasing is similar to debt financing.
  - The cash flows have relatively low risk; most are fixed by contract.
  - Therefore, the firm's 10% cost of debt is a good candidate.
- The tax shield of interest payments must be recognized, so the discount rate is

10%(1 - T) = 10%(1 - 0.4) = 6.0%.

20 - 12

Time Line: After-Tax Cost of Leasing (In Thousands)

	0	1	2	3	4
Lease pmt	-280	-280	-280	-280	
Tax sav	112	112	112	112	
NCF	-168	-168	-168	-168	

PV cost of leasing @ 6% = -$617,066.

20 - 13

What is the net advantage to leasing (NAL)?

- NAL = PV cost of leasing - PV cost of owning
  = - $617,066 - (-$639,267)
  = $22,201.
- Should the firm lease or buy the equipment? Why?

20 - 14

- Note that we have assumed the company will not continue to use the asset after the lease expires; that is, project life is the same as the term of the lease.
- What changes to the analysis would be required if the lessee planned to continue using the equipment after the lease expired?

20 - 15

Assume the RV could be $0 or $200,000, with an expected value of $100,000. How could this risk be reflected?

- The discount rate applied to the residual value inflow (a positive CF) should be increased to account for the increased risk.
- All other cash flows should be discounted at the original 6% rate.

(More...)

20 - 16

- If the residual value were included as an outflow (a *negative* CF) in the cost of leasing cash flows, the increased risk would be reflected by applying a lower discount rate to the residual value cash flow.
- Again, all other cash flows have relatively low risk, and hence would be discounted at the 6% rate.

20 - 17

What effect would increased uncertainty about the residual value have on the lessee's decision?

- The lessor owns the equipment when the lease expires.
- Therefore, residual value risk is passed from the lessee to the lessor.
- Increased residual value risk makes the lease more attractive to the lessee.

20 - 18

How should the lessor analyze the lease transaction?

- To the lessor, writing the lease is an investment.
- Therefore, the lessor must compare the return on the lease investment with the return available on alternative investments of similar risk.

20 - 19

Assume the following data for Consolidated Leasing, the lessor:

- $300,000 rental payment instead of $280,000.
- All other data are the same as for the lessee.

20 - 20

Time Line: Lessor's Analysis (In Thousands)

	0	1	2	3	4
Cost	-1,000				
Dep shld		132	180	60	28
Maint	-20	-20	-20	-20	
Tax sav	8	8	8	8	
Lse pmt	300	300	300	300	
Tax	-120	-120	-120	-120	
RV					100
RV tax					-40
NCF	-832	300	348	228	88

20 - 21

- The NPV of the net cash flows, when discounted at 6%, is $21,875.
- The IRR is 7.35%.
- Should the lessor write the lease? Why?

20 - 22

Find the lessor's NPV if the lease payment were $280,000.

- With lease payments of $280,000, the lessor's cash flows would be equal, but opposite in sign, to the lessee's NAL.
- Thus, lessor's NPV = -$22,201.
- If all inputs are symmetrical, leasing is a zero-sum game.
- What are the implications?

20 - 23

What impact would a cancellation clause have on the lease's riskiness from the lessee's standpoint? From the lessor's standpoint?

- A cancellation clause would lower the risk of the lease to the lessee but raise the lessor's risk.
- To account for this, the lessor would increase the annual lease payment or else impose a penalty for early cancellation.

20 - 24

Other Issues in Lease Analysis

- Do higher residual values make leasing less attractive to the lessee?
- Is lease financing more available or "better" than debt financing?
- Is the lease analysis presented here applicable to real estate leases? To auto leases?

(More...)

20 - 25

- Would spreadsheet models be useful in lease analyses?
- What impact do tax laws have on the attractiveness of leasing? Consider the following provisions:
  - Investment tax credit (when available)
  - Tax rate differentials between the lessee and the lessor
  - Alternative minimum tax (AMT)

20 - 26

Numerical analyses often indicate that owning is less costly than leasing. Why, then, is leasing so popular?

- Provision of maintenance services.
- Risk reduction for the lessee.
  - Project life
  - Residual value
  - Operating risk
- Portfolio risk reduction enables lessor to better bear these risks.

BLUEPRINTS: CHAPTER 21

HYBRID FINANCING: PREFERRED STOCK, WARRANTS, AND CONVERTIBLES

Paul Duncan, financial manager of Edusoft Inc., is facing a dilemma. The firm was founded five years ago to provide educational software for the rapidly expanding primary and secondary school markets. Although Edusoft has done well, the firm's founder believes that an industry shakeout is imminent. To survive, Edusoft must grab market share now, and this will require a large infusion of new capital.

Because he expects earnings to continue rising sharply and looks for the stock price to follow suit, Mr. Duncan does not think it would be wise to issue new common stock at this time. On the other hand, interest rates are currently high by historical standards, and with the firm's B rating, the interest payments on a new debt issue would be prohibitive. Thus, he has narrowed his choice of financing alternatives to two securities: (1) bonds with warrants or (2) convertible bonds. As Duncan's assistant, you have been asked to help in the decision process by answering the following questions:

a. How does preferred stock differ from both common equity and debt? Is preferred stock more risky than common stock? What is floating rate preferred stock?

b. How can a knowledge of call options help a financial manager to better understand warrants and convertibles?

c. One of the firm's alternatives is to issue a bond with warrants attached. EduSoft's current stock price is $20, and its investment banker estimates that the cost of a 20-year, annual coupon bond without warrants would be 12 percent. The bankers suggest attaching 50 warrants, each with an exercise price of $25, to each $1,000 bond. It is estimated that each warrant, when detached and traded separately, would have a value of $3.

   (1) What coupon rate should be set on the bond with warrants if the total package is to sell for $1,000?

   (2) Suppose the bonds were issued and the warrants immediately traded on the open market for $5 each. What would this imply about the terms of the issue? Did the company "win" or "lose"?

   (3) When would you expect the warrants to be exercised? Assume they have a 10-year life; that is, they expire 10 years after issue.

   (4) Will the warrants bring in additional capital when exercised? If so, how much, and what type of capital?

(5) Since warrants lower the cost of the accompanying debt issue, shouldn't all debt be issued with warrants? What is the expected return to the holders of the bond with warrants (or the expected cost to the company) if the warrants are expected to be exercised in five years, when EduSoft's stock price is expected to be $36.75? How would you expect the cost of the bond with warrants to compare with the cost of straight debt? With the cost of common stock?

d. As an alternative to the bond with warrants, Mr. Duncan is considering convertible bonds. The firm's investment bankers estimate that EduSoft could sell a 20-year, 10.5 percent annual coupon, callable convertible bond for its $1,000 par value, whereas a straight-debt issue would require a 12 percent coupon. The convertibles would be call protected for 5 years, the call price would be $1,100, and the company would probably call the bonds as soon as possible after their conversion value exceeds $1,200. Note, though, that the call must occur on an issue date anniversary. EduSoft's current stock price is $20, its last dividend was $1.48, and the dividend is expected to grow at a constant 8 percent rate. The convertible could be converted into 40 shares of EduSoft stock at the owner's option.

(1) What conversion price is built into the bond?

(2) What is the convertible's straight-debt value? What is the implied value of the convertibility feature?

(3) What is the formula for the bond's expected conversion value in any year? What is its conversion value at Year 0? At Year 10?

(4) What is meant by the "floor value" of a convertible? What is the convertible's expected floor value at Year 0? At Year 10?

(5) Assume that EduSoft intends to force conversion by calling the bond as soon as possible after its conversion value exceeds 20 percent above its par value, or 1.2($1,000) = $1,200. When is the issue expected to be called? (Hint: Recall that the call must be made on an anniversary date of the issue.)

(6) What is the expected cost of capital for the convertible to EduSoft? Does this cost appear to be consistent with the riskiness of the issue?

e. EduSoft's market value capital structure is as follows (in millions of dollars):

Debt	$ 50
Equity	50
	$100

If the company raises $20 million in additional capital by selling (1) convertibles or (2) bonds with warrants, what would its WACC be, and how would those figures compare with its current WACC? EduSoft's tax rate is 40 percent.

f. Mr. Duncan believes that the costs of both the bond with warrants and the convertible bond are close enough to one another to call them even, and also consistent with the risks involved. Thus, he will make his decision based on other factors. What are some of the factors which he should consider?

g. How do convertible bonds help reduce agency costs?

21 - 1

CHAPTER 21
Hybrid Financing: Preferred Stock, Warrants, and Convertibles

- Types of hybrid securities
  - Preferred stock
  - Warrants
  - Convertibles
- Features and risk
- Cost of capital to issuers

21 - 2

How does preferred stock differ from common stock and debt?

- Preferred dividends are specified by contract, but they may be omitted without placing the firm in default.
- Most preferred stocks prohibit the firm from paying common dividends when the preferred is in arrears.
- Usually cumulative up to a limit.

(More...)

21 - 3

- Some preferred stock is perpetual, but most new issues have sinking fund or call provisions which limit maturities.
- Preferred stock has no voting rights, but may require companies to place preferred stockholders on the board (sometimes a majority) if the dividend is passed.
- Is preferred stock closer to debt or common stock? What is its risk to investors? To issuers?

21 - 4

What are the advantages and disadvantages of preferred stock financing?

- Advantages
  - Dividend obligation not contractual
  - Avoids dilution of common stock
  - Avoids large repayment of principal
- Disadvantages
  - Preferred dividends not tax deductible, so typically costs more than debt
  - Increases financial leverage, and hence the firm's cost of common equity

21 - 5

What is floating rate preferred?

- Dividends are indexed to the rate on treasury securities instead of being fixed.
- Excellent S-T corporate investment:
  - Only 30% of dividends are taxable to corporations.
  - The floating rate generally keeps issue trading near par.

21 - 6

- However, if the issuer is risky, the floating rate preferred stock may have too much price instability for the liquid asset portfolios of many corporate investors.

21 - 7

How can a knowledge of call options help one understand warrants and convertibles?

- A warrant is a long-term call option.
- A convertible consists of a fixed rate bond (or preferred stock)plus a long-term call option.

21 - 8

Given the following facts, what coupon rate must be set on a bond with warrants if the total package is to sell for $1,000?

- P_0 = $20.
- k_d of 20-year annual payment bond without warrants = 12%.
- 50 warrants with an exercise price of $25 each are attached to bond.
- Each warrant's value is estimated to be $3.

21 - 9

Step 1: Calculate V_{Bond}

$$V_{Package} = V_{Bond} + V_{Warrants} = \$1,000.$$

$$V_{Warrants} = 50(\$3) = \$150.$$

$$V_{Bond} + \$150 = \$1,000$$

$$V_{Bond} = \$850.$$

21 - 10

Step 2: Find Coupon Payment and Rate

20	12	-850		1000
N	I/YR	PV	PMT	FV

Solve for payment = 100

Therefore, the required coupon rate is \$100/\$1,000 = 10%.

21 - 11

If after issue the warrants immediately sell for \$5 each, what would this imply about the value of the package?

- At issue, the package was actually worth

  $V_{Package}$ = \$850 + 50(\$5) = \$1,100,

  which is \$100 more than the selling price.

(More...)

21 - 12

- The firm could have set lower interest payments whose PV would be smaller by \$100 per bond, or it could have offered fewer warrants and/or set a higher exercise price.
- Under the original assumptions, current stockholders would be losing value to the bond/warrant purchasers.

21 - 13

Assume that the warrants expire 10 years after issue. When would you expect them to be exercised?

- Generally, a warrant will sell in the open market at a premium above its value if exercised (it can't sell for less).
- Therefore, warrants tend not to be exercised until just before expiration.

(More...)

21 - 14

- In a stepped-up exercise price, the exercise price increases in steps over the warrant's life. Because the value of the warrant falls when the exercise price is increased, step-up provisions encourage in-the-money warrant holders to exercise just prior to the step-up.
- Since no dividends are earned on the warrant , holders will tend to exercise voluntarily if a stock's payout ratio rises enough.

21 - 15

Will the warrants bring in additional capital when exercised?

- When exercised, each warrant will bring in the exercise price, $25.
- This is equity capital and holders will receive one share of common stock per warrant.
- The exercise price is typically set some 20% to 30% above the current stock price when the warrants are issued.

21 - 16

Because warrants lower the cost of the accompanying debt issue, should all debt be issued with warrants?

No. As we shall see, the warrants have a cost which must be added to the coupon interest cost.

21 - 17

What is the expected return to the bond-with-warrant holders (and cost to the issuer) if the warrants are expected to be exercised in 5 years when P = $36.75?

- The company will exchange stock worth $36.75 for one warrant plus $25. The opportunity cost to the company is $36.75 - $25.00 = $11.75 per warrant.
- Bond has 50 warrants, so the opportunity cost per bond = 50($11.75) = $587.50.

(More...)

21 - 18

- Here are the cash flows on a time line:

0	1	…	4	5	6	…	19	20
+1,000	-100		-100	-100	-100		-100	-100
				-587.50				-1,000
				-687.50				-1,100

Input the cash flows into a calculator to find IRR = 14.7%. This is the pre-tax cost of the bond and warrant package.

(More...)

21 - 19

- The cost of the bond with warrants package is higher than the 12% cost of straight debt because part of the expected return is from capital gains, which are riskier than interest income.
- The cost is lower than the cost of equity because part of the return is fixed by contract.

(More...)

21 - 20

- When the warrants are exercised, there is a wealth transfer from existing stockholders to exercising warrant holders.
- But, bondholders previously transferred wealth to existing stockholders, in the form of a low coupon rate, when the bond was issued.

21 - 21

- At the time of exercise, either more or less wealth than expected may be transferred from the existing shareholders to the warrant holders, depending upon the stock price.
- At the time of issue, on a risk-adjusted basis, the expected cost of a bond-with-warrants issue is the same as the cost of a straight-debt issue.

21 - 22

Assume the following convertible bond data:

- 20-year, 10.5% annual coupon, callable convertible bond will sell at its $1,000 par value; straight debt issue would require a 12% coupon.
- Call protection = 5 years and call price = $1,100. Call the bonds when conversion value > $1,200, but the call must occur on the issue date anniversary.
- P_0 = $20; D_0 = $1.48; g = 8%.
- Conversion ratio = CR = 40 shares.

21 - 23

What conversion price (P_c) is built into the bond?

$$P_c = \frac{\text{Par value}}{\text{\# Shares received}}$$

$$= \frac{\$1,000}{40} = \$25.$$

Like with warrants, the conversion price is typically set 20%-30% above the stock price on the issue date.

21 - 24

Examples of real convertible bonds issued by Internet companies

Issuer	Size of issue	Cvt Price	Price at issue
Amazon.com	$1,250 mil	$156.05	$122
Beyond.com	55 mil	18.34	16
CNET	173 mil	74.81	84
DoubleClick	250 mil	165	134
Mindspring	180 mil	62.5	60
NetBank	100 mil	35.67	32
PSINet	400 mil	62.36	55
SportsLine.com	150 mil	65.12	52

21 - 25

What is (1) the convertible's straight debt value and (2) the implied value of the convertibility feature?

Straight debt value:

20	12		105	1000
N	I/YR	PV	PMT	FV

Solution: -887.96

21 - 26

Implied Convertibility Value

- Because the convertibles will sell for \$1,000, the implied value of the convertibility feature is

  \$1,000 - \$887.96 = \$112.04.

- The convertibility value corresponds to the warrant value in the previous example.

21 - 27

What is the formula for the bond's expected conversion value in any year?

Conversion value = $CV_t = CR(P_0)(1 + g)^t$.

t = 0

$CV_0 = 40(\$20)(1.08)^0 = \$800.$

t = 10

$CV_{10} = 40(\$20)(1.08)^{10}$
$= \$1{,}727.14.$

21 - 28

What is meant by the floor value of a convertible? What is the floor value at t = 0? At t = 10?

- The floor value is the higher of the straight debt value and the conversion value.
- Straight debt value$_0$ = $887.96.
- CV_0 = $800.

Floor value at Year 0 = $887.96.

21 - 29

- Straight debt value$_{10}$ = $915.25.
- CV_{10} = $1,727.14.

Floor value$_{10}$ = $1,727.14.

- A convertible will generally sell above its floor value prior to maturity because convertibility constitutes a call option that has value.

21 - 30

If the firm intends to force conversion on the first anniversary date after CV > $1,200, when is the issue expected to be called?

	8	-800	0	1200
N	I/YR	PV	PMT	FV

Solution: n = 5.27

Bond would be called at t = 6 since call must occur on anniversary date.

21 - 31

What is the convertible's expected cost of capital to the firm?

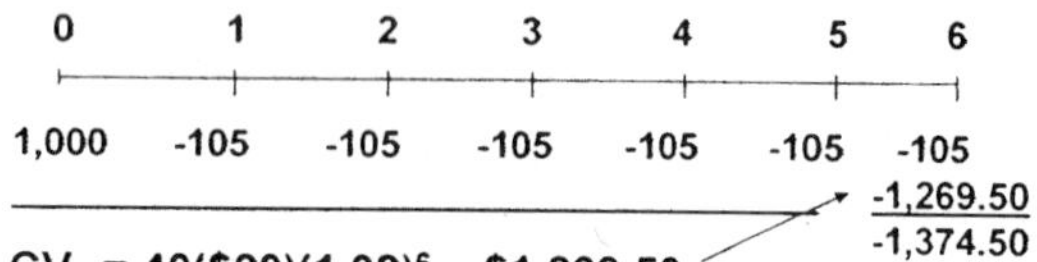

$CV_6 = 40(\$20)(1.08)^6 = \$1,269.50.$

Input the cash flows in the calculator and solve for IRR = 13.7%.

21 - 32

Does the cost of the convertible appear to be consistent with the costs of debt and equity?

- For consistency, need $k_d < k_c < k_s$.
- Why?

(More...)

21 - 33

- Check the values:

$k_d = 12\%$ and $k_c = 13.7\%$.

$$k_s = \frac{D_0(1 + g)}{P_0} + g = \frac{\$1.48(1.08)}{\$20} + 0.08$$

$$= 16.0\%.$$

Since k_c is between k_d and k_s, the costs are consistent with the risks.

21 - 34

WACC Effects

Assume the firm's tax rate is 40% and its debt ratio is 50%. Now suppose the firm is considering either:

(1) issuing convertibles, or

(2) issuing bonds with warrants.

Its new target capital structure will have 40% straight debt, 40% common equity and 20% convertibles or bonds with warrants. What effect will the two financing alternatives have on the firm's WACC?

21 - 35

Convertibles Step 1: Find the after-tax cost of the convertibles.

0	1	2	3	4	5	6
1,000	-63	-63	-63	-63	-63	-63
						-1,269.50
						-1,332.50

INT(1 - T) = \$105(0.6) = \$63.

With a calculator, find:

k_c (AT) = IRR = 9.81%.

21 - 36

Convertibles Step 2: Find the after-tax cost of straight debt.

k_d (AT) = 12%(0.06) = 7.2%.

21 - 37

Convertibles Step 3: Calculate the WACC.

WACC (with convertibles) = 0.4(7.2%) + 0.2(9.81%) + 0.4(16%)
= 11.24%.

WACC (without convertibles) = 0.5(7.2%) + 0.5(16%)
= 11.60%.

21 - 38

- Some notes:
  - We have assumed that k_s is not affected by the addition of convertible debt.
  - In practice, most convertibles are subordinated to the other debt, which muddies our assumption of k_d = 12% when convertibles are used.
  - When the convertible is converted, the debt ratio would decrease and the firm's financial risk would decline.

21 - 39

Warrants Step 1: Find the after-tax cost of the bond with warrants.

0	1 ...	4	5	6 ...	19	20
+1,000	-60	-60	-60	-60	-60	-60
			-587.50			-1,000
			-647.50			-1,060

INT(1 - T) = $100(0.60) = $60.

Warrants(Opportunity loss per warrant)
= 50($11.75) = $587.50.

Solve for: k_w (AT) = 10.32%.

21 - 40

Warrants Step 2: Calculate the WACC if the firm uses warrants.

WACC (with warrants) = 0.4(7.2%) + 0.2(10.32%) + 0.4(16%) = 11.34%.

WACC (without warrants) = 0.5(7.2%) + 0.5(16%)

= 11.60%.

21 - 41

Besides cost, what other factors should be considered?

- The firm's future needs for equity capital:
  - Exercise of warrants brings in new equity capital.
  - Convertible conversion brings in no new funds.
  - In either case, new lower debt ratio can support more financial leverage.

(More...)

21 - 42

- Does the firm want to commit to 20 years of debt?
  - Convertible conversion removes debt, while the exercise of warrants does not.
  - If stock price does not rise over time, then neither warrants nor convertibles would be exercised. Debt would remain outstanding.

EXTENSION

21 - 43

Recap the differences between warrants and convertibles.

- Warrants bring in new capital, while convertibles do not.
- Most convertibles are callable, while warrants are not.
- Warrants typically have shorter maturities than convertibles, and expire before the accompanying debt.

(More...)

21 - 44

- Warrants usually provide for fewer common shares than do convertibles.
- Bonds with warrants typically have much higher flotation costs than do convertible issues.
- Bonds with warrants are often used by small start-up firms. Why?

21 - 45

How do convertibles help minimize agency costs?

- Agency costs due to conflicts between shareholders and bondholders
  - Asset substitution (or bait-and-switch). Firm issues low cost straight debt, then invests in risky projects
  - Bondholders suspect this, so they charge high interest rates
  - Convertible debt allows bondholders to share in upside potential, so it has low rate.

21 - 46

Agency Costs Between Current Shareholders and New Shareholders

- Information asymmetry: company knows its future prospects better than outside investors
  - Otside investors think company will issue new stock only if future prospects are not as good as market anticipates
  - Issuing new stock send negative signal to market, causing stock price to fall

21 - 47

- Company with good future prospects can issue stock "through the back door" by issuing convertible bonds
  - Avoids negative signal of issuing stock directly
  - Since prospects are good, bonds will likely be converted into equity, which is what the company wants to issue

BLUEPRINTS: CHAPTER 22
CURRENT ASSET MANAGEMENT

Dan Barnes, financial manager of Ski Equipment Inc. (SKI), is excited, but apprehensive. The company's founder recently sold his 51 percent controlling block of stock to Kent Koren, who is a big fan of EVA (Economic Value Added). EVA is found by taking the after-tax operating profit and then subtracting the dollar cost of all the capital the firm uses:

$$\begin{aligned} EVA &= NOPAT - \text{Capital costs} \\ &= EBIT(1 - T) - WACC\ (\text{Operating capital}). \end{aligned}$$

If EVA is positive, then the firm is creating value. On the other hand, if EVA is negative, the firm is not covering its cost of capital, and stockholders' value is being eroded. Koren rewards managers handsomely if they create value, but those whose operations produce negative EVAs are soon looking for work. Koren frequently points out that if a company can generate its current level of sales with less assets, it would need less capital. That would, other things held constant, lower capital costs and increase its EVA.

Shortly after he took control of SKI, Kent Koren met with SKI's senior executives to tell them of his plans for the company. First, he presented some EVA data which convinced everyone that SKI had not been creating value in recent years. He then stated, in no uncertain terms, that this situation must change. He noted that SKI's designs of skis, boots, and clothing are acclaimed throughout the industry, but something is seriously amiss elsewhere in the company. Costs are too high, prices are too low, or the company employs too much capital, and he wants SKI's managers to correct the problem or else.

Barnes has long felt that SKI's working capital situation should be studied--the company may have the optimal amounts of cash, securities, receivables, and inventories, but it may also have too much or too little of these items. In the past, the production manager resisted Dan's efforts to question his holdings of raw materials inventories, the marketing manager resisted questions about finished goods, the sales staff resisted questions about credit policy (which affects accounts receivable), and the treasurer did not want to talk about her cash and securities balances. Koren's speech made it clear that such resistance would no longer be tolerated.

Dan also knows that decisions about working capital cannot be made in a vacuum. For example, if inventories could be lowered without adversely affecting operations, then less capital would be required, the dollar cost of capital would decline, and EVA would increase. However, lower raw materials inventories might lead to production slowdowns and higher costs, while lower finished goods inventories might lead to the loss of profitable sales. So, before inventories are changed, it will be necessary to study operating as well as financial effects. The situation is the same with regard to cash and receivables. Following are some ratios for SKI:

	SKI	Industry
Current	1.75	2.25
Quick	0.83	1.20
Debt/assets	58.76%	50.00%
Turnover of cash and securities	16.67	22.22
Days sales outstanding	45.00	32.00
Inventory turnover	4.82	7.00
Fixed assets turnover	11.35	12.00
Total assets turnover	2.08	3.00
Profit margin on sales	2.07%	3.50%
Return on equity (ROE)	10.45%	21.00%
Payables deferral period	30.00	33.00

a. Dan plans to use the preceding ratios as the starting point for discussions with SKI's operating executives. He wants everyone to think about the pros and cons of changing each type of current asset and how changes would interact to affect profits and EVA. Based on the data in the table, does SKI seem to be following a relaxed, moderate, or restricted working capital policy?

b. How can one distinguish between a relaxed but rational working capital policy and a situation where a firm simply has a lot of current assets because it is inefficient? Does SKI's working capital policy seem appropriate?

c. Calculate SKI's cash conversion cycle, assuming all calculations use a 360-day year.

d. What might SKI do to reduce its cash and securities without harming operations?

e. What is "float," and how is it affected by the firm's cash manager (treasurer)?

In an attempt to better understand SKI's cash position, Dan developed a cash budget. Data for the first two months of the year are shown at the end of this mini case. (Note that Dan's preliminary cash budget does not account for interest income or interest expense.) He has the figures for the other months, but they are not shown in this mini case.

f. Should depreciation expense be explicitly included in the cash budget? Why or why not?

g. In his preliminary cash budget, Dan has assumed that all sales are collected and, thus, that SKI has no bad debts. Is this realistic? If not, how would bad debts be dealt with in a cash budgeting sense? (Hint: Bad debts will affect collections but not purchases.)

h. Dan's cash budget for the entire year, although not given here, is based heavily on his forecast for monthly sales. Sales are expected to be extremely low between May and September but then increase dramatically in the fall and winter. November is typically the firm's best month, when SKI ships equipment to retailers for the holiday season. Interestingly, Dan's forecasted cash budget indicates that the company's cash holdings will exceed the targeted cash balance every month except for October and November, when shipments will be high but collections will not be coming in until later. Based on the ratios in the first table, does it appear that SKI's target cash balance is appropriate? In addition to possibly lowering the target cash balance, what actions might SKI take to better improve its cash management policies, and how might that affect its EVA?

i. What reasons might SKI have for maintaining a relatively high amount of cash?

j. What are the three categories of inventory costs? If the company takes steps to reduce its inventory, what effect would this have on the various costs of holding inventory?

k. Is there any reason to think that SKI may be holding too much inventory? If so, how would that affect EVA and ROE?

l. If the company reduces its inventory without adversely affecting sales, what effect should this have on the company's cash position (1) in the short run and (2) in the long run? Explain in terms of the cash budget and the balance sheet.

m. Dan knows that SKI sells on the same credit terms as other firms in its industry. Use the ratios presented in the first table to explain whether SKI's customers pay more or less promptly than those of its competitors. If there are differences, does that suggest that SKI should tighten or loosen its credit policy? What four variables make up a firm's credit policy, and in what direction should each be changed by SKI?

n. Does SKI face any risks if it tightens its credit policy?

o. If the company reduces its DSO without seriously affecting sales, what effect would this have on its cash position (1) in the short run and (2) in the long run? Answer in terms of the cash budget and the balance sheet. What effect should this have on EVA in the long run?

		Nov	Dec	Jan	Feb	Mar	Apr
I. COLLECTIONS AND PURCHASES WORKSHEET							
(1)	Sales (gross)	$71,218	$68,212.00	$65,213.00	$52,475.00	$42,909	$30,524
Collections							
(2)	During month of sale (0.2)(0.98)(month's sales)			12,781.75	10,285.10		
(3)	During first month after sale 0.7(previous month's sales)			47,748.40	45,649.10		
(4)	During second month after sale 0.1(sales 2 months ago)			7,121.80	6,821.20		
(5)	Total collections (Lines 2 + 3 + 4)			$67,651.95	$62,755.40		
Purchases							
(6)	0.85(forecasted sales 2 months from now)		$44,603.75	$36,472.65	$25,945.40		
(7)	Payments (1-month lag)			44,603.75	36,472.65		
II. CASH GAIN OR LOSS FOR MONTH							
(8)	Collections (from Section I)			$67,651.95	$62,755.40		
(9)	Payments for purchases (from Section I)			44,603.75	36,472.65		
(10)	Wages and salaries			6,690.56	5,470.90		
(11)	Rent			2,500.00	2,500.00		
(12)	Taxes						
(13)	Total payments			$53,794.31	$44,443.55		
(14)	Net cash gain (loss) during month (Line 8 - Line 13)			$13,857.64	$18,311.85		
III. CASH SURPLUS OR LOAN REQUIREMENT							
(15)	Cash at beginning of month if no borrowing is done			$ 3,000.00	$16,857.64		
(16)	Cumulative cash (cash at start + gain or - loss = Line 14 + Line 15)			16,857.64	35,169.49		
(17)	Target cash balance			1,500.00	1,500.00		
(18)	Cumulative surplus cash or loans outstanding to maintain $1,500 target cash balance (Line 16 - Line 17)			$15,357.64	$33,669.49		

22 - 1

CHAPTER 22
Current Asset Management

- Alternative working capital policies
- Cash management
- Inventory management
- Accounts receivable management

22 - 2

Basic Definitions

- Gross working capital:
  Total current assets.
- Net working capital:
  Current assets - Current liabilities.
- Working capital policy:
  - The level of each current asset.
  - How current assets are financed.

(More...)

22 - 3

- Working capital management:

  Includes both establishing working capital policy and then the day-to-day control of:
  - Cash
  - Inventories
  - Receivables
  - Short-term liabilities

22 - 4

Selected Ratios for SKI Incorporated

	SKI	Industry
Current	1.75x	2.25x
Quick	0.83x	1.20x
Debt/Assets	58.76%	50.00%
Turnover of cash & securities	16.67x	22.22x
DSO (days)	45.00	32.00
Inv. turnover	4.82x	7.00x
F.A. turnover	11.35x	12.00x
T.A. turnover	2.08x	3.00x
Profit margin	2.07%	3.50%
ROE	10.45%	21.00%
Pay. deferral period	30.00	33.00

22 - 5

How does SKI's working capital policy compare with the industry?

- Working capital policy is reflected in a firm's current ratio, quick ratio, turnover of cash and securities, inventory turnover, and DSO.
- These ratios indicate SKI has large amounts of working capital relative to its level of sales. Thus, SKI is following a relaxed (fat cat) policy.

22 - 6

Alternative Current Asset Investment Policies

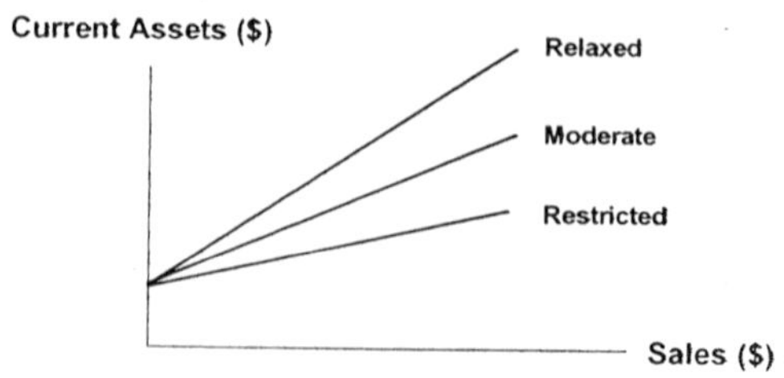

22 - 7

Is SKI inefficient or just conservative?

- A relaxed policy may be appropriate if it reduces risk more than profitability.
- However, SKI is much less profitable than the average firm in the industry. This suggests that the company probably has excessive working capital.

22 - 8

Cash Conversion Cycle

The cash conversion cycle focuses on the time between payments made for materials and labor and payments received from sales:

$$\text{Cash conversion cycle} = \text{Inventory conversion period} + \text{Receivables collection period} - \text{Payables deferral period}.$$

22 - 9

Cash Conversion Cycle (Cont.)

$$\text{CCC} = \frac{\text{Days per year}}{\text{Inv. turnover}} + \text{Days sales outstanding} - \text{Payables deferral period}$$

$$\text{CCC} = \frac{360}{4.82} + 45 - 30$$

$$\text{CCC} = 75 + 45 - 30$$

$$\text{CCC} = 90 \text{ days.}$$

22 - 10

Cash Conversion Cycle

The cash conversion cycle focuses on the time between payments made for materials and labor and payments received from sales:

Cash conversion cycle	=	Inventory conversion period	+	Receivables collection period	-	Payables deferral period .

What does the cash conversion cycle tell us about working capital management?

22 - 11

Cash Management: Cash doesn't earn interest, so why hold it?

- Transactions: **Must have some cash to pay current bills.**
- Precaution: **"Safety stock." But lessened by credit line and marketable securities.**
- Compensating balances: **For loans and/or services provided.**
- Speculation: **To take advantage of bargains, to take discounts, and so on. Reduced by credit line, marketable securities.**

22 - 12

What's the goal of cash management?

- **To have sufficient cash on hand to meet the needs listed on the previous slide.**
- **However, since cash is a non-earning asset, to have not one dollar more.**

22 - 13

Ways to Minimize Cash Holdings

- Use lockboxes.
- Insist on wire transfers from customers.
- Synchronize inflows and outflows.
- Use a remote disbursement account.

(More...)

22 - 14

- Increase forecast accuracy to reduce the need for a cash "safety stock."
- Hold marketable securities instead of a cash "safety stock."
- Negotiate a line of credit (also reduces need for a "safety stock").

22 - 15

What is float and how can it be affected by cash management?

- Net float is the difference between cash as shown on the firm's books and on its bank's books.
- If it takes SKI 1 day to deposit checks it receives and it takes its bank another day to clear those checks, SKI has 2 days of collections float.

22 - 16

- If it takes 6 days for the checks that SKI writes to clear and be deducted from SKI's account, SKI has 6 days of disbursement float.
- SKI's net float is the difference between the disbursement float and the collections float:

  Net float = 6 days - 2 days = 4 days.
- If SKI wrote and received $1 million of checks per day, it would be able to operate with $4 million less working capital than if it had zero net float.

22 - 17

Cash Budget: The Primary Cash Management Tool

- Purpose: Uses forecasts of cash inflows, outflows, and ending cash balances to predict loan needs and funds available for temporary investment.
- Timing: Daily, weekly, or monthly, depending upon budget's purpose. Monthly for annual planning, daily for actual cash management.

22 - 18

Data Required for Cash Budget

1. Sales forecast.
2. Information on collections delay.
3. Forecast of purchases and payment terms.
4. Forecast of cash expenses: wages, taxes, utilities, and so on.
5. Initial cash on hand.
6. Target cash balance.

22 - 19

SKI's Cash Budget for January and February

	Net Cash Flows	
	January	February
Collections	$67,651.95	$62,755.40
Purchases	$44,603.75	$36,472.65
Wages	6,690.56	5,470.90
Rent	2,500.00	2,500.00
Total payments	$53,794.31	$44,443.55
Net CF	$13,857.64	$18,311.85

22 - 20

Cash Budget (Continued)

	January	February
Cash at start	$ 3,000.00	$16,857.64
Net CF	13,857.64	18,311.85
Cumulative cash	$16,857.64	$35,169.49
Less: target cash	1,500.00	1,500.00
Surplus	$15,357.64	$33,669.49

22 - 21

Should depreciation be explicitly included in the cash budget?

- No. Depreciation is a noncash charge. Only cash payments and receipts appear on cash budget.
- However, depreciation does affect taxes, which do appear in the cash budget.

22 - 22

What are some other potential cash inflows besides collections?

- Proceeds from fixed asset sales.
- Proceeds from stock and bond sales.
- Interest earned.
- Court settlements.

22 - 23

How can interest earned or paid on short-term securities or loans be incorporated in the cash budget?

- Interest earned: Add line in the collections section.
- Interest paid: Add line in the payments section.
- Found as interest rate x surplus/loan line of cash budget for preceding month.
- Note: Interest on any other debt would need to be incorporated as well.

22 - 24

How could bad debts be worked into the cash budget?

- Collections would be reduced by the amount of bad debt losses.
- For example, if the firm had 3% bad debt losses, collections would total only 97% of sales.
- Lower collections would lead to lower surpluses and higher borrowing requirements.

22 - 25

SKI's forecasted cash budget indicates that the company's cash holdings will exceed the targeted cash balance every month, except for October and November.

- Cash budget indicates the company probably is holding too much cash.
- SKI could improve its EVA by either investing its excess cash in more productive assets or by paying it out to the firm's shareholders.

22 - 26

What reasons might SKI have for maintaining a relatively high amount of cash?

- If sales turn out to be considerably less than expected, SKI could face a cash shortfall.
- A company may choose to hold large amounts of cash if it does not have much faith in its sales forecast, or if it is very conservative.
- The cash may be there, in part, to fund a planned fixed asset acquisition.

22 - 27

Inventory Management: Categories of Inventory Costs

- Carrying Costs: Storage and handling costs, insurance, property taxes, depreciation, and obsolescence.
- Ordering Costs: Cost of placing orders, shipping, and handling costs.
- Costs of Running Short: Loss of sales, loss of customer goodwill, and the disruption of production schedules.

22 - 28

Effect of Inventory Size on Costs

Reducing the average amount of inventory held generally:

- Reduces carrying costs.
- Increases ordering costs.
- Increases probability of a stockout.

22 - 29

Is SKI holding too much inventory?

- SKI's inventory turnover (4.82) is considerably lower than the industry average (7.00). The firm is carrying a lot of inventory per dollar of sales.
- By holding excessive inventory, the firm is increasing its operating costs which reduces its NOPAT. Moreover, the excess inventory must be financed, so EVA is further lowered.

22 - 30

If SKI reduces its inventory, without adversely affecting sales, what effect will this have on its cash position?

- Short run: Cash will increase as inventory purchases decline.
- Long run: Company is likely to then take steps to reduce its cash holdings.

22 - 31

Accounts Receivable Management: Do SKI's customers pay more or less promptly than those of its competitors?

- SKI's days' sales outstanding (DSO) of 45 days is well above the industry average (32 days).
- SKI's customers are paying less promptly.
- SKI should consider tightening its credit policy to reduce its DSO.

22 - 32

Elements of Credit Policy

- Cash Discounts: Lowers price. Attracts new customers and reduces DSO.
- Credit Period: How long to pay? Shorter period reduces DSO and average A/R, but it may discourage sales.

(More...)

22 - 33

- Credit Standards: Tighter standards reduce bad debt losses, but may reduce sales. Fewer bad debts reduces DSO.
- Collection Policy: Tougher policy will reduce DSO, but may damage customer relationships.

22 - 34

Does SKI face any risk if it tightens its credit policy?

YES! A tighter credit policy may discourage sales. Some customers may choose to go elsewhere if they are pressured to pay their bills sooner.

22 - 35

If SKI succeeds in reducing DSO without adversely affecting sales, what effect would this have on its cash position?

- Short run: If customers pay sooner, this increases cash holdings.
- Long run: Over time, the company would hopefully invest the cash in more productive assets, or pay it out to shareholders. Both of these actions would increase EVA.

BLUEPRINTS: CHAPTER 23
SHORT-TERM FINANCING

Bats and Balls (B&B) Inc., a baseball equipment manufacturer, is a small company with seasonal sales. Each year before the baseball season, B&B purchases inventory which is financed through a combination of trade credit and short-term bank loans. At the end of the season, B&B uses sales revenues to repay its short-term obligations. The company is always looking for ways to become more profitable, and senior management has asked one of its employees, Ann Taylor, to review the company's current asset financing policies. Putting together her report, Ann is trying to answer each of the following questions:

a. B&B tries to match the maturity of its assets and liabilities. Describe how B&B could adopt either a more aggressive or more conservative financing policy.

b. What are the advantages and disadvantages of using short-term credit as a source of financing?

c. Is it likely that B&B could make significantly greater use of accruals?

d. Assume that B&B buys on terms of 1/10, net 30, but that it can get away with paying on the 40th day if it chooses not to take discounts. Also, assume that it purchases $3 million of components per year, net of discounts. How much free trade credit can the company get, how much costly trade credit can it get, and what is the percentage cost of the costly credit? Should B&B take discounts?

e. What is commercial paper? Would it be feasible for B&B to finance with commercial paper?

f. Suppose B&B decided to raise an additional $100,000 as a 1-year loan from its bank, for which it was quoted a rate of 8 percent. What is the effective annual cost rate assuming (1) simple interest, (2) discount interest, (3) discount interest with a 10 percent compensating balance, and (4) add-on interest on a 12-month installment loan? For the first three of these assumptions, would it matter if the loan were for 90 days, but renewable, rather than for a year?

g. How large would the loan actually be in each of the cases in Part f?

h. What are the pros and cons of borrowing on a secured versus an unsecured basis?

23 - 1

CHAPTER 23
Short-Term Financing

- Working capital financing policies
- Accounts payable (trade credit)
- Commercial paper
- Short-term bank loans
- Secured short-term credit

23 - 2

Working Capital Financing Policies

- Maturity Matching: Matches the maturity of the assets with the maturity of the financing.
- Aggressive: Uses short-term (temporary) capital to finance some permanent assets.
- Conservative: Uses long-term (permanent) capital to finance some temporary assets.

23 - 3

Maturity Matching Financing Policy

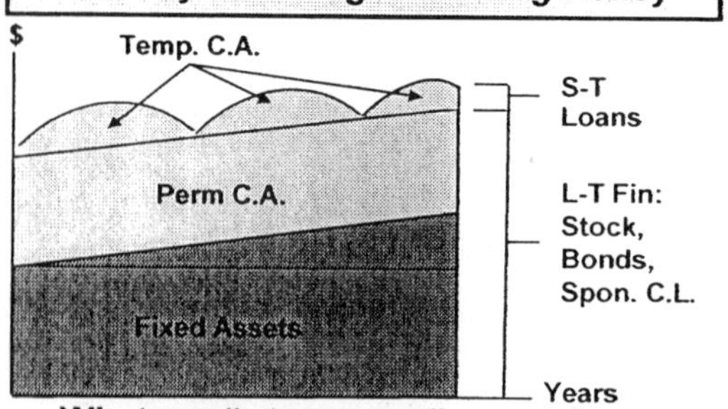

What are "permanent" assets?

23 - 4

Aggressive Financing Policy

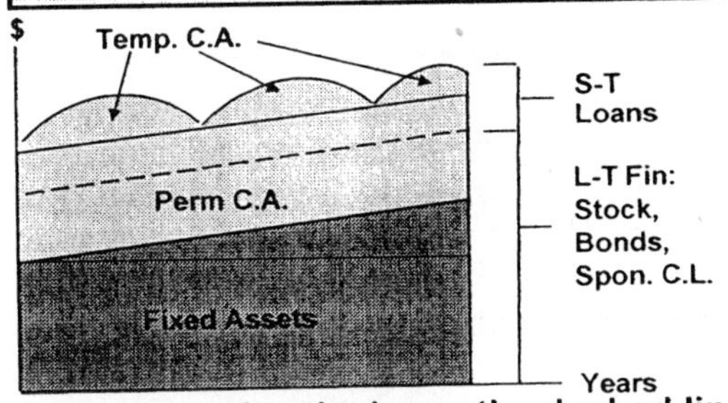

More aggressive the lower the dashed line.

23 - 5

Conservative Financing Policy

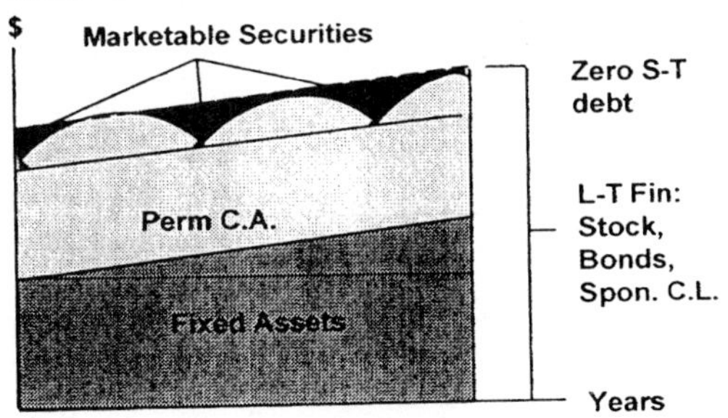

23 - 6

- The choice of working capital policy is a classic risk/return tradeoff.
- The aggressive policy promises the highest return but carries the greatest risk.
- The conservative policy has the least risk but also the lowest expected return.
- The moderate (maturity matching) policy falls between the two extremes.

23 - 7

What is short-term credit? What are the major sources?

- Short-term credit: Debt requiring repayment within one year.
- Major sources:
  - Accruals
  - Accounts payable (trade credit)
  - Commercial paper
  - Bank loans

23 - 8

- Short-term debt is riskier than long-term debt for the borrower.
  - Short-term rates may rise.
  - May have trouble rolling debt over.
- Advantages of short-term debt.
  - Typically lower cost.
  - Can get funds relatively quickly with low transactions costs.
  - Can repay without penalty.

23 - 9

Is there a cost to accruals? Do firms have much control over amount of accruals?

- Accruals are free in the sense that no explicit interest is charged.
- However, firms have little control over accrual levels, which are influenced more by industry custom, economic factors, and tax laws than by managerial actions.

23 - 10

What is trade credit?

- Trade credit is credit furnished by a firm's suppliers.
- Trade credit is often the largest source of short-term credit for small firms.
- Trade credit is spontaneous and relatively easy to get, but the cost can be high.

23 - 11

B&B buys $3,030,303 gross, or $3,000,000 net, on terms of 1/10, net 30. However, the firm pays on Day 40.

How much free and costly trade credit are they getting?

What is the cost of the costly trade credit?

23 - 12

Gross/Net Breakdown

- Company buys goods worth $3,000,000. That's the cash price.
- They must pay $30,303 more over the year if they forego the discount.
- Think of the extra $30,303 as a financing cost similar to the interest on a loan.
- Must compare that cost with the cost of alternative credit.

23 - 13

Net daily purchases = $3,000,000/360
= $8,333.

Payables level if discount is taken:
Payables = $8,333 (10) = $83,333.

Payables level if don't take discount:
Payables = $8,333 (40) = $333,333.

Credit Breakdown:

Total trade credit	= $333,333
Free trade credit	= 83,333
Costly trade credit	= $250,000

23 - 14

Nominal Cost of Costly Trade Credit

Firm loses 0.01($3,030,303) = $30,303 of discounts to obtain $250,000 in extra trade credit, so

$$k_{Nom} = \frac{\$30,303}{\$250,000} = 0.1212 = 12.12\%.$$

But the $30,303 in lost discounts is paid all during the year, not just at year-end, so the EAR is higher.

23 - 15

Nominal Cost Formula, 1/10, net 40

$$k_{Nom} = \frac{\text{Discount \%}}{1 - \text{Discount \%}} \times \frac{360}{\text{Days taken - Discount period}}$$

$$= \frac{1}{99} \times \frac{360}{30} = 0.0101 \times 12$$

$$= 0.1212 = 12.12\%.$$

Pays 1.01% 12 times per year.

23 - 16

Effective Annual Rate, 1/10, net 40

Periodic rate = 0.01/0.99 = 1.01%.

Periods/year = 360/(40 - 10) = 12.

EAR = $(1 + \text{Periodic rate})^n - 1.0$
$= (1.0101)^{12} - 1.0 = 12.82\%$.

23 - 17

Commercial Paper (CP)

- CP are short term notes issued by large, strong companies. B&B could not issue CP; the company is too small.
- CP trades in the market at rates just above the T-bill rate.
- CP is bought by banks and other companies, then held as marketable securities for liquidity purposes.

23 - 18

A bank is willing to lend B&B $100,000 for 1 year at an 8 percent nominal rate. What is the EAR under the following five loans?

1. Simple annual interest, 1 year.
2. Simple interest, paid monthly.
3. Discount interest.
4. Discount interest with 10 percent compensating balance.
5. Installment loan, add-on, 12 months.

23 - 19

Why must we use Effective Annual Rates (EARs) to evaluate the loans?

- In our examples, the nominal (quoted) rate is 8% in all cases.
- We want to compare loan cost rates and choose the alternative with the lowest cost.
- Because the loans have different terms, we must make the comparison on the basis of EARs.

23 - 20

Simple Annual Interest, 1-Year Loan

"Simple interest" means not discount or add-on.

Interest = 0.08($100,000) = $8,000.

$$k_{Nom} = EAR = \frac{\$8,000}{\$100,000} = 0.08 = 8.0\%.$$

On a simple interest loan of one year, k_{Nom} = EAR.

23 - 21

Simple Interest, Paid Monthly

Monthly interest = (0.08/12)($100,000)
= $666.67.

0   1   ...   12

100,000   -666.67   ...   -667.67
-100,000.00

12		100000	-666.67	-100000
N	I/YR	PV	PMT	FV
	0.66667			

(More...)

23 - 22

k_{Nom} = (Monthly rate)(12)
= 0.66667%(12) = 8.00%.

$$EAR = \left(1 + \frac{0.08}{12}\right)^{12} - 1 = 8.30\%.$$

or: 8 ■ NOM%, 12 ■ P/YR, ■ EFF% = 8.30%.

Note: If interest were paid quarterly, then:

$$EAR = \left(1 + \frac{0.08}{4}\right)^{4} - 1 = 8.24\%.$$

Daily, EAR = 8.33%.

23 - 23

8% Discount Interest, 1 Year

Interest deductible = 0.08($100,000)
= $8,000.

Usable funds = $100,000 - $8,000
= $92,000.

0	i = ?	1
92,000		-100,000

1		92	0	-100
N	I/YR	PV	PMT	FV
	8.6957% = EAR			

23 - 24

Discount Interest (Continued)

$$\text{Amt. borrowed} = \frac{\text{Amount needed}}{1 - \text{Nominal rate (decimal)}}$$

$$= \frac{\$100{,}000}{0.92} = \$108{,}696.$$

23 - 25

Need \$100,000. Offered loan with terms of 8% discount interest, 10% compensating balance.

$$\text{Face amount of loan} = \frac{\text{Amount needed}}{1 - \text{Nominal rate} - \text{CB}}$$

$$= \frac{\$100{,}000}{1 - 0.08 - 0.1} = \$121{,}951.$$

(More...)

23 - 26

Interest = 0.08 (\$121,951) = \$9,756.

$$\text{Cost} = \frac{\text{Interest paid}}{\text{Amount received}}.$$

$$\text{EAR} = \frac{\$9{,}756}{\$100{,}000} = 9.756\%.$$

EAR correct only if amount is borrowed for 1 year.

(More...)

23 - 27

8% Discount Interest with 10% Compensating Balance (Continued)

0 ——— i = ? ——— 1

121,951	Loan	-121,951
-9,756	Prepaid interest	+ 12,195
-12,195	CB	-109,756
100,000	Usable funds	

1 [N] [I/YR] 100000 [PV] 0 [PMT] -109756 [FV]

9.756% = EAR

This procedure can handle variations.

23 - 28

1-Year Installment Loan, 8% "Add-On"

Interest = 0.08($100,000) = $8,000.

Face amount = $100,000 + $8,000 = $108,000.

Monthly payment = $108,000/12 = $9,000.

Average loan outstanding = $100,000/2 = $50,000.

Approximate cost = $8,000/$50,000 = 16.0%.

(More...)

23 - 29

Installment Loan

To find the EAR, recognize that the firm has received $100,000 and must make monthly payments of $9,000. This constitutes an ordinary annuity as shown below:

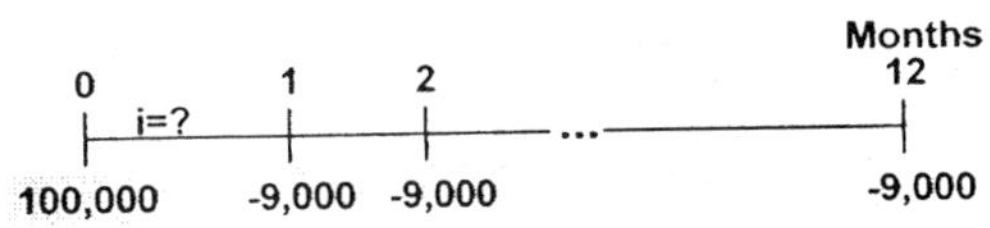

23 - 30

12		100000	-9000	0
N	I/YR	PV	PMT	FV

1.2043% = rate per month

k_{Nom} = APR = (1.2043%)(12) = 14.45%.
EAR = $(1.012043)^{12}$ - 1 = 15.45%.

14.45 ■ NOM ⟶ enters nominal rate
12 ■ P/YR ⟶ enters 12 pmts/yr
■ EFF% = 15.4489 = 15.45%.

1 ■ P/YR to reset calculator.

23 - 31

What is a secured loan?

- In a secured loan, the borrower pledges assets as collateral for the loan.
- For short-term loans, the most commonly pledged assets are receivables and inventories.
- Securities are great collateral, but generally firms needing short-term loans generally do not have securities.

23 - 32

What are the differences between pledging and factoring receivables?

- If receivables are pledged, the lender has recourse against both the original buyer of the goods and the borrower.
- When receivables are factored, they are generally sold, and the buyer (lender) has no recourse to the borrower.

23 - 33

What are three forms of inventory financing?

- Blanket lien.
- Trust receipt.
- Warehouse receipt.
- The form used depends on the type of inventory and situation at hand.

23 - 34

Legal stuff is vital.

- **Security agreement: Standard form under Uniform Commercial Code. Describes when lender can claim collateral.**
- **UCC Form-1: Filed with Secretary of State to establish claim. Future lenders do search, won't lend if prior UCC-1 is on file.**

BLUEPRINTS: CHAPTER 24
DERIVATIVES AND RISK MANAGEMENT

Assume that you have just been hired as a financial analyst by Tennessee Sunshine Inc., a mid-sized Tennessee company that specializes in creating exotic sauces from imported fruits and vegetables. The firm's CEO, Bill Stooksbury, recently returned from an industry corporate executive conference in San Francisco, and one of the sessions he attended was on the pressing need for smaller companies to institute corporate risk management programs. Since no one at Tennessee Sunshine is familiar with the basics of derivatives and corporate risk management, Stooksbury has asked you to prepare a brief report that the firm's executives could use to gain at least a cursory understanding of the topics.

To begin, you gathered some outside materials on derivatives and corporate risk management and used these materials to draft a list of pertinent questions that need to be answered. In fact, one possible approach to the paper is to use a question-and-answer format. Now that the questions have been drafted, you have to develop the answers.

a. Why might stockholders be indifferent whether or not a firm reduces the volatility of its cash flows?

b. What are six reasons risk management might increase the value of a corporation?

c. What is corporate risk management? Why is it important to all firms?

c. Risks that firms face can be categorized in many ways. Define the following types of risk: (1) speculative risks; (2) pure risks; (3) demand risks; (4) input risks; (5) financial risks; (6) property risks; (7) personnel risks; (8) environmental risks; (9) liability risks; and (10) insurable risks.

e. What are the three steps of corporate risk management?

f. What are some actions that companies can take to minimize or reduce risk exposures?

g. What is financial risk exposure? Describe the following concepts and techniques that can be used to reduce financial risks: (1) derivatives; (2) futures markets; (3) hedging; and (4) swaps.

h. Describe how commodity futures markets can be used to reduce input price risk.

24 - 1

CHAPTER 24
Derivatives and Risk Management

- Risk management and stock value maximization.
- Derivative securities.
- Fundamentals of risk management.
- Using derivatives to reduce interest rate risk.

24 - 2

Do stockholders care about volatile cash flows?

- If volatility in cash flows is not caused by systematic risk, then stockholders can eliminate the risk of volatile cash flows by diversifying their portfolios.
- Stockholders might be able to reduce impact of volatile cash flows by using risk management techniques in their own portfolios.

24 - 3

How can risk management increase the value of a corporation?

Risk management allows firms to:

- Have greater debt capacity, which has a larger tax shield of interest payments.
- Implement the optimal capital budget without having to raise external equity in years that would have had low cash flow due to volatility. (More...)

24 - 4

Risk management allows firms to:

- Avoid costs of financial distress.
  - Weakened relationships with suppliers.
  - Loss of potential customers.
  - Distractions to managers.
- Utilize comparative advantage in hedging relative to hedging ability of investors.

(More...)

24 - 5

Risk management allows firms to:

- Reduce borrowing costs by using interest rate swaps.

  Example: Two firms with different credit ratings, Hi and Lo:

  Hi can borrow fixed at 11% and floating at LIBOR + 1%.

  Lo can borrow fixed at 11.4% and floating at LIBOR + 1.5%.

(More...)

24 - 6

Hi wants fixed rate, but it will issue floating and "swap" with Lo. Lo wants floating rate, but it will issue fixed and swap with Hi. Lo also makes "side payment" of 0.45% to Hi.

CF to lender	-(LIBOR+1%)	-11.40%
CF Hi to Lo	-11.40%	+11.40%
CF Lo to Hi	+(LIBOR+1%)	-(LIBOR+1%)
CF Lo to Hi	+0.45%	-0.45%
Net CF	-10.95%	-(LIBOR+1.45%)

(More...)

24 - 7

Risk management allows firms to:

- Minimize negative tax effects due to convexity in tax code.

  Example: EBT of $50K in Years 1 and 2, total EBT of $100K,

  Tax = $7.5K each year, total tax of $15.

  EBT of $0K in Year 1 and $100K in Year 2,

  Tax = $0K in Year 1 and $22.5K in Year 2.

24 - 8

What is corporate risk management?

Corporate risk management is the management of unpredictable events that would have adverse consequences for the firm.

24 - 9

Definitions of Different Types of Risk

- **Speculative risks:** Those that offer the chance of a gain as well as a loss.
- **Pure risks:** Those that offer only the prospect of a loss.
- **Demand risks:** Those associated with the demand for a firm's products or services.
- **Input risks:** Those associated with a firm's input costs.

(More...)

24 - 10

- **Financial risks:** Those that result from financial transactions.
- **Property risks:** Those associated with loss of a firm's productive assets.
- **Personnel risk:** Risks that result from human actions.
- **Environmental risk:** Risk associated with polluting the environment.
- **Liability risks:** Connected with product, service, or employee liability.
- **Insurable risks:** Those which typically can be covered by insurance.

24 - 11

What are the three steps of corporate risk management?

Step 1. Identify the risks faced by the firm.

Step 2. Measure the potential impact of the identified risks.

Step 3. Decide how each relevant risk should be dealt with.

24 - 12

What are some actions that companies can take to minimize or reduce risk exposures?

- Transfer risk to an insurance company by paying periodic premiums.
- Transfer functions which produce risk to third parties.
- Purchase derivatives contracts to reduce input and financial risks.

(More...)

24 - 13

- Take actions to reduce the probability of occurrence of adverse events.
- Take actions to reduce the magnitude of the loss associated with adverse events.
- Avoid the activities that give rise to risk.

24 - 14

What is a financial risk exposure?

- Financial risk exposure refers to the risk inherent in the financial markets due to price fluctuations.
- Example: A firm holds a portfolio of bonds, interest rates rise, and the value of the bonds falls.

24 - 15

Financial Risk Management Concepts

- Derivative: Security whose value stems or is derived from the value of other assets. Swaps, options, and futures are used to manage financial risk exposures.
- Futures: Contracts which call for the purchase or sale of a financial (or real) asset at some future date, but at a price determined today. Futures (and other derivatives) can be used either as highly leveraged speculations or to hedge and thus reduce risk. (More...)

24 - 16

- **Hedging:** Generally conducted where a price change could negatively affect a firm's profits.
  - **Long hedge:** Involves the purchase of a futures contract to guard against a price increase.
  - **Short hedge:** Involves the sale of a futures contract to protect against a price decline in commodities or financial securities.

(More...)

24 - 17

- **Swaps:** Involve the exchange of cash payment obligations between two parties, usually because each party prefers the terms of the other's debt contract. Swaps can reduce each party's financial risk.

24 - 18

How can commodity futures markets be used to reduce input price risk?

The purchase of a commodity futures contract will allow a firm to make a future purchase of the input at today's price, even if the market price on the item has risen substantially in the interim.

24 - 19

Chapter 24 Extension: Insurance and Bond Portfolio Risk Management

- Risk identification and measurement
- Property loss, liability loss, and financial loss exposures
- Bond portfolio risk management

24 - 20

How are risk exposures identified and measured?

- Large corporations have risk management personnel which have the responsibility to identify and measure risks facing the firm.
- Checklists are used to identify risks.
- Small firms can obtain risk management services from insurance companies or risk management consulting firms.

24 - 21

Describe (1) "property" loss and (2) "liability" loss exposures.

- Property loss exposures: Result from various perils which threaten a firm's real and personal properties.
  - Physical perils: Natural events
  - Social perils: Related to human actions
  - Economic perils: Stem from external economic events

24 - 22

- Liability loss exposures: Result from penalties imposed when responsibilities are not met.
  - Bailee exposure: Risks associated with having temporary possession of another's property while some service is being performed. (Cleaners ruin your new suit.)
  - Ownership exposure: Risks inherent in the ownership of property. (Customer is injured from fall in store.)

24 - 23

- Business operation exposure: Risks arising from business practices or operations. (Airline sued following crash.)
- Professional liability exposure: Stems from the risks inherent in professions requiring advanced training and licensing. (Doctor sued when patient dies, or accounting firm sued for not detecting overstated profits.)

24 - 24

What actions can companies take to reduce property and liability exposures?

- Both property and liability exposures can be accommodated by either self-insurance or passing the risk on to an insurance company.
- The more risk passed on to an insurer, the higher the cost of the policy. Insurers like high deductibles, both to lower their losses and to reduce moral hazard.

24 - 25

How can diversification reduce business risk?

- By appropriately spreading business risk over several activities or operations, the firm can significantly reduce the impact of a single random event on corporate performance.
- Examples: Geographic and product diversification.

24 - 26

What is a financial risk exposure?

- Financial risk exposure refers to the risk inherent in the financial markets due to price fluctuations.
- Example: A firm holds a portfolio of bonds, interest rates rise, and the value of the bonds falls.

24 - 27

Financial risk management concepts:

- **Duration:** Average time to bondholders' receipt of cash flows, including interest and principal repayment. Duration is used to help assess interest rate and reinvestment rate risks.
- **Immunization:** Process of selecting durations for bonds in a portfolio such that gains or losses from reinvestment exactly match gains or losses from price changes.

BLUEPRINTS: CHAPTER 25
BANKRUPTCY, REORGANIZATION, AND LIQUIDATION

Kimberly MacKenzie, president of Kim's Clothes Inc., a medium-sized manufacturer of women's casual clothing, is worried. Her firm has been selling clothes to Russ Brothers Department Store for more than ten years, and she has never experienced any problems in collecting payment for the merchandise sold. Currently, Russ Brothers owes Kim's Clothes $65,000 for spring sportswear that was delivered to the store just two weeks ago. Kim's concern was brought about by an article that appeared in yesterday's *Wall Street Journal* that indicated that Russ Brothers was having serious financial problems. Further, the article stated that Russ Brothers' management was considering filing for reorganization, or even liquidation, with a federal bankruptcy court.

Kim's immediate concern was whether or not her firm would collect its receivables if Russ Brothers went bankrupt. In pondering the situation, Kim also realized that she knew nothing about the process that firms go through when they encounter severe financial distress. To learn more about bankruptcy, reorganization, and liquidation, Kim asked Ron Mitchell, the firm's chief financial officer, to prepare a briefing on the subject for the entire board of directors. In turn, Ron asked you, a newly hired financial analyst, to do the groundwork for the briefing by answering the following questions:

a. (1) What are the major causes of business failure?

   (2) Do business failures occur evenly over time?

   (3) Which size of firm, large or small, is more prone to business failure? Why?

b. What key issues must managers face in the financial distress process?

c. What informal remedies are available to firms in financial distress? In answering this question, define the following terms:

   (1) Workout

   (2) Restructuring

   (3) Extension

   (4) Composition

   (5) Assignment

   (6) Assignee (trustee)

d. Briefly describe U.S. bankruptcy law, including the following terms:

(1) Chapter 11

(2) Chapter 7

(3) Trustee

(4) Voluntary bankruptcy

(5) Involuntary bankruptcy

e. What are the major differences between an informal reorganization and reorganization in bankruptcy? In answering this question, be sure to discuss the following items:

(1) Common pool problem

(2) Holdout problem

(3) Automatic stay

(4) Cramdown

(5) Fraudulent conveyance

f. What is a prepackaged bankruptcy? Why have prepackaged bankruptcies become more popular in recent years?

g. Briefly describe the priority of claims in a Chapter 7 liquidation.

h. Assume that Russ Brothers did indeed fail, and that it had the following balance sheet when it was liquidated (in millions of dollars):

Current assets	$40.0	Accounts payable	$10.0
Net fixed assets	5.0	Notes payable (to banks)	5.0
		Accrued wages	0.3
		Federal taxes	0.5
		State and local taxes	0.2
		Current liabilities	$16.0
		First mortgage	$ 3.0
		Second mortgage	0.5
		Subordinated debentures[a]	4.0
		Total long-term debt	$ 7.5
		Preferred stock	$ 1.0
		Common stock	13.0
		Paid-in capital	2.0
		Retained earnings	5.5
		Total equity	$21.5
Total assets	$45.0	Total claims	$45.0

[a]The debentures are subordinated to the notes payable.

The liquidation sale resulted in the following proceeds:

From sale of current assets	$14,000,000
From sale of fixed assets	2,500,000
Total receipts	$16,500,000

For simplicity, assume that there were no trustee's fees or any other claims against the liquidation proceeds. Also, assume that the mortgage bonds are secured by the entire amount of fixed assets. What would each claimant receive from the liquidation distribution?

25 - 1

CHAPTER 25
Bankruptcy, Reorganization, and Liquidation

- Financial distress process
- Federal bankruptcy law
- Reorganization
- Liquidation

25 - 2

What are the major causes of business failure?

- Economic factors
  - industry weakness
  - poor location/product
- Financial factors
  - too much debt
  - insufficient capital

Most failures occur because a number of factors combine to make the business unsustainable.

25 - 3

Do business failures occur evenly over time?

- A large number of businesses fail each year, but the number in any one year has never been a large percentage of the total business population.
- The failure rate of businesses has tended to fluctuate with the state of the economy.

25 - 4

What size firm, large or small, is more prone to business failure?

- Bankruptcy is more frequent among smaller firms.
- Large firms tend to get more help from external sources to avoid bankruptcy, given their greater impact on the economy.

25 - 5

What key issues must managers face in the financial distress process?

- Is it a temporary problem (technical insolvency) or a permanent problem caused by asset values below debt obligations (insolvency in bankruptcy)?
- Who should bear the losses?
- Would the firm be more valuable if it continued to operate or if it were liquidated?

(More...)

25 - 6

- Should the firm file for bankruptcy, or should it try to use informal procedures?
- Who would control the firm during liquidation or reorganization?

25 - 7

What informal remedies are available to firms in financial distress?

- Informal reorganization
- Informal liquidation
- Why might informal remedies be preferable to formal bankruptcy?
- What types of companies are most suitable for informal remedies?

25 - 8

Informal Bankruptcy Terminology

- Workout: Voluntary informal reorganization plan.
- Restructuring: Current debt terms are revised to facilitate the firm's ability to pay.
  - Extension: Creditors postpone the dates of required interest or principal payments, or both. Creditors prefer extension because they are promised eventual payment in full. (More...)

25 - 9

  - Composition: Creditors voluntarily reduce their fixed claims on the debtor by either accepting a lower principal amount or accepting equity in lieu of debt repayment.
- Assignment: An informal procedure for liquidating a firm's assets. Title to the debtor's assets is transferred to a third party, called a trustee or assignee, and then the assets are sold off.

25 - 10

Describe the following terms related to U.S. bankruptcy law:

- **Chapter 11: Business reorganization guidelines.**
- **Chapter 7: Liquidation procedures.**
- **Trustee:**
  - **Appointed to control the company when current management is incompetent or fraud is suspected.**
  - **Used only in unusual circumstances.** (More...)

25 - 11

- **Voluntary bankruptcy: A bankruptcy petition filed in federal court by the distressed firm's management.**
- **Involuntary bankruptcy: A bankruptcy petition filed in federal court by the distressed firm's creditors.**

25 - 12

What are the major differences between an informal reorganization and reorganization in bankruptcy?

- **Informal Reorganization:**
  - **Less costly**
  - **Relatively simple to create**
  - **Typically allows creditors to recover more money and sooner.**

(More...)

25 - 13

- Reorganization in Bankruptcy
  - Avoids holdout problems.
  - Due to automatic stay provision, avoids common pool problem.
  - Interest and principal payments may be delayed without penalty until reorganization plan is approved.

(More...)

25 - 14

- Permits the firm to issue debtor in possession (DIP) financing.
- Gives debtor exclusive right to submit a proposed reorganization plan for agreement from the parties involved.
- Reduces fraudulent conveyance problem.
- Cramdown if majority in each creditor class approve plan.

25 - 15

What is a prepackaged bankruptcy?

- New type of reorganization
  - Combines the advantages of both formal and informal reorganizations.
  - Avoids holdout problems
  - Preserves creditors' claims
  - Favorable tax treatment.
- Agreement to plan obtained from creditors prior to filing for bankruptcy.
- Plan filed with bankruptcy petition.

25 - 16

List the priority of claims in a Chapter 7 liquidation.

- Secured creditors.
- Trustee's administrative costs.
- Expenses incurred after involuntary case begun but before trustee appointed.
- Wages due workers within 3 months prior to filing.

(More...)

25 - 17

- Unpaid contributions to employee benefit plans that should have been paid within 6 months prior to filing.
- Unsecured claims for customer deposits.
- Taxes due.
- Unfunded pension plan liabilities.
- General (unsecured) creditors.
- Preferred stockholders.
- Common stockholders.

25 - 18

Liquidation Illustration Data (millions of $)

Creditor Claims:	
Accounts payable	$10.0
Notes payable	5.0
Accrued wages	0.3
Federal taxes	0.5
State and local taxes	0.2
First mortgage	3.0
Second mortgage	0.5
Subordinated debentures*	4.0
	$23.5

*Subordinated to notes payable.

(More...)

25 - 19

Proceeds from liquidation:

From current assets	$14.0
From fixed assets*	2.5
Total receipts	$16.5

* All fixed assets pledged as collateral to mortgage holders.

25 - 20

Priority Distribution (millions of $)

Creditor	Claim	Distribution	Unsatisfied
Accrued wages	$0.3	$0.3	$0.0
Federal taxes	0.5	0.5	0.0
Other taxes	0.2	0.2	0.0
First mortgage	3.0	2.5	0.5
Second mortgage	0.5	0.0	0.5
	$4.5	$3.5	$1.0

Notes: (1) First mortgage receives entire proceeds from sale of fixed assets, leaving $0 for the second mortgage.
(2) $16.5 - $3.5 = $13.0 remains for distribution to general creditors.

25 - 21

General Creditor Distribution (millions of $)

Creditor	Remaining GC Claim	Initial Distrib.[a]	Final Amount[b]	Percent Received
Accounts payable	$10.0	$6.500	$6.500	65.0%
Notes payable	5.0	3.250	5.000	100.0
Accrued wages	0.0		0.300	100.0
Federal taxes	0.0		0.500	100.0
Other taxes	0.0		0.200	100.0
First mortgage	0.5	0.325	2.825	94.2
Second mortgage	0.5	0.325	0.325	65.0
Sub. deb.	4.0	2.600	0.850	21.2
	$20.0	$13.000	$16.500	

[a] Pro rata amount = $13/$20 = 0.65.
[b] Includes priority distribution and $1.75 transfer from subordinated debentures.

25 - 22

Other Motivations for Bankruptcy

- Normally, bankruptcy is motivated by serious current financial problems.
- However, some companies have used bankruptcy proceedings for other purposes:
  - To break union contracts
  - To hasten liability settlements

25 - 23

Some Criticisms of Bankruptcy Laws

- Critics contend that current (1978) bankruptcy laws are flawed.
- Too much value is siphoned off by lawyers, managers, and trustees.
- Companies that have no hope remain alive too long, leaving little for creditors when liquidation does occur.
- Companies in bankruptcy can hurt other companies in industry.

25 - 24

Chapter 25 Extension

- MDA to predict bankruptcy
- Recent business failures

25 - 25

What is MDA, and how can it be used to predict bankruptcy?

- Multiple discriminant analysis (MDA) is a statistical technique similar to multiple regression.
- It identifies the characteristics of firms that went bankrupt in the past.
- Then, data from any firm can be entered into the model to assess the likelihood of future bankruptcy.

25 - 26

MDA Illustration

- Assume you have the following 1997 data for 12 companies:
  - Current ratio
  - Debt ratio
- Six of the companies (marked by Xs) went bankrupt in 1998 while six (marked by dots) remained solvent.

(More...)

25 - 27

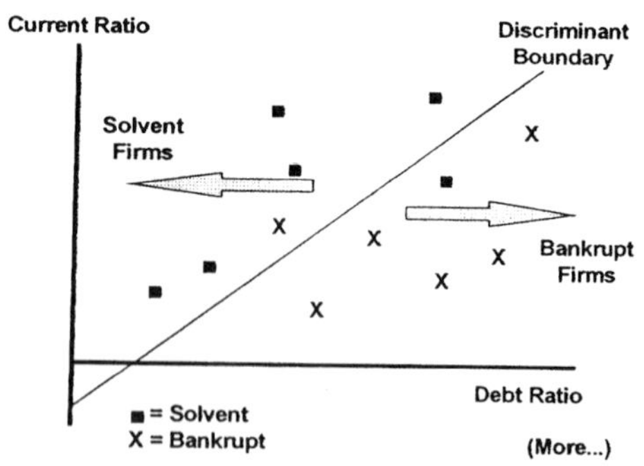

(More...)

25 - 28

- The discriminant boundary, or Z line, statistically separates the bankrupt and solvent companies.
- Note that two companies have been misclassified by the MDA program: One bankrupt company falls on the solvent (left) side and one solvent company falls on the bankrupt (right) side.

(More...)

25 - 29

- Assume the equation for the boundary line is

  Z = -2 + 1.5(Current ratio) - 5.0(Debt ratio).

- Furthermore, if Z = -1 to +1, the future of the company is uncertain. If Z > 1, bankruptcy is unlikely; if Z < -1, bankruptcy is likely to occur.

25 - 30

Using MDA To Predict Bankruptcy

- Suppose Firm S has CR = 4.0 and DR = 0.40. Then,

  Z = -2 + 1.5(4.0) - 5.0(0.40) = +2.0,

  and firm is unlikely to go bankrupt.

- Suppose Firm B has CR = 1.5 and DR = 0.75. Then,

  Z = -2 + 1.5(1.5) - 5.0(0.75) = -3.5,

  and firm is likely to go bankrupt.

25 - 31

Some Final Points

- The most well-known bankruptcy prediction model is Edward Altman's five factor model.
- Such models tend to work relatively well, but only for the near term.
- The more similar the historical sample to the firm being evaluated, the better the prediction.

BLUEPRINTS: CHAPTER 26

MERGERS, LBOs, DIVESTITURES, AND HOLDING COMPANIES

Smitty's Home Repair Company, a regional hardware chain which specializes in "do-it-yourself" materials and equipment rentals, is cash rich because of several consecutive good years. One of the alternative uses for the excess funds is an acquisition. Linda Wade, Smitty's treasurer and you boss, has been asked to place a value on a potential target, Hill's Hardware, a small chain which operates in an adjacent state, and she has enlisted your help.

The table below indicates Wade's estimates of Hill's earnings potential if it came under Smitty's management (in millions of dollars). The interest expense listed here includes the interest (1) on Hill's existing debt and on (2) on new debt expected to be issued over time to help finance expansion within the new "H division," the code name given to the target firm. The retentions represent earnings that will be reinvested within the H division to help finance its growth.

Security analysts estimate Hill's beta to be 1.3. The acquisition would not change Hill's capital structure or tax rate. Wade realizes that Hill's Hardware also generates depreciation cash flows, but she believes that these funds would have to be reinvested within the division to replace worn-out equipment.

Wade estimates the risk-free rate to be 9 percent and the market risk premium to be 4 percent. She also estimates that net cash flows after 2005 will grow at a constant rate of 6 percent. Following are projections for sales and other items.

	2002	2003	2004	2005
Net sales	$60.0	$90.0	$112.5	$127.5
Cost of goods sold (60%)	36.0	54.0	67.5	76.5
Selling/administrative expense	4.5	6.0	7.5	9.0
Interest expense	3.0	4.5	4.5	6.0
Necessary retained earnings	0.0	7.5	6.0	4.5

Smitty's management is new to the merger game, so Wade has been asked to answer some basic questions about mergers as well as to perform the merger analysis. To structure the task, Wade has developed the following questions, which you must answer and then defend to Smitty's board.

a. Several reasons have been proposed to justify mergers. Among the more prominent are (1) tax considerations, (2) risk reduction, (3) control, (4) purchase of assets at below-replacement cost, (5) synergy, and (6) globalization. In general, which of the reasons are economically justifiable? Which are not? Which fit the situation at hand? Explain.

b. Briefly describe the differences between a hostile merger and a friendly merger.

c. Use the data developed previously to construct the H division's cash flow statements for 2002 through 2005. Why is interest expense deducted in merger cash flow statements, whereas it is not normally deducted in capital budgeting cash flow analysis? Why are earnings retentions deducted in the cash flow statement?

d. Conceptually, what is the appropriate discount rate to apply to the cash flows developed in Part c? What is your actual estimate of this discount rate?

e. What is the estimated horizon, or continuing, value of the acquisition; that is, what is the estimated value of the H division's cash flows beyond 2005? What is Hill's value to Smitty's shareholders? Suppose another firm were evaluating Hill's as an acquisition candidate. Would they obtain the same value? Explain.

f. Assume that Hill's has 10 million shares outstanding. These shares are traded relatively infrequently, but the last trade, made several weeks ago, was at a price of $9 per share. Should Smitty's make an offer for Hill's? If so, how much should it offer per share?

g. Assume that publicly traded companies in Hill's line of business have stock prices in the range of 12 to 14 times earnings per share (EPS). Use the market multiple approach to value the target company.

h. There has been considerable research undertaken to determine whether mergers really create value, and, if so, how this value is shared between the parties involved. What are the results of this research?

i. What are the two methods of accounting for mergers?

j. What merger-related activities are undertaken by investment bankers?

k. What is a leveraged buyout (LBO)? What are some of the advantages and disadvantages of going private?

l. What are the major types of divestitures? What motivates firms to divest assets?

m. What are holding companies? What are their advantages and disadvantages?

26 - 1

CHAPTER 26
Mergers, LBOs, Divestitures, and Holding Companies

- Types of mergers
- Merger analysis
- Role of investment bankers
- LBOs, divestitures, and holding companies

26 - 2

What are some valid economic justifications for mergers?

- Synergy: Value of the whole exceeds sum of the parts. Could arise from:
  - Operating economies
  - Financial economies
  - Differential management efficiency
  - Taxes (use accumulated losses)

(More...)

26 - 3

- Break-up value: Assets would be more valuable if broken up and sold to other companies.

26 - 4

What are some questionable reasons for mergers?

- Diversification
- Purchase of assets at below replacement cost
- Acquire other firms to increase size, thus making it more difficult to be acquired

26 - 5

Five Largest Completed Mergers (as of January 2001)

BUYER	TARGET	VALUE (Billion)
Vodafone AirTouch	Mannesman	$161
Pfizer	Warner-Lambert	116
America Online	Time Warner	106
Exxon	Mobil	81
Glaxo Wellcome	SmithKline Beecham	74

26 - 6

Differentiate between hostile and friendly mergers

- Friendly merger:
  - The merger is supported by the managements of both firms.

(More...)

- Hostile merger:
  - Target firm's management resists the merger.
  - Acquirer must go directly to the target firm's stockholders, try to get 51% to tender their shares.
  - Often, mergers that start out hostile end up as friendly, when offer price is raised.

Reasons why alliances can make more sense than acquisitions

- Access to new markets and technologies
- Multiple parties share risks and expenses
- Rivals can often work together harmoniously
- Antitrust laws can shelter cooperative R&D activities

DCF Valuation Analysis (In Millions)

Cash Flow Statements after Merger Occurs

	2002	2003	2004	2005
Net sales	$60.0	$90.0	$112.5	$127.5
Cost of goods sold (60%)	36.0	54.0	67.5	76.5
Selling/admin. expenses	4.5	6.0	7.5	9.0
Interest expense	3.0	4.5	4.5	6.0
EBT	$16.5	$25.5	$ 33.0	$ 36.0
Taxes (40%)	6.6	10.2	13.2	14.4
Net income	$ 9.9	$15.3	$ 19.8	$ 21.6
Retentions	0.0	7.5	6.0	4.5
Cash flow	$ 9.9	$ 7.8	$ 13.8	$ 17.1

26 - 10

Conceptually, what is the appropriate discount rate to apply to the target's cash flows?

- Estimated cash flows are residuals that belong to the shareholders of the acquiring firm.
- They are riskier than the typical capital budgeting cash flows, because including fixed interest charges increases the volatility.

(More...)

26 - 11

- Because the cash flows are equity flows, they should be discounted using a cost of equity rather than an overall cost of capital.
- Note that the cash flows reflect the target's business risk, not the acquiring company's.
- However, if the merger will affect the target's leverage and tax rate, then it will affect its financial risk.

26 - 12

Discount Rate Calculation

$$k_{s(Target)} = k_{RF} + (k_M - k_{RF})b_{Target}$$
$$= 9\% + (4\%)1.3 = 14.2\%.$$

26 - 13

Horizon, or Continuing, Value

$$\text{Horizon value} = \frac{(2005\text{ Cash flow})(1+g)}{k_s - g}$$

$$= \frac{\$17.1(1.06)}{0.142 - 0.06}$$

= $221.0 million.

26 - 14

What Is the Value of the Target Firm to the Acquiring Shareholders? (In Millions)

	2002	2003	2004	2005
Annual cash flow	$9.9	$7.8	$13.8	$ 17.1
Terminal value				221.0
Net cash flow	$9.9	$7.8	$13.8	$238.1

$$\text{Value} = \frac{\$9.9}{(1.142)^1} + \frac{\$7.8}{(1.142)^2} + \frac{\$13.8}{(1.142)^3} + \frac{\$238.1}{(1.142)^4}$$

= $163.9 million.

26 - 15

Would another potential acquirer obtain the same value?

- No. The cash flow estimates would be different, both due to forecasting inaccuracies and to differential synergies.
- Further, a different beta estimate, financing mix, or tax rate would change the discount rate.

26 - 16

Assume the target company has 10 million shares outstanding. The stock last traded at $9 per share, which reflects the target's value on a stand-alone basis. How much should the acquiring firm offer?

26 - 17

Estimate of target's value	**= $163.9 million**
Target's current value	**= $ 90.0 million**
Merger premium	**= $ 73.9 million**

Presumably, the target's value is increased by $73.9 million due to merger synergies, although realizing such synergies has been problematic in many mergers.

(More...)

26 - 18

- **The offer could range from $9 to $163.9/10 = $16.39 per share.**
- **At $9, all merger benefits would go to the acquiring firm's shareholders.**
- **At $16.39, all value added would go to the target firm's shareholders.**
- **The graph on the next slide summarizes the situation.**

26 - 19

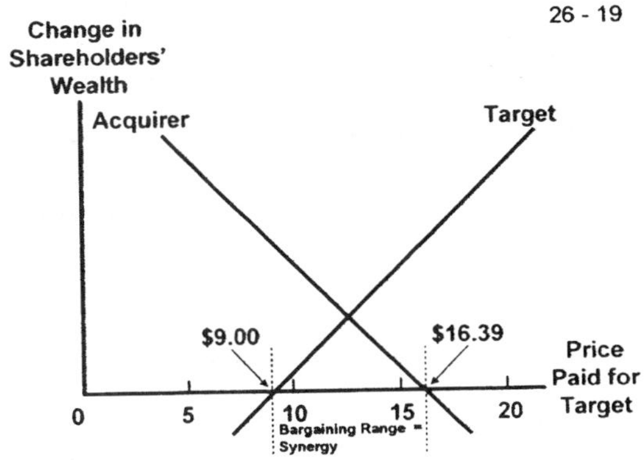

26 - 20

Points About Graph

- Nothing magic about crossover price.
- Actual price would be determined by bargaining. Higher if target is in better bargaining position, lower if acquirer is.
- If target is good fit for many acquirers, other firms will come in, price will be bid up. If not, could be close to $9.

(More...)

26 - 21

- Acquirer might want to make high "preemptive" bid to ward off other bidders, or low bid and then plan to go up. Strategy is important.
- Do target's managers have 51% of stock and want to remain in control?
- What kind of personal deal will target's managers get?

26 - 22

Assuming a market multiple of 12-14 times EPS, use the market multiple method to value the stock.

2002 EPS	= $	9.90 million
2003 EPS	=	15.30
		$ 25.20 million
Divided by 2 = Average	=	$ 12.60 million
12 x Avg. EPS	=	$151.20 million
14 x Avg. EPS	=	$176.40 million

26 - 23

Which valuation method is better, DCF or market multiple?

Both methods have significant implementation problems.

- Confidence in DCF cash flow forecasts and discount rate is often low.
- Validity of market multiple method depends on comparability of firms and ability of EPS to capture synergies.
- Judgment is key to final valuation.

26 - 24

Do mergers really create value?

- According to empirical evidence, acquisitions do create value as a result of economies of scale, other synergies, and/or better management.
- Shareholders of target firms reap most of the benefits, that is, the final price is close to full value.
  - Target management can always say no.
  - Competing bidders often push up prices.

26 - 25

What are the two methods of accounting for mergers?

- Pooling of interests:
  - Assumes a merger among equals.
  - New balance sheet is merely the sum of the two existing balance sheets.
  - No income statement effects other than summing the two income statements.

(More...)

26 - 26

- Purchase:
  - The assets of the acquired firm are "written up" to reflect purchase price if it is greater than the net asset value.
  - Goodwill is often created, which appears as an asset on the balance sheet.
  - Common equity account is increased to balance assets and claims.
  - Goodwill is amortized and expensed over time, thus reducing future reported earnings.

26 - 27

What are some merger-related activities of investment bankers?

- Identifying targets
- Arranging mergers
- Developing defensive tactics
- Establishing a fair value
- Financing mergers
- Arbitrage operations

26 - 28

What is a leveraged buyout (LB0)?

- In an LBO, a small group of investors, normally including management, buys all of the publicly held stock, and hence takes the firm private.
- Purchase often financed with debt.
- After operating privately for a number of years, investors take the firm public to "cash out."

26 - 29

What are are the advantages and disadvantages of going private?

- Advantages:
  - Administrative cost savings
  - Increased managerial incentives
  - Increased managerial flexibility
  - Increased shareholder participation
- Disadvantages:
  - Limited access to equity capital
  - No way to capture return on investment

26 - 30

What are the major types of divestitures?

- Sale of an entire subsidiary to another firm.
- Spinning off a corporate subsidiary by giving the stock to existing shareholders.
- Carving out a corporate subsidiary by selling a minority interest.
- Outright liquidation of assets.

26 - 31

What motivates firms to divest assets?

- Subsidiary worth more to buyer than when operated by current owner.
- To settle antitrust issues.
- Subsidiary's value increased if it operates independently.
- To change strategic direction.
- To shed money losers.
- To get needed cash when distressed.

26 - 32

What are holding companies?

- A holding company is a corporation formed for the sole purpose of owning the stocks of other companies.
- In a typical holding company, the subsidiary companies issue their own debt, but their equity is held by the holding company, which, in turn, sells stock to individual investors.

26 - 33

What are the advantages and disadvantages of holding companies?

- Advantages:
  - Control with fractional ownership.
  - Isolation of risks.
- Disadvantages:
  - Partial multiple taxation.
  - Ease of enforced dissolution.

BLUEPRINTS: CHAPTER 27

MULTINATIONAL FINANCIAL MANAGEMENT

Citrus Products Inc. is a medium-sized producer of citrus juice drinks with groves in Indian River County, Florida. Until now, the company has confined its operations and sales to the United States, but its CEO, George Gaynor, wants to expand into Europe. The first step would be to set up sales subsidiaries in Spain and Sweden, then to set up a production plant in Spain, and, finally, to distribute the product throughout the European common market. The firm's financial manager, Ruth Schmidt, is enthusiastic about the plan, but she is worried about the implications of the foreign expansion on the firm's financial management process. She has asked you, the firm's most recently hired financial analyst, to develop a 1-hour tutorial package that explains the basics of multinational financial management. The tutorial will be presented at the next board of directors meeting. To get you started, Schmidt has supplied you with the following list of questions.

a. What is a multinational corporation? Why do firms expand into other countries?

b. What are the six major factors which distinguish multinational financial management from financial management as practiced by a purely domestic firm?

c. Consider the following illustrative exchange rates.

	U.S. Dollars Required to Buy One Unit of Foreign Currency
Spanish peseta	0.0050
Swedish krona	0.0985

(1) Are these currency prices direct quotations or indirect quotations?

(2) Calculate the indirect quotations for pesetas and kronas.

(3) What is a cross rate? Calculate the two cross rates between pesetas and kronas.

(4) Assume Citrus Products can produce a liter of orange juice and ship it to Spain for $1.75. If the firm wants a 50 percent markup on the product, what should the orange juice sell for in Spain?

(5) Now, assume Citrus Products begins producing the same liter of orange juice in Spain. The product costs 240 pesetas to produce and ship to Sweden, where it can be sold for 20 kronas. What is the dollar profit on the sale?

(6) What is exchange rate risk?

d. Briefly describe the current international monetary system. How does the current system differ from the system that was in place prior to August 1971?

e. What is a convertible currency? What problems arise when a multinational company operates in a country whose currency is not convertible?

f. What is the difference between spot rates and forward rates? When is the forward rate at a premium to the spot rate? At a discount?

g. What is interest rate parity? Currently, you can exchange 1 peseta for 0.00505 dollar in the 30-day forward market, and the risk-free rate on 30-day securities is 6 percent in the United States and 4 percent in Spain. Does interest rate parity hold? If not, which securities offer the highest expected return?

h. What is purchasing power parity? If grapefruit juice costs $2.00 a liter in the United States and purchasing power parity holds, what should be the price of grapefruit juice in Spain?

i. What impact does relative inflation have on interest rates and exchange rates?

j. Briefly discuss the international capital markets.

k. To what extent do average capital structures vary across different countries?

l. What is the impact of multinational operations on each of the following financial management topics?

(1) Cash management.

(2) Capital budgeting decisions.

(3) Credit management.

(4) Inventory management.

27 - 1

CHAPTER 27
Multinational Financial Management

- Factors that make multinational financial management different
- Exchange rates and trading
- International monetary system
- International financial markets
- Specific features of multinational financial management

27 - 2

What is a multinational corporation?

- A multinational corporation is one that operates in two or more countries.
- At one time, most multinationals produced and sold in just a few countries.
- Today, many multinationals have world-wide production and sales.

27 - 3

Why do firms expand into other countries?

- To seek new markets.
- To seek new supplies of raw materials.
- To gain new technologies.
- To gain production efficiencies.
- To avoid political and regulatory obstacles.
- To reduce risk by diversification.

27 - 4

What are the major factors that distinguish multinational from domestic financial management?

- Currency differences
- Economic and legal differences
- Language differences
- Cultural differences
- Government roles
- Political risk

27 - 5

Consider the following exchange rates:

	U.S. $ to buy 1 Unit
Spanish peseta	0.0050
Swedish krona	0.0985

Are these currency prices direct or indirect quotations?

Since they are prices of foreign currencies expressed in U.S. dollars, they are direct quotations.

27 - 6

What is an indirect quotation?

- An indirect quotation gives the amount of a foreign currency required to buy one U.S. dollar.
- Note than an indirect quotation is the reciprocal of a direct quotation.

27 - 7

Calculate the indirect quotations for pesetas and kronas.

	# of Units of Foreign Currency per U.S. $
Spanish peseta	200.00
Swedish krona	10.15

Peseta: 1/0.0050 = 200.00.
Krona: 1/0.0985 = 10.15.

27 - 8

What is a cross rate?

- A cross rate is the exchange rate between any two currencies not involving U.S. dollars.
- In practice, cross rates are usually calculated from direct or indirect rates. That is, on the basis of U.S. dollar exchange rates.

27 - 9

Calculate the two cross rates between pesetas and kronas.

- Cross rate $= \frac{\text{Pesetas}}{\text{Dollar}} \times \frac{\text{Dollars}}{\text{Krona}}$

  = 200.00 x 0.0985
  = 19.70 pesetas/krona.

- Cross rate $= \frac{\text{Kronas}}{\text{Dollar}} \times \frac{\text{Dollars}}{\text{Peseta}}$

  = 10.15 x 0.0050
  = 0.051 kronas/peseta.

27 - 10

Note:

- **The two cross rates are reciprocals of one another.**
- **They can be calculated by dividing either the direct or indirect quotations.**

27 - 11

Assume the firm can produce a liter of orange juice in the U.S. and ship it to Spain for $1.75. If the firm wants a 50% markup on the product, what should the juice sell for in Spain?

Target price = ($1.75)(1.50)=$2.625

Spanish price = ($2.625)(200.00 pesetas/$)

= 525.00 pesetas.

27 - 12

Now the firm begins producing the orange juice in Spain. The product costs 240 pesetas to produce and ship to Sweden, where it can be sold for 20 kronas. What is the dollar profit on the sale?

240 pesetas = 240(0.051) = 12.24 kronas.

20 - 12.24 = 7.76 kronas profit.

Dollar profit = 7.76 kronas(0.0985 dollars per krona) = $0.76.

27 - 13

What is exchange rate risk?

Exchange rate risk is the risk that the value of a cash flow in one currency translated from another currency will decline due to a change in exchange rates.

For example, in the last slide, a weakening krona (strengthening dollar) would lower the dollar profit.

27 - 14

Describe the current and former international monetary systems.

- The current system is a floating rate system.
- Prior to 1971, a fixed exchange rate system was in effect.
  - The U.S. dollar was tied to gold.
  - Other currencies were tied to the dollar.

27 - 15

The European Monetary Union

In 2002, the full implementation of the "euro" is expected to be complete. The national currencies of the 11 participating countries will be phased out in favor of the "euro." The newly formed European Central Bank will control the monetary policy of the EMU.

27 - 16

The 11 Member Nations of the European Monetary Union

Austria	Germany	Netherlands
Belgium	Ireland	Portugal
Finland	Italy	Spain
France	Luxembourg	

European Union countries not in the EMU:
Britain Sweden Denmark Greece

27 - 17

What is a convertible currency?

- A currency is convertible when the issuing country promises to redeem the currency at current market rates.
- Convertible currencies are traded in world currency markets.

27 - 18

What problems arise when a firm operates in a country whose currency is not convertible?

- It becomes very difficult for multinational companies to conduct business because there is no easy way to take profits out of the country.
- Often, firms will barter for goods to export to their home countries.

27 - 19

What is the difference between spot rates and forward rates?

- A spot rate is the rate applied to buy currency for immediate delivery.
- A forward rate is the rate applied to buy currency at some agreed-upon future date.

27 - 20

When is the forward rate at a premium to the spot rate?

- If the U.S. dollar buys fewer units of a foreign currency in the forward than in the spot market, the foreign currency is selling at a premium.
- In the opposite situation, the foreign currency is selling at a discount.
- The primary determinant of the spot/forward rate relationship is relative interest rates.

27 - 21

What is interest rate parity?

Interest rate parity implies that investors should expect to earn the same return on similar-risk securities in all countries:

$$\frac{\text{Forward rate}}{\text{Spot rate}} = \frac{1 + k_h}{1 + k_f}.$$

Here,

k_h = periodic interest rate in the home country.

k_f = periodic interest rate in the foreign country.

27 - 22

Assume 1 peseta = $0.00505 in the 30-day forward market and and 30-day risk-free rate is 6% in the U.S. and 4% in Spain.

Does interest rate parity hold?

Forward rate = $0.00505.
k_h = 6%/12 = 0.500%.
k_f = 4%/12 = 0.333%.

(More...)

27 - 23

$$\frac{\text{Forward rate}}{\text{Spot rate}} = \frac{1 + k_h}{1 + k_f}$$

$$\frac{0.00505}{\text{Spot rate}} = \frac{1.00500}{1.00333}$$

Spot rate = 0.00504.

If interest rate parity holds, the computed spot rate would be 0.0055 dollars/peseta. However, the observed spot rate is 0.0050 dollars/peseta.

27 - 24

Which 30-day security (U.S. or Spanish) offers the higher return?

- **A U.S. investor could directly invest in the U.S. security and earn an annualized rate of 6%.**
- **Alternatively, the U.S. investor could convert dollars to pesetas, invest in the Spanish security, and then convert profit back into dollars. If the return on this strategy is higher than 6%, then the Spanish security has the higher rate.**

27 - 25

What is the return to a U.S. investor in the Spanish security?

- **Buy $1,000 worth of pesetas in the spot market:**

  1,000(200 $/peseta) = 200,000 pesetas.

- **Spanish investment return (in pesetas):**

  200,000(1.00333)=200,666.67 pesetas.

(More...)

27 - 26

- **Buy contract today to exchange 200,666.67 pesetas in 30 days at forward rate of 0.00505 dollars/peseta.**
- **At end of 30 days, convert peseta investment to dollars:**

  200,666.67(0.00505) = $1,013.37.

- **Calculate the rate of return:**

  $13.37/$1,000 = 1.337% **per 30 days.**

(More...)

27 - 27

The Spanish security has the highest return, even though it has a lower interest rate.

- **U.S. 30-day rate is 0.500%, so Spanish securities at 1.337% offer a higher rate of return to U.S. investors.**
- **But could such a situation exist for very long?**

27 - 28

Arbitrage

- Traders could borrow at the U.S. rate, convert to pesetas at the spot rate, and simultaneously lock in the forward rate and invest in Spanish securities.
- This would produce arbitrage: a positive cash flow, with no risk and none of the traders own money invested.

27 - 29

Impact of Arbitrage Activities

- Traders would recognize the arbitrage opportunity and make huge investments.
- Their actions would tend to move interest rates, forward rates, and spot rates to parity.

27 - 30

What is purchasing power parity?

Purchasing power parity implies that the level of exchange rates adjusts so that identical goods cost the same amount in different countries.

$$P_h = P_f(\text{Spot rate}),$$

or

$$\text{Spot rate} = P_h/P_f.$$

27 - 31

If grapefruit juice costs \$2.00/liter in the U.S. and purchasing power parity holds, what is price in Spain?

$$\text{Spot rate} = P_h/P_f.$$
$$\$0.005 = \$2.00/P_f$$
$$P_f = \$2.00/\$0.005$$
$$= 400 \text{ pesetas.}$$

- Do interest rate and purchasing power parity hold exactly at any point in time?

27 - 32

What impact does relative inflation have on interest rates and exchange rates?

- Lower inflation leads to lower interest rates, so borrowing in low-interest countries may appear attractive to multinational firms.
- However, currencies in low-inflation countries tend to appreciate against those in high-inflation rate countries, so the true interest cost increases over the life of the loan.

27 - 33

Describe the international money and capital markets.

- Eurodollar markets
  - Dollars held outside the U.S.
  - Mostly Europe, but also elsewhere
- International bonds
  - Foreign bonds: Sold by foreign borrower, but denominated in the currency of the country of issue.
  - Eurobonds: Sold in country other than the one in whose currency it is denominated.

27 - 34

To what extent do capital structures vary across different countries?

- Early studies suggested that average capital structures varied widely among the large industrial countries.
- However, a recent study, which controlled for differences in accounting practices, suggests that capital structures are more similar across different countries than previously thought.

27 - 35

What is the impact of multinational operations on each of the following topics?

Cash Management

- Distances are greater.
- Access to more markets for loans and for temporary investments.
- Cash is often denominated in different currencies.

27 - 36

Capital Budgeting Decisions

- Foreign operations are taxed locally, and then funds repatriated may be subject to U.S. taxes.
- Foreign projects are subject to political risk.
- Funds repatriated must be converted to U.S. dollars, so exchange rate risk must be taken into account.

27 - 37

Credit Management

- Credit is more important, because commerce to lesser-developed countries often relies on credit.
- Credit for future payment may be subject to exchange rate risk.

27 - 38

Inventory Management

- Inventory decisions can be more complex, especially when inventory can be stored in locations in different countries.
- Some factors to consider are shipping times, carrying costs, taxes, import duties, and exchange rates.

27 - 39

Capital Budgeting in Foreign Countries

Country	Method	Comment
Singapore	Average Accounting Return (AAR)	Divides the average Net Income of a project by that project's average book value of equity.
India & Thailand	Payback Period	Preferred by Indian and Thai financial managers because of relative simplicity.